Governing Transboundary Waters

With almost the entire world's water basins crossing political borders of some kind, understanding how to cooperate with one's neighbor is of global relevance. For Indigenous communities, whose traditional homelands may predate and challenge the current borders, and whose relationships to water sources are linked to the protection of traditional lifeways (or "ways of life"), transboundary water governance is deeply political.

This book explores the nuances of transboundary water governance through an in-depth examination of the Canada–U.S. border, with an emphasis on the leadership of Indigenous actors (First Nations and Native Americans). The inclusion of this "third sovereign" in the discussion of Canada–U.S. relations provides an important avenue to challenge borders as fixed, both in terms of natural resource governance and citizenship, and highlights the role of non-state actors in charting new territory in water governance. The volume widens the conversation to provide a rich analysis of the cultural politics of transboundary water governance.

In this context, the book explores the issue of what makes a good upstream neighbor and analyzes the rescaling of transboundary water governance. Through narrative, the book explores how these governance mechanisms are linked to wider issues of environmental justice, decolonization, and self-determination. To highlight the changing patterns of water governance, it focuses on six case studies that grapple with transboundary water issues at different scales and with different constructions of border politics, from the Pacific coastline to the Great Lakes.

Emma S. Norman is Chair of the Science Department/Native Environmental Science Program at Northwest Indian College, Bellingham, Washington State, USA. She is also a Research Associate with the Smithsonian Institution, National Museum of the American Indian, USA, and a long-term collaborator with the Program on Water Governance at the University of British Columbia, Canada.

Earthscan Studies in Water Resource Management

Water Management, Food Security and Sustainable Agriculture in Developing Economies
Edited by M. Dinesh Kumar, M.V.K. Sivamohan and Nitin Bassi

Governing International Watercourses
River Basin Organizations and the Sustainable Governance of Internationally Shared Rivers and Lakes
Susanne Schmeier

Transferable Groundwater Rights
Integrating Hydrogeology, Law and Economics
Andreas N. Charalambous

Contemporary Water Governance in the Global South
Scarcity, Marketization and Participation
Edited by Leila Harris, Jacqueline Goldin and Christopher Sneddon

Water Governance, Policy and Knowledge Transfer
International Studies on Contextual Water Management
Edited by Cheryl de Boer, Joanne Vinke-de Kruijf, Gül Özerol and Hans Th. A. Bressers

Water as a Catalyst for Peace
Transboundary Water Management and Conflict Resolution
Ahmed Abukhater

Sustainable Water and Sanitation Services
The Life-cycle Approach to Planning and Management
Livelihoods & Natural Resource Management Institute, International Water & Sanitation Centre, Centre for Economic and Social Studies, Watershed Support Services & Activities Network

Water for Food Security and Well-being in Latin America and the Caribbean
Social and Environmental Implications for a Globalized Economy
Edited by Bárbara A. Willaarts, Alberto Garrido and M. Ramón Llamas

Water Scarcity, Livelihoods and Food Security
Research and Innovation for Development
Edited by Larry W. Harrington and Myles J. Fisher

Adaptation to Climate Change through Water Resources Management
Capacity, Equity and Sustainability
Edited by Dominic Stucker and Elena Lopez-Gunn

Hydropower Devleopment in the Mekong Region
Political, Socio-economic and Environmental Perspectives
Edited by Nathanial Matthews and Kim Geheb

Governing Transboundary Waters
Canada, the United States and Indigenous Communities
Emma S. Norman

For more information and to view forthcoming titles in this series, please visit the Routledge website: www.routledge.com/books/series/ECWRM/

"Norman provides a much-needed re-framing of transboundary governance from Indigenous peoples' perspectives and celebrates the achievements made by First Nations and Tribes to date in successfully re-uniting communities across state borders and rescaling transboundary watersheds. A compelling read and one that should be required reading for anyone working in watershed governance at the border."

– Jennifer L. Archer, Rivers without Borders, Vancouver, Canada

"Bringing together politics of coloniality and Indigenous struggles for territorial, cultural and resource rights with water politics at the U.S.-Canada border, this work makes significant conceptual and policy relevant contributions. Skillfully weaving diverse narratives, experiences, and moments of relevance for Indigenous communities on both sides of the border, the book makes for an inspiring read that explores key debates for contemporary water governance."

– Karen Bakker and Leila Harris, Co-Directors, Program on Water Governance, University of British Columbia, Canada

"For anyone interested in the future of our waters and how we can truly care for them, Emma Norman's book is vitally important. It illuminates in fresh ways the challenges of 'transborder' water governance, and in particular the function of borders themselves to distort how we understand, treat, and value water – as divisible, bounded, owned – and to reiterate power relationships of exclusion and alienation from our water 'neighbors'. In accessible and hopeful case studies, Norman shows how Indigenous communities and their allies are re-asserting the meaning of ecological boundaries, reweaving communities around them, and creating leadership structures capable of sharing and protecting water."

– Alexa Bradley, Co-Director, Great Lakes Commons, www.greatlakescommons.org

"*Governing Transboundary Waters* marks an important contribution to scholarship on water governance, transboundary resource management, and border studies. Whereas most studies of transboundary water management focus on state interaction, Norman brings the study down to earth, engaging with the communities involved in resource management around the international border itself. As such, she reminds us that the international border is a colonial relic that continues divide traditionally connected Indigenous communities. Rejecting the international border as the essential arbiter of resource management is a first step in moving towards environmental justice in transboundary resource management."

– Kathryn Furlong, Department of Geography, Université de Montréal, Canada

"Water territorialities may be the next frontier to roam in order to progress in our understanding of socio-spatial relations, and this book indeed shows that labile environments reveal a lot about multi-tier decision making. Through a very convincing demonstration based on extensive field knowledge, E. Norman presents the disruptions in territorial hierarchies which are at stake when maritime management overlaps both international limits and sets of autochthonous rights. Her thorough analysis of the now-called 'Salish sea', over the U.S.–Canada border, escapes easy conclusions and interestingly recalls to us that the semantic transfer from government to governance does not mean that the state has been kicked out of politics!"

– Anne-Laure Amilhat Szary, Professor, Université Grenoble-Alpes, France

"E. Norman's *Governing Transboundary Waters* captures genuine progress in restoring boundary environments. Her eloquently written book analyzes how through patient, determined Indigenous led efforts, legal rights to access culturally relevant food are being secured. This book is a timely guide for critically needed environmental action."

– Melvin J. Visser, author of *Cold, Clear, and Deadly: Unravelling a Toxic Legacy*

Governing Transboundary Waters

Canada, the United States, and Indigenous communities

Emma S. Norman

Routledge
Taylor & Francis Group
LONDON AND NEW YORK

First published 2015
by Routledge
2 Park Square, Milton Park, Abingdon, Oxon OX14 4RN

and by Routledge
711 Third Avenue, New York, NY 10017

Routledge is an imprint of the Taylor & Francis Group, an informa business

British Library Cataloguing-in-Publication Data
A catalogue record for this book is available from the British Library

Library of Congress Cataloging-in-Publication Data
Norman, Emma S.
Governing transboundary waters: Canada, the United States and indigenous communities/Emma S. Norman.
pages cm. – (Earthscan studies in water resource management)
Includes bibliographical references and index.
1. Water rights – Canada. 2. Water rights – United States. 3. Water – Government policy –Canada. 4. Water – Government policy – United States. 5. Indians of North America – Legal status, laws, etc. I. Title.
HD1696.C2N67 2014
341.4′480973 – dc23
2014020382

ISBN: 978-0-415-83859-7 (hbk)
ISBN: 978-0-203-78145-6 (ebk)

Typeset in Bembo
by Florence Production Ltd, Stoodleigh, Devon, UK

Cover images:
Middle: Canoe Reflecting In Water by Jeff Bear, used with permission from Urbanrez Productions, Producer of Water Stories and www.samaqan.ca

Left: North fork of the Nooksack River; and *right*: San Juan Island, Salish Sea; both by Emma S. Norman

Contents

Figures

Tables

Acknowledgements

I was recently asked how long it took to write this book. I paused because there was no straightforward answer to this question. On the one hand, I wrote much of this book over the course of an idyllic summer on San Juan Island, Washington. As a scholar-in-residence at the University of Washington's Whiteley Center, I took this book from a collection of ideas and essays to the first full draft. I was able to work productively that summer – waking up early every morning and walking to my office along the rocky shoreline trail that I would often share with deer or fox. Those days, I lost myself in the words that are now this book. As a perfect antidote to the hours of writing in solitude, I spent the late afternoons and evenings exploring the tidal flats with my family. The editing took place in Michigan, where I revised the manuscript during the busy school year, where I watched the landscape change outside of my office window – from green leaves, to brown leaves, to a snowy (very snowy) winterland.

On the other hand, the genesis of this book was, perhaps, when I started studying transboundary water governance as a graduate student at Western Washington University, and then at The University of British Columbia (UBC). But, in reality, the start of the book could be pushed back further – perhaps it was the 2 years in the Peace Corps, where I worked along the Malawi–Zambia border. Or perhaps it was the high school trip to Germany, where I saw the Berlin Wall, just months after it fell. In essence, there is a lifetime of experiences that shape the words found in this book.

Although it is difficult to know exactly *how long* this book took to write, a fundamental component of this process is the number of people that helped along the way, both in terms of shaping ideas or directly commenting on text.

First, my work at Northwest Indian College (NWIC) has influenced me deeply, in particular, understanding the importance of "a line" that divides historically connected communities, intact ecosystems to sustain communities, and oral histories to motivate change and honor traditions. As a faculty member for 10 years at NWIC teaching in the Native Environmental Science Program (and now as Chair of the Science Department), I have been exposed to scores of inspirational community leaders, resilient students, and dedicated colleagues, in particular, the leadership of Cheryl Crazy Bull, Justin Guillory, Sharon Kinley, Dave Oreiro, Bernice Portervint, and Carol Rave. The grounding of inspirational leaders such as Greg Cajete, Tom

Sampson, Dan Wildcat, Dave Wilkins, and the late Billy Frank Jr. all helped provide context for this discussion, and my colleagues, Ane Berrett, Brian Compton, Jon Davis, Mark Moss, Steve Pavlik, Terri Plake, John Rombold, Jessica Urbanec, Ted Williams, Skye Augustine, and Marco Hatch (among many others!) who helped explore the edges of Indigenous Environmental Science.

Certainly, those that were part of my educational training had a significant role in shaping my ideas. In particular, I am thankful to my advisors, Karen Bakker and Matthew Evenden at The University of British Columbia, and my committee members Doug Harris and Trevor Barnes. At Western Washington University: Jean Melious, Don Alper, Gigi Berardi, and Lynn Robbins; and at Colby College, James Webb all provided generous mentorship. Numerous other colleagues and mentors were influential as I entered into this work: Juliet Fall, Leila Harris, Jessica Budds, Bonnie Kaserman, Jayme Walenta, Alice Cohen, Christina Cook, Gemma Dunn, James Loucky and David Kennedy all helped shape this project at various stages.

In addition, my affiliation with Michigan Technological University as an Assistant Professor in the Social Sciences Department and the Great Lakes Research Center lent me new appreciation of the power of the "Freshwater Nation". I am thankful to the "crazy smart" students, wonderful colleagues and passionate community members that I had the pleasure of working with – particularly Guy Meadows, Nancy Langston, Audrey Mayer, Hugh Gorman, Judith Perlinger, Noel Urban, Val Gagnon, Maggie Morrison, Melissa Baird, Kari Henquinet, Carol MacLennon, and Richelle Winkler.

Of course, I express heartfelt thanks to my wonderful publishers at Routledge: Tim Hardwick for support and guidance from the prospectus to the first print, and Ashley Wright for her keen attention to detail and gracious assistance in getting this through the many stages of the publication process. The team at Routledge has been nothing but supportive, and for that, I am truly appreciative.

In addition, I am humbled and amazed by the generosity of people who graciously agreed to read this book in draft form. It was essential for me that this book was not only academically sound, but also reached people beyond the academy. For those working "in the trenches" in environmental governance and Indigenous governance, I wanted to make sure the book was accurate, respectful, thoughtful *and* push the boundaries of previous work related to transboundary water governance. To help accomplish this, I called upon many people to read drafts of this book at various stages. I am deeply moved by the number of people who dove into these drafts without pause or hesitation.

For those that read drafts of this book from cover-to-cover, I am especially grateful. I appreciate their keen insights that helped to ultimately strengthen this book. Thank you to Jennifer Archer, Frank Ettawageshik, Kathryn Furlong, Jessica Koski, Merrell-Ann Phare, Tom Sampson, and Mel Visser. Thanks also to those that commented on specific chapters related to their area of expertise – Murray Clamen, Suzanne Chisholm, Jamie James, Val Gagnon, Jamie Donatuto, Alix Foster, Justin Finkbonner, Daryl Williams, Charlene Krise, Jon Waterhouse, Nick Wilson, Leila Harris, Alice Cohen, Christina Cook, Rosemary Collard, Karen Bakker, and Matthew Evenden. Any remaining errors, of course, remain mine.

A special thanks to the amazing people who let me recount their stories as a way to give depth (and heart) to the discussions: Grandmother Josephine Mandamin – her dedication to and honoring of water is an inspiration; Justin Finkbonner – his leadership at Lummi Nation and in the Canoe Journey is key; Jamie James, Suzanne Chisholm, and Mike Parfett for their amazing work standing up for the rights of those that do not have the voice to do so themselves. Thanks also to Joanne Charles whose story about Boundary Bay inspired me to write Chapter 5.

In addition, two people: Tom Sampson, revered elder and former Chief of Tsartlip First Nation and the late Billy Frank Jr., intellectual leader and famed fishing rights activists of the coastal pacific tribes, read the chapters associated with the Coast Salish Gathering. Knowing that I have their blessing means the world to me. Although Billy has since walked into the next world, his work will continue to inspire generations to come.

Several people contributed to the figures that appear in this book. Thanks to Eric Leinberger, who, since I started graduate school at UBC, has been an amazing support through his cartographic genius. For this project, he contributed to Figures 3.2, 3.3, 4.4, 5.1, 6.1 and 9.1. Many thanks to Jeff Bear for permission to use the image of the Coast Salish canoe that appears on the cover of the book and the photograph of the Canoe Journey at sunset (Figure 7.1). Thanks also to the Associated Press for permission to use the photograph of Alexander receiving the Presidential Citizen's Award (Figure 3.4), the International Joint Commission, for providing the photograph of the first meeting of the IJC (Figure 3.1) and the data harmonization process images (Figures 4.2 and 4.3); Caroline Edwards for permission to use the image of the paddlers waiting to land (Figure 7.2); Tanvir Khan for the adaption to Figure 8.2; Brent Wesley and Grandmother Josephine Mandamin for the use of image 8.1; and Suzanne Chisholm for graciously letting me reproduce her amazing photographs of *Tsu-xiit* (Figures 9.2 and 9.3).

Thanks also to Dan Cole from the Smithsonian Institution, who graciously produced maps 2.2 and 2.3. In addition, through this work, Dan Cole and his colleague, Doug Herman, brought me into the Smithsonian family as a Research Associate with the National Museum of American Indian. This new affiliation will undoubtedly continue to foster meaningful collaborations that weave together issues of social and environmental justice into the work of water governance – a testament to the power of maps!

Thanks to the Department of Anthropology at the Smithsonian Institution for permission to reproduce the Ives Goddard map (Figure 2.1). In addition, thanks to the Royal Geographical Society for permission to reprint a revised version of Chapter 5. Thanks also to the editors of *Water Alternatives* for permission to reprint a portion of Chapter 6. In addition, a very special thank you to Chief Dean Sayers (Batchewana First Nation), President Levi Carrick (Bay Mills Chippewa Indian Community), Chairman Aaron Payment (Sault Sainte Marie Tribe of Chippewa), and Chiefs Sayers (Garden River First Nation) for permission to print a copy of the Treaty found in Appendix A.

Financial support is gratefully acknowledged from the American Indian College Fund, Mellon Foundation, the Canadian Embassy and the Seattle Canadian

Consulate General who generously funded portions of this research that contributed to this book. Thanks also to Michigan Technological University (who provided funding to help complete this manuscript through the Research Excellence Fund) and for deferring costs of production.

Perhaps less directly, but equally as important, is my support network. Throughout the years, my running partners, book club (yay, Bella Chica!), and mothers' group friends provided an important testimony to how essential it is to have a supportive community to discuss all aspects of life! In particular, thanks to Kimberly Peters, Rebecca Krueger, Vicki Hsueh, Jennifer Seltz, Becky Donatuto, Jennifer Berdinka, Lisa Shrake Perry, Terry Drussell, Amy Hamlin, and Ruth Sofield.

My family, of course, continues to be my greatest support and motivation. Thanks, first, to my parents, whose early adventures in life helped to shape my worldview and whose continued support and encouragement gave me confidence to think big, without losing sight of the steps that it takes to get there; my sister, Polly, and brothers, Brett and Adam, for their good humor and cheer, who can make me laugh only the way family can; to my children – Parker and Luke – whose sense of wonder is contagious and whose attention to the here-and-now is both refreshing and grounding. Their propensity to ask the question, "why", challenges me to continue to seek out better answers, while their unconditional love keeps my metaphorical cup filled to the brim; and, of course, my husband, Chad, who has been on this journey with me since we first met in Naples, Florida, in 1998 – he, just back from teaching in India, me, from the Peace Corps in Malawi – ready to start a new chapter. With Chad, I am able to see the deeper meaning of it all.

Thanks to you all (and so many more!).

Emma S. Norman
Bellingham, Washington

1 Introduction

Water, borders, scale, and power

Our relationship to water is intimate. It is one of the few things in this world that connects all human beings. In many cultures, water is revered as a gift from the Creator, to be protected and sustained for generations. Given the universal need for survival, one could easily argue that water is simply too important to politicize. Yet, the very nature of water – changing states and crossing boundaries of all kinds – makes this vital substance inherently political.

Nowhere is water more political than at the site of an international border, where sets of laws, regulations, and rules terminate abruptly and where notions of "insiders" and "outsiders" are delineated. As an interloper between jurisdictions, water provides a challenge for governance systems that are delineated by fixed political boundaries.

Looking at water governance from the site of the international border is a telling exercise. Like a roadside geologist you can see the nested scales of governance: federal, tribal, provincial, state, and municipal, each operating within (seemingly) neatly defined responsibilities and purviews. Yet, looking closely at these borders (and the process of border-making) one often sees entrenched colonial legacies, which fosters both exclusion and privileging (Said, 1979; Harris, 2002; Braun, 2002; Gregory, 2004). The act of drawing a line bounds territory and ultimately sets a trajectory for a relationship between people and their environment. As water transgresses in and out and through jurisdictions, it becomes integrated into wider social–political contexts that are wrought with power dynamics, historical legacies, and asymmetries. This line, in turn, can be revealed as scale, power, and justice.

Thus, the governance challenge is a "*hydrosocial*" one – that is, it relates both to the physical and the material processes of water, as well as the social and the political context around which it is governed (Swyngedouw, 1999; Bakker, 2003a, 2003b; Harris, 2006; Loftus, 2007; Budds, 2008). When the communities and the resources in question span political borders, these processes become further complicated. For Indigenous communities, whose traditional homelands often span and pre-date contemporary nation-state borders and whose relationship to water sources are linked to the protection of traditional lifeways (or "ways of life"), transboundary water governance is deeply political.[1] In fact, even the word "transboundary" implies a colonial legacy. For many Indigenous communities that live within borderlands, transboundary water governance, therefore, is linked to issues of environmental justice, decolonization, and self-determination.

This leads us to a dilemma: how are we to govern water resources that span political borders when our institutions and frameworks are bound within fixed jurisdictions and nation-state frameworks? Furthermore, how are these governance systems able to equitably represent (and protect) diverse populations when the systems themselves are wrought with power-dynamics and colonial legacies, and the impacts of degraded environments are unevenly felt across populations?

This book grapples with these dilemmas by analyzing the social and political contexts of transboundary water governance, and highlighting the rescaling of governance mechanisms and emerging strategies of Indigenous communities to address transboundary water issues. It asks three interrelated questions: "How are governance mechanisms changing to address the social, political, and ecological aspects of transboundary water?", "How are the Indigenous-led governance mechanisms linked to the twinned goals of ecosystem protection and processes of self-determination, empowerment, and decolonization?", and the last question, which is generalizable across populations and asks, simply "What makes a good upstream neighbor?"

To answer the first question, I look into institutional changes related to transboundary water governance. To answer the second question, I look at the different tools and methods Indigenous communities have adopted to address water issues of shared concern. To answer the last question, I seek to identify universal principles that foster equitability and justice as it relates to governing transboundary – or *shared* – waters.

These questions are of global relevance. With almost the entire world's water basins crossing political borders of some kind, and almost all major water basins crossing nation-state boundaries, understanding the hydrosocial complexities of transboundary water is of universal importance (Wolf, 1999; Conca, 2006; Norman *et al.*, 2013). The issue becomes an urgent one in the face of declining water supplies, failing infrastructure, increased pollution, stressed ecosystems, and global climate change. Despite the ongoing international campaign to make access to clean water a fundamental human right, the United Nations estimates that 768 million people do not have access to clean drinking water and 2.5 billion have inadequate sanitation services (Brichieri-Colombi, 2009; Mirosa and Harris, 2012; United Nations, 2013). Indigenous communities are particularly vulnerable to water-related issues. In Canada, for example, both rural and remote Indigenous communities as well as those in urban settings face higher incidence of health issues related to inadequate drinking water than the rest of the population (Phare, 2009, 2013; White *et al.*, 2012). However, the issues go beyond drinking water.

For many Indigenous communities throughout the world, protecting water sources is foundational to preserving and protecting traditional lifeways (La Duke, 1999; Holifield *et al.*, 2009; Holifield, 2010). Yet these water sources are threatened due to extraterritorial pollution, and are exacerbated by fixed geographic spaces located on historically marginalized lands (Harris, 2002). The environmental stressors are particularly pronounced for Indigenous communities whose traditional lifeways are intricately linked to the protection of intact ecosystems for food sources. In the Arctic, for example, Indigenous communities are exposed to significantly higher concentrations of pollutants, due to atmospheric deposition of pollutants such as polychlorinated biphenyls (PCBs) (AMAP, 2011; Perlinger *et al.*, 2014). These chemicals biointensify in marine mammals such as seals and coldwater fish that are integral to the diet of many Northern communities (El-Hayek, 2007; AMAP, 2011; Selin, 2011). As a result of the extraterritorial pollutants, Indigenous populations are experiencing devastating health impacts, including increased cancer rates, stunted growth, miscarriages, and deformities (Epstein, 1978; Visser, 2007; Langston, 2010a, 2010b; Selin, 2010; AMAP, 2011). In addition, many of the health impacts are proving to be multigenerational – appearing as disorders, cancers, and diseases in the daughters, granddaughters, sons, and grandsons of the exposed person (Langston, 2010a, 2010b).

As discussed in the chapters that follow, populations in the coastal Pacific of North America (Salish Sea Basin) and the Great Lakes Basins are experiencing similar issues related to degraded environments and health concerns. Because of the mismatch of governance mechanisms to address extraterritorial pollutants, and the lack of adequate frameworks to address these issues that asymmetrically impact communities, many of these issues become environmental and social justice issues.

To this aim, this book explores the changing dynamics of transboundary water governance. In Part One, I document how formal governance mechanisms are changing, and, in Part Two, how Indigenous communities, who have previously been outside of the purview of formal governance mechanisms, are increasingly becoming involved in leadership roles in transboundary waters. I employ a political ecology approach, in which the issues of governance are intricately linked to power dynamics, colonial legacies, and environmental justice. I seek to find solutions that are meaningful and applicable to diverse populations by identifying qualities of "good upstream neighbors".

Conceptual approach

Exploring transboundary water governance in the context of Indigenous communities is an important contribution to the scholarship on transboundary water governance because it: 1) fills a gap in the existing transboundary water governance literature; 2) brings the politics of colonial boundary-making into the discussions of transboundary water governance; 3) highlights the Indigenous-led work to address water issues of shared concern; and 4) opens up space to insert discussions of environmental justice into discussions of transboundary water governance. These points provide the rationale and guiding framework for this book.

Filling a gap/key theoretical contribution

While a growing body of literature has made great strides in understanding, predicting, and explaining the nuances of transboundary water governance – particularly in relation to water scarcity and water wars,[2] transboundary river basins,[3] integrated water resources management,[4] and international water courses,[5] little attention has been paid to Indigenous-led transboundary movements and impacts of colonial borders on water resources (which are central themes found throughout this volume). Zietoun *et al.* (2013) is a notable exception, with their work on the Jordan River Basin.

In the last decade, more attention to power dynamics and environmental justice has been included in discussions of water governance. Muehlmann's (2013) recent ethnography related to the cultural-social-economic impacts of upstream diversion on the Indigenous populations of the Colorado River Delta is also a notable contribution to the transboundary environmental justice literature. In addition, the rich literature on the politics of scale has helped to connect issues of power, decision-making, and jurisdictional scale.[6] The politics-of-scale literature has helped to refine thinking about human-environmental and hydrosocial relations.[7] In addition, issues related to Indigenous communities and environmental justice (Holifield, 2010; Ranco *et al.*, 2011), hydrohegemony (Zeitoun *et al.*, 2013) and conceptual tools such as waterscapes (Budds and Hinojosa, 2012), hydrosocial networks (Swyngedouw 2004), political economy (Bakker, 2003a, 2003b; Furlong and Bakker, 2010), and performativity (Harris and Alatout, 2010; Cohen and Harris, 2014) all provide important contributions to understanding the complexities of water politics and governance.

In particular, a waterscape approach, which sees water and society as co-producing, is a useful tool for this analysis. A waterscape, as Molle (2009, p. 2) defines it, is an "expression of the interaction between humans and their environment and encompasses all of the social, economic and political processes through which water in nature is conceived of and manipulated by societies". Thus, to help link water and social power relations, Budds and Hinojosa suggest that the waterscape approach usefully allows you to "explore the ways in which flows of water, power, and capital converge to produce uneven socio-ecological arrangements over space and time, the particular characteristics of which reflect the power relations that shaped their production" (2012, p. 124).

While these previous studies have helped understand the dynamics associated with hydrosocial networks, a dearth in research remains where these processes are explored through the lens of Indigenous communities impacted by and involved in transboundary water governance.

My theoretical contribution, in my mind, relates to reframing the dominant narrative related to transboundary water governance. This reframing helps to unpack the "border" in transborder as an active colonizing act, which continues to shape and influence water policy and decision-making. Reframing the narrative so that Indigenous communities are in the center of the discussion (rather than the periphery or not in the dialogue at all) provides an avenue to explore how governance of water (a lifesource) can lead to wider projects such as decolonization and self-determination. Mainstream dialogue reinforces colonial borders as fixed, ahistorical, and unproblematized, while Indigenous spaces are often seen as a historical relic. Thus, I use narrative to gently re-center the dialogue and open up conceptual space for a more critical look at transborder water governance.

Thus, it is the goal of this volume to explicitly engage with the cultural and political aspects of transborder water governance by highlighting the counter-hegemonic activities that are emerging throughout Indigenous communities. This is happening the world over; however, this work engages with the borderland I am most familiar with – the Canada–U.S. border.

Canada–U.S. transboundary water governance

To fill these gaps, I turn to a border that has been part of the backdrop of my life for the last 15 years. The Canada–U.S. border provides a useful platform to analyze transboundary water governance. Because of the length of the border (the largest continuous international border spanning 5,525 miles/8,891 kilometers including Alaska and the Yukon Territory), it has hundreds of rivers, lakes, and aquifers that flow across, under or serve as the political border.

In addition, the Canada–U.S. border is often celebrated as having the most robust transboundary water mechanisms (often linked to the 1909 Boundary Waters Treaty and the subsequent creation of the binational International Joint Commission (IJC)). Over the last 30 years, however, there has been a shift – a rescaling – of water governance (Norman *et al.*, 2013). Under this new paradigm, subnational, regional, and local actors are more involved in transnational environmental governance activities (Norman and Bakker, 2009). This process occurs through processes of decentralization, in which the State is downloading much of its responsibility to the subnational actors (at the provincial, state, or local level). However, these processes often do not include support or infrastructure. Initially, the shift in responsibility downwards to the local was celebrated as empowering for community members and local actors; however, without proper support this devolution of responsibility and "hollowing out of the state" can leave the communities less protected than with State control (Jessop, 2004). Thus, to understand fully the complex rescaling of water governance, it is important to look at the wider trends. For transboundary water governance, it is also important to look at the politics and colonial legacies of the border itself, as well as the border-making process. Thus, looking at the waterscape as complex relationships between scale, power, and justice (or, environmental politics, colonial legacies, and environmental justice) helps to provide nuance to the discussions on transboundary water governance.

Thus, I attempt to widen the conversation away from the notion that borders of sovereign nations are fixed and naturalized (a "Westphalian" view that dominates much of the International Relations literature) to an understanding that borders are actively produced and wrought with power dynamics. Thus, although nation-state borders are "fixed" in one sense (as they relate to legal structures and policies), they are also "fluid" in another sense (as they relate to the permeability of the border for both people and nature) – both of which are linked to power dynamics.

For transboundary governance of water, the literature has largely focused on the formal legal mechanisms established through treaty processes (Wolf, 1999), with a growing attention on sub-state actors (Norman and Bakker, 2009) and watershed mechanisms (Cohen and Davidson, 2011). Little attention, however, has been paid to the growing number of Indigenous communities that are participating in, developing, and influencing transboundary water governance. Some attention has been paid to the growing inter-governmental agreements between Aboriginal governments and provincial governments within Canada (Nelles and Alcantara, 2011; Alcantara and Nelles, 2014), but this analysis rarely extends into international agreements).

Divergent management systems

Management systems in place to govern transboundary water and resources (as well as other environmental issues) largely operate within established political and cultural frameworks that reinforce dominant narratives and networks. For those outside of these established systems – either by choice or by circumstance – it can prove challenging to have your needs met. For Indigenous communities, the borders pose a set of challenges that are often invisible to those operating within the dominant governance framework.

Culturally, the border impacts travel between communities that reside on either side of the border, between traditional homelands that span the nation-state boundary (Miller, 1997, 2006). The international border also impacts the trading of culturally relevant goods and subjects them to tariffs that make traditional practices such as potlatching cost-prohibitive (Miller, 1997; Thom, 2010). It confines territory to reservations (or reserves in Canada). For those that were non-signatories on the original treaties, such as the Samish Nation in western Washington, it leaves them without a federally recognized space to call home (with protected status). Although the tribes still have a "homeland" in the sense that they have traditional territory, access to these lands are not preserved as they chose not to engage in the original Treaty process (Harmon, 2000).

The international border also poses significant impacts to harvesting migrating species of fish. The infamous "fish wars" between Canada and the U.S. show how the restructuring of jurisdictions impacts access to flow resources such as migrating salmon (Taylor, 1999). Similarly, international rivers such as the Columbia, which flows south from British Columbia, Canada into Washington State, are altered by political decisions and hydropolitics. The decisions to prioritize energy over intact fisheries can be "read" by the dams and reservoirs spanning the length of the river. When the Columbia River Treaty was negotiated in the early 1960s, Indigenous communities were excluded from the discussions. In the Treaty renegotiation process (which, at the time of writing, is underway), the dynamics have become more inclusive. The hydropolitics of waterways are visible the world over. The Mekong Basin, for example, is a dramatic example of privileging hydropower over protecting traditional homelands and ecosystems (Sneddon and Fox, 2006). The Los Angeles River – which people more often identify as the drag-racing scene in the classic film *Grease* than an actual river – is often portrayed as a cautionary tale of what can go wrong when we turn our back on waterways. The Colorado

River, whose waters fail to reach the sea as a consequence of dramatic upstream diversions, remains a story of inequity and egregious Indigenous injustices (Muehlmann, 2013). However, in a recent historiography of six rivers, Peter Coates (2013) shows the range of outcomes related to hydropolitics, ranging from the over-industrialized Los Angeles River to the wild and largely unaltered Yukon River. Coates takes care not to privilege one type of river over another. Rather, he characterizes the relationships between humans and nature as reflexive and dynamic – showing how rivers influence people and civilizations, just as people influence the shape and character of rivers. Seeing this "reflexivity" between humans and water is an important lens to understand transboundary water governance.

Indigenous leadership

In many ways, Indigenous communities that span international borders are in a unique position to provide leadership and visioning for the governance of transboundary waters. In fact, throughout this book, I suggest that Indigenous communities are well poised to provide leadership roles in transboundary water governance because: their traditional territories are not bound by contemporary nation-state borders; their traditional boundaries often follow river basins and watersheds, rather than Cartesian borders; and their approach to water issues is often more holistic and integrated (and includes protection of both ecosystem and human health). In addition, many Indigenous communities have a deep and sustained connection with their waterways, and protecting the water (and the marine resources) is integral to preserving their livelihood and lifeways.

In the pages that follow, I highlight some of the innovative ways in which Indigenous communities address transboundary water issues and assume leadership roles in reshaping transboundary water governance. This occurs both within formal governance mechanisms, as well as through education, and advocacy work. Furthermore, I also show that addressing environmental issues for Indigenous communities is often intertwined with decolonization and counter-hegemonic activities (such as increased capacity to govern, teach-ins, and canoe journeys). I also highlight the partnerships emerging between government agencies, citizens, and Indigenous communities to address issues facing transboundary waters. Although there is no "magic bullet" for improving water for human and ecosystem health, governance systems that support diverse worldviews are crucial.

What makes a good upstream neighbor?

Under this context, the underlying (and generalizable) question for this book is, "What makes a good upstream neighbor".[8] This misleadingly simple question is important for two reasons. First, the term "neighbor" reflects relationships that are both spatial and temporal – that is, the relationship is proximate and ongoing. The term elicits a small-scale relationship (the relationship with your *next-door* neighbor, perhaps). However, it can just as easily be scaled up to municipal neighbors, nation-state neighbors, or even "global citizenship". Second, the term connotes neutrality – a relationship in which all parties are on equal footing. In this case, when I refer to "Canada", "the United States", and "Indigenous communities" I also am speaking of neighbor-to-neighbor relationships, nation-to-nation relationships.

Throughout the text, I will continue to refine and deepen the exploration of this question of being a good neighbor. However, to start the conversation, I have outlined a handful of key ingredients that I believe (and others in the field believe) to be foundational for a "successful neighborly relationship"(see Warry, 2008; Boyd 2012, for example):

- transparency
- ongoing communication
- respect
- empathy
- equality
- equity.

In fact, these characteristics are foundational to many treaties designed to prepare for and mitigate transboundary water issues, such as the 1909 Canada–U.S. Boundary Waters Treaty and the 1964 Columbia River Treaty. In those treaties, however, a key problem was the scope of signatories and the narrow purview; Indigenous communities were not included as "neighbors" in the development of these mechanisms, nor was ecosystem health a consideration. This absence is slowly becoming rectified, for example with the Columbia River Treaty renegotiation in which Tribes and First Nations are playing a more prominent role in the decision-making process (Shurts and Paisley, 2013). The IJC International Watersheds Initiative (discussed in Chapter 4) also holds an opportunity for greater inclusion of people living in the watershed, including Indigenous communities (although early reports indicate much more needs to be done). The concept of a good neighbor also appears in legal mechanisms such as the Trail Smelter Arbitration, in which the legal mechanism *sic utere tuo ut alienum non laedas*, which translates to "use your property so that the property of others is not damaged" is the underlying principle whereby the State has a duty to *prevent* transboundary harm (precautionary principle) and the State should compensate for the transboundary harm it has caused (polluter pays principle) (Wirth, 1996).

Taking these themes as pillars of a good neighborly relationship, we can identify the shortcomings (and strengths) of the relationship between Canada, the United States, and Indigenous communities, in terms of governing shared waters. To do this, I explore several cases of transboundary water governance along the Canada–U.S. borderland and make explicit the links between borders, water, governance, scale, and power. This new lens of inquiry provides an opportunity to reframe transboundary water governance in a postcolonial and political ecological framework.

Methodology and narrative

> *Now that I am in the field, everything is fieldwork.*
>
> —Paul Rabinow (1977)

The process of going into the "field" to "collect" information to analyze is a curious business. Whatmore likens data "collection" to squirrels hoarding their acorns for winter use:

> Whether interviewing actors *in situ*, manipulating the digital population of census returns, or trawling documentary archives for traces of past lives, data collection mimics this squirrel–acorn relationship as you scurry about after nuggets of "evidence" just waiting to be picked up, brought home and feasted on at a later date.
>
> (Whatmore, 2003, p. 89)

Similarly, Latour (1999) artfully describes the process of collecting immutable objects and bringing them back to sites of analysis in *Pandora's hope*, where he emphasizes the complex space–time of the research event. This physical act of gathering and storing information has politics surrounding it and is, in itself, not passive. Rose (2000) maintains, for example, that the archive is a place where information is not just stored; it is rather where ideas are also shaped.[9] After all, "We all know that field data (or any other kind of data in the human studies for that matter) are not *Dinge an sich*[10] but are constructs of the process by which we acquire them" (Bellah, 1977, p. xi).

I started this project with the recognition that, in research, pure objectivity and total immersion are impossibilities. As Massey (2003, p. 75) reflects, "there is no such thing as total immersion; there will always still be a perspective, some things will be missed". Certainly, my positionality, i.e., as a female researcher trained at the University of British Columbia and Western Washington University, my role as a faculty member at Northwest Indian College and Michigan Technological University, and my role as a mother, wife, sister, daughter, and friend, all influence my dealings with people in the field. For example, my role as a graduate student studying transboundary environmental issues helped me gain access to meetings with certain environmental groups who were interested in gaining feedback on their own organization. Also, my role as faculty member at NWIC introduced me to several Indigenous leaders who have generously provided comments and insight into this long-term project. In addition, the many hours of conversations with students, colleagues, and friends has helped me to see border politics through a more informed and critical lens.

Throughout my work, I attempt to remain cognizant of the politics of my position. To help mitigate possible dichotomies inherent in many research projects, I strive for transparency with all of those that I work with. Part of this certainly includes ongoing peer-review and community reviews.

I am also very inspired by and informed by Indigenous knowledge and theories – particularly drawing on the work of Shawn Wilson (2008), Linda Tuiwai Smith

(2012), Margaret Kovach (2010), and Greg Cajete (2000), who strive to have research practice as a part of wider projects of decolonization. Smith, Wilson, Kovach, and Cajete each show how inserting "Indigenous Ways of Knowing" into research practices can help identify alternative and multiple ways of seeing problems and identifying solutions. For me, these insights translate into a deep appreciation for place and an understanding of the relationship of humans and their environment over time.

Overall, my research is based on a triangulation approach, where I have employed interviews, participant observation techniques, hosted transboundary water symposia, and analyzed scores of primary and secondary sources over the past decade. The triangulation approach serves to cross-check materials – which is increasingly common in historical geography and environmental governance studies (Zimmerer and Bassett, 2003; Wynn, 2010).

The geographic scope of this project is throughout the North American borderland of Canada and the United States (with an emphasis on the basins that I am most familiar with – the Salish Sea and the Great Lakes and, to a lesser degree, the Yuquot and Yukon Basins). My work is inherently place-based and – as I discuss in my "parable of discovery" – my experiences of living, working, going to school, and exploring the waterways of these basins situate me within the wider hydrosocial politics that I discuss throughout this volume.

I approach many of the issues in a narrative form. These narratives suggest both success and stumbling in the governance of shared waters. The narratives are rooted in stories of overcoming, of hard work, of vision, of engagement, and of reconnections. They are also rooted in building allies.

Because there is so much at stake for the Indigenous communities highlighted in this book, the stories are not *just* about protecting water or improving water governance. Rather, the cases demonstrate the importance of strengthening community to address transboundary water issues. It is also a lens in which the work cannot be done in isolation. The extraterritorial nature of environmental issues makes this work equally about maintaining and fostering allies.

The changing political fabric provides challenges for governance across borders, yet has created opportunities to rethink the mechanisms in place to govern water, particularly in a postcolonial context. The increased leadership of Indigenous actors in the governance of transnational environmental resources – particularly water – is important to document. This provides important avenues to challenge borders as "fixed", both in terms of natural resource governance and citizenship. Thus, the inclusion of a "third sovereign" in the discussion of Canada–U.S. relations provides a rich opportunity to analyze the cultural politics of transboundary water governance.

Structure of book and key themes

To help answer my central questions, the book is organized into two parts: "Rescaling transboundary water governance" and "Indigenous water governance: re/ordering transnational space". In the first part, I contextualize the material through a literature of key texts and studies related to transboundary water governance. In particular, I focus on identifying the links between borders (colonial bordering), water governance, and the politics of scale. I outline key transboundary water governance mechanisms in the Canada–U.S. context and highlight how one of the original binational institutions – the International Joint Commission – has begun to implement changes to address changing environments and political cultures. I also highlight opportunities for greater inclusion, particularly in relation to recognizing Treaty rights and formalizing processes for meaningful decision-making processes.

In the second part, I examine the cultural politics of transboundary water governance, as it pertains to Indigenous communities that live "between borders". I first highlight the ongoing impacts of colonial bordering and how contemporary governance mechanisms fall short in protecting Indigenous communities (particularly as these mechanisms are rooted in a nation-state framework and treat the borders as fixed). I also highlight environmental issues that impact all people, but have a particular impact on Indigenous communities because of the traditional reliance on marine-based resources for sustenance (for example, the politics of shellfish contamination discussed in Chapter 5). I also show how power dynamics are often built into state-run governance mechanisms.

Through narrative, I explore the second question: how Indigenous-led mechanisms are meeting goals of environmental protection and self-determination. The stories include both governance structures (such as the Coast Salish Gathering of Chapter 6) as well as performative techniques that strengthen communities and build allies (such as the Canoe Journey of Chapter 7 and the Water Walkers of Chapter 8). The cases also examine how counter-hegemonic techniques such as "strategic essentialism", "performativity", and "critical cartography" are changing the dynamics of transboundary water governance. The case of Luna, the "lost whale", demonstrates the complexities of boundaries, both in terms of political boundaries and cultural (animal–human) boundaries. All cases encourage a more nuanced approach and critical inquiry into transboundary governance.

Chapter descriptions

In Chapter 2, I provide the conceptual tools necessary to analyze the complex hydrosocial network as it relates to the cultural politics of transboundary water governance. I situate key literature related to borders, scales, and governance. I also introduce the literature that frames water issues and management as a hydrosocial context.

In Chapter 3, I introduce the reader to a range of formal governance mechanisms in the Canada–U.S. context. I provide an introductory overview and analysis of four transboundary institutions, operating at different scales that govern water along the Canada–U.S. border: The International Joint Commission (IJC), the North American Free Trade Agreement's Commission for Environmental Cooperation (CEC), the British Columbia–Washington Environmental Cooperation Council (ECC), and the Yukon River Inter-Tribal Watershed Council (YRITWC).

Analyzing these transboundary institutions provides insight into how governance processes play out at various jurisdictional and administrative scales and operate within different governance frameworks. Understanding how these governance mechanisms emerged, the purview and scope of their frameworks, and how they have changed over time is an important foundation for the chapters that follow.

In Chapter 4, I explore the changing role of the International Joint Commission, the administrative arm of the Boundary Waters Treaty. The IJC has been celebrated for its long-standing role in transboundary water governance. It has also been criticized for its lack of enforcement capacity and its reactive (rather than proactive) capacity. This chapter documents the rise of the International Watersheds Initiative, which was developed, in part, as a response to the IJC criticisms. This chapter shows how formal, binational mechanisms are attempting to change in response to increased demand for regional actors. However, the struggles that the IJC Watersheds Initiative faces suggests that further work is required for equitable participation of basin members, particularly meaningful and consistent participation of Indigenous actors.

Chapter 5 marks the first chapter in Part Two, which begins the narratives of "Indigenous water governance: re/ordering transnational space". In this chapter, I turn to a case of shellfish harvesting in Boundary Bay, whose jurisdiction is half in Canada and half in the United States, yet is part of the traditional territory of the Coast Salish peoples. In this chapter, I explore the ways that historically connected Indigenous communities are divergently impacted by shellfish regulations and water pollution. I describe how ecocolonialism employs a series of political technologies (including calculative techniques such as the enumeration of contamination levels) that have significant political effects on Indigenous communities. This chapter helps to establish the link between environmental justice issues, ecosystem protection, and access to traditional food resources. By asking the simple question "who's counting?", both in terms of shellfish numbers and pollution inputs, I explore the spatial politics of ecosystem management, particularly in relation to Indigenous rights to access culturally relevant food.

Chapter 6 explores the case of the Coast Salish Gathering, a newly developed governance mechanism designed by Indigenous leaders of the coastal Pacific of North America to protect and restore aquatic ecosystems. The Coast Salish – whose traditional territory spans and pre-dates the Canada and U.S. border – are natural leaders for the protection of salmon habitat, as the species holds great economic and cultural significance. The creation of the Gathering represents an important shift in the governance of shared resources, as it exemplifies not only greater participation of Indigenous communities as a "third sovereign", but it also marks a moment where the creation of the governance mechanism reinforces a shared Coast Salish identity.

Chapter 7 highlights the intertribal Canoe Journeys that occur every summer throughout the Coast Salish territory. I show how the Canoe Journeys help to promote effective water governance both internally (through increased self-determination, cultural revitalization, and empowerment) and externally (through partnerships and creation of allies). I show how participating in (and training for) the journey helps to strengthen community ties, rebuild networks, reconnect with the water, and expose the youth to positive life experiences that celebrate traditional cohesion and respect for each other and themselves. The material connections between the participants and the environment viscerally connect the participants with the ecosystem. Second, the role of partners and allies provides stronger community importance. This occurs informally through interpersonal relations and formally through curriculum development and partnerships with agencies such as the United States Geological Survey. Thus, this chapter highlights the performativities of transboundary water governance through traditional practices, and acts of self-determination through partnerships and allies.

Chapter 8 moves from the Salish Sea context to the Great Lakes. In this chapter, I show how performative techniques of the Water Walkers raise awareness of environmental pollution. The chapter highlights the environmental issues facing the Great Lakes, particularly in relation to contaminated fish and extraterritorial pollution such as PCBs and mercury. However, the lessons that the Grandmother Water Walkers highlight in this chapter shifts the responsibility back to the individual. They suggest that it is everyone's responsibility to work towards the solution. Taking responsibility as individuals to address transboundary water issues is also a way to reclaim power through self-determination. The media attention brought through their high-profile walks (first around the Great Lakes, then from the Four Corners of North America) has helped to raise awareness of pressing water-related issues, with the aim of policy change and reform. It is also a way to honor the waters as living beings. The fact that the leaders of the movements are part of the Ojibwa Nation, which spans Canada and the United States, contributes to the dialogue of a "connected" cultural ecosystem.

Chapter 9, the penultimate chapter, widens the conversation of transboundary water governance to include boundaries beyond just political. The chapter details the story of a "lost whale" that crossed from the "American waters" of the San Juan Islands in Washington State to the "Canadian waters" in the remote waters of outer Vancouver Island, British Columbia. The whale attracted international attention as environmental groups encouraged the relocation of the whale with its pod for preservation purposes, while local fisherpeople were motivated to steer the whale away from the waters and away from their boats due to increasing boat damage. The Mowachaht/Muchalaht First Nation successfully halted the high-profile international transfer as they contended the whale was not "lost" at all, rather it had come "home" as their chief reincarnate. This highly compelling story raises a number of questions related to transnational environmental governance in a postcolonial context. The case takes the questions beyond the territorial transgressions. Rather, Luna's *Tsu-xiit's* Story prompts us to ask the critical question: "what happens when the *being* itself is contested" – in this case the animal–human/nature–culture boundary.

In Chapter 10, I conclude by revisiting the key themes and reflecting on how the chapters help to answer the guiding questions. I explore how this work contributes to the ongoing work on transborder water governance and postcolonial theory and urge readers to continue to widen their interpretation of transboundary water governance to include social and political contexts. In closing, I present a list of lessons learned that help answer the question, "What makes a good upstream neighbor".

An interlude – my parable of discovery

How I came to be working on transboundary water justice is a long and winding path. Early in life, I was positioned to think beyond the constructs of "nationality" and "citizenship". Although I didn't realize this until much later, my early beginnings in life had a profound impact on my worldview.

I was born a foreigner. My parents moved from Chicago, Illinois to Sydney, Australia in their early twenties. Many things influenced their decision to leave, but the tragic events at Kent State University – where four unarmed college students were killed and nine injured by national guardsmen while protesting about the Vietnam War – was their tipping point. The Kent State shootings so angered and saddened my parents that they felt compelled to leave their home in search of a better life. Although they had no immediate plans beyond "leaving", my father eventually secured a job with the sales division of British Airways. It was a job that, it turned out, took him – and us – around the world many times over.

Being born "abroad" positioned me early in life to think of myself more as a global citizen than a person tied to a particular country. Although my family eventually moved back to North America, the early imprinting of being born *somewhere else* – and experiencing different cultures at an early age – tended to make me slightly aloof to the concepts of nationalism and citizenship and the concept of sticking within the delineations of a single home country. Because of my parents' political sensibilities, I was also sensitized early on to ideas of "justice" and "political action".

I am sure that this early exposure in life led me down my academic path. As an undergraduate at a small liberal arts college in Maine, I chose International Studies as my major, partly because of the interdisciplinary nature of its offerings and partly because of the opportunity to study abroad. The history, economics, anthropology, and environmental policy courses provided tools to start understanding the complexities and asymmetries of the world order. But, it was not until my junior year study abroad in Nepal that a new piece of the world puzzle was presented to me – a piece that had (and continues to have) profound impacts on me. At the age of 20, living in the outskirts of Kathmandu with a family of six who had 2 hours of electricity per week and no running water, influenced me in ways that no textbook ever could. What I learned in Nepal are lessons that I carry with me today. I learned about the tremendous discrepancies of wealth and standards of living, and the struggles many face just to survive on a daily basis.

Living in Nepal, I also learned that access to clean water should not be taken for granted. Living for 3 months without running water, I saw what it meant to rely on the local stream for everything – your weekly wash, your drinking water, washing dishes, and bathing. Getting severely sick as a result of contaminated water also made me understand – viscerally – the physical impacts of poverty. However, having access to healthcare – something that my host family did not have – made me acutely aware of asymmetries and power dynamics, even in my weakened state.

Academically, it also made me understand that environmental issues cannot be separated from health issues – something that carries through my work today. I saw this on my daily walk into the city. Walking from the rural outskirts into the heart of the city, I witnessed different forms of poverty along the way. I also saw this on my trek deep into the Himalayas and my fieldwork in the remote Terai – where the bucolic poverty, on the surface, looked a lot more palatable than the poverty I had witnessed in the densely populated Kathmandu.

After Nepal, I was left with more questions than answers. I was also left with the unshakeable desire to be part of the solution that would address some of the environmental and social issues that I had just experienced. With this new fire, I spent my summer volunteering as an adult literacy instructor in inner-city Chicago, and my free-time in my senior year at Colby College teaching adult literacy in rural Maine – both experiences bringing the consequences of poverty much closer to home.

So, when it was time to graduate and many of my friends were applying for jobs on Wall Street, I applied to the Peace Corps. This experience, not surprisingly, deepened my interest in equity, justice, and the environment.

I served as a Peace Corps volunteer in Northern Malawi, along the rift valley of southern Africa. It was my time in Malawi that helped me to start thinking critically about borders – seeing them as active constructs, rather than passive delineations. In Africa, the history of border-making is so raw and so clearly linked to colonial processes and resource extraction, you can't help but think about their history; that African countries were delineated through processes of colonization, and that the current geopolitical borders do not follow language groups or clan groups. Examples of how gifts of land were given to royalty – such as Mt. Kilimanjaro – seemed unbelievable, but the stories of power were all right there on the map. The lines on the map, for the first time, started coming to life – representing stories of power struggles, victims and victors, haves and have-nots, colonizers and colonized. I witnessed the ongoing struggles related to access to land and cultural fragmentation in postcolonial Africa.

Working as an educator with the Department of Parks and Wildlife further entrenched my interests in borders – borders of a different kind. One of the parks that I worked in, Nyika National Park (which means "where the water comes from"), straddles the northern border of Malawi and the southern border of Zambia. I spent many hours walking along the lines of the park – one foot in Malawi, one in Zambia – seeing zebras, elands, hyenas, and elephants walking between these geopolitical spaces. This imagery was my first rub with the concept of "nature knows no boundaries" – a concept that I see now is not entirely true, thanks to a rich body of geographic literature on the matter (e.g., Fall, 2005; Agnew, 2007; Budds, 2008).

But, coming in and out of the national park, passing through the big arches welcoming guests into a National Wilderness Area, made me think about issues of power, privilege, borders, and historical legacies. On one side of the park, it is "legal" to kill wildlife if it is in your garden (viewed as self-defense). On the other side, it is "illegal" to kill the same animal (viewed as poaching). Anti-poaching activities tend to be full-time jobs for the park rangers. Many of the villagers living alongside the park's boundary would argue that before the park's boundaries were delineated, this was their traditional hunting ground. However, this argument held little weight in the current laws (although many parks in South Africa are now implementing buffer zones to try to mediate the fixity of these borders). Transgressing these spaces and being an outsider to the system incited curiosity about how rules and regulations are applied inside and outside bounded spaces of wilderness. This experience helped me realize that the "winners" and "losers" in this construct are certainly not clear-cut.

I also found that the national parks, although "public places", are places of privilege. I found irony in the fact that many of the national parks in Africa were originally delineated as hunting preserves for the colonial elite. What were once quintessential colonial relics, are now seen as national treasures and, even today, the parks are places of exclusion. For most Malawians, a visit to the national parks is outside of their realm of possibility. As one of the poorest countries in the world, the option to do anything other than directly work towards daily survival is limited. The parks, then, become places for tourists, expatriates, and national elites.

To help bridge this gap, part of my job at the Department of Parks and Wildlife was to take school wildlife clubs on weekend visits into the national parks. For most, including the lorry drivers who transported the children, this was their first time inside the park, with the distance being too far and the expense too great for most to do such a trip independently. So these subsidized trips exposed children to "exotic places" in their own homeland. The goal was to inspire the students to build a conservation ethic into their lives and ultimately become environmental leaders for their community. But the harsh realities that the youth faced – of chronic malnutrition, illnesses associated with malaria, cholera and dengue fever, and the growing pandemic of AIDS (with upwards of 35 percent of the population infected with HIV when I was a volunteer) – tended to overshadow the conservation practices. How could these youth become environmental leaders, if they did not make it past their twenty-fifth birthday? This was another harsh reminder that human health and ecosystem health cannot be addressed independently.

Ironically, it was also my time in Malawi that helped bridge my work back into the North American context. It was my Malawian counterpart – Andrew Bwanali – who posed the simple question: what is the state of the Indigenous people in the United States, the Native Americans? It was not until his question that I ever really considered the impacts of colonization on Indigenous peoples in North America. In my mind's eye, colonial legacies occurred somewhere else, mostly in the Global South.

Having no answer to the question, I turned red with shame. So, with that powerful moment, I was sensitized to issues of colonization and marginalization in a North American context. I made a vow to educate myself about these issues and to work with, or alongside, Indigenous communities as an ally. My first opportunity occurred shortly after returning from Malawi, while I was working as a policy intern with the Conservancy of Southwest Florida.

At that time, the Miccosukee Tribe was in a struggle over water quality rights with the State of Florida. The Tribe was arguing that the nutrient runoff from the upstream sugar plantations was causing damage to their water quality and the ecosystem health of their home territory in the Everglades. Although the downstream water was within the "legal limits" set by the U.S. and upheld by the State, the Miccosukee Tribe successfully argued that the nutrient load was causing severe damage to their coastal ecosystems and negatively impacting their way of life. Participating in the public meetings brought to light the issues of cultural preservation, environmental justice, sovereignty, and water quality (topics that are central to this book).

Wanting to pursue these issues further, I decided to continue my education and joined one of the few environmental programs in the nation that explicitly linked environmental policy and environmental science, at the Huxley College of the Environment at Western Washington University.

So I moved to Bellingham, Washington, which sits in the northwesternmost corner of the United States, with my now-husband, Chad, who had also worked at the Conservancy and had, himself, been heavily influenced by his previous experience teaching along the India–Pakistan border.

I started my degree in Geography with every intention to go back to Africa to pursue my studies. However, along the way, a persuasive mentor, Dr. Don Alper, pulled me aside one day and said: "you know, you could go back to Africa for your studies, or, you have an international border right here, in your backyard." With that simple nudge, I oriented my compass to the Canada–U.S. border, curious as to how I could address "international issues" that were simultaneously "local issues".

For my master's thesis, I studied a small aquifer – the Abbotsford-Sumas Aquifer that was half in Canada and half in the United States. I saw how people living on the aquifer were quick to blame "the other side" for environmental pollutants. I also saw the dedication of people on task forces and working groups to help remedy the issues associated with the elevated nitrate pollutants of the aquifer (the pollutants from dairy and chicken farms, and raspberry fields). What struck me the most, though, was how the two communities – who literally stared at each other across Double Ditch Road, which serves as the international border – had little or no shared identity with each other, and that the people residing on one side of the road considered themselves distinctly "Canadian", while those on the other side of the road were distinctly "American", with one group looking towards Ottawa and the other towards Washington, DC for their political leadership. The different currencies, political systems, fiscal calendars, and migration patterns, all within a few miles/kilometers radius left me scratching my head. Although the population, for the most part, shared the same language, the immigrant populations were distinct; on the northern side of the border, Punjabi immigrants were settling in the lower mainland of British Columbia, while Latino and Russian immigrants were settling in northern Washington State.

Looking at the mechanisms in place to manage water, I was also surprised to see how much work, and how much ongoing collaboration, it took to get people who are part of distinct political systems to work together. This experience, made me start questioning, how are we to govern resources that span political borders when our institutions and frameworks are so bound within a nation-state framework?

This question became central to my dissertation work at the University of British Columbia, where I continued my work on transborder water governance. For my research, I set out to understand the wider trends of the rescaling of transnational water governance along the Canada–U.S. border.

I was surprised to see that the "rise of the local" was often celebrated in environmental governance literature; and more often than not, participation was conflated with decision-making capacity. From my previous work relating to local, transborder groups, such as the Abbotsford-Sumas Aquifer, I had come to know that these groups were certainly engaged in environmental governance activities, but I was not convinced that it was linked to increased capacity or decision-making capability. I was also surprised to see how little discussion was focused on the colonial histories of the border itself; that the border had different histories according to your worldview. The border was largely treated as apolitical and ahistorical in much of the transboundary literature and discussions. So my work sought to bring the border (and the act of bordering) more to the front of the conversation. This was particularly salient for the Indigenous communities whose traditional territories span the international border.

I therefore set out to do a few things with my research: first, to document (and quantify) the rescaling of water governance mechanisms along the Canada–U.S. border, through a survey of supranational, national, regional, and local governance mechanisms over a 100-year period (something I was surprised to see had not been done before)[11] and second, to look at the social construction of borders and the impact of colonial constructs (border-making) on transborder water governance, which was important, particularly – but not solely – in a postcolonial context.[12]

But what really helped me to bring nuance to these questions and to start looking at the issues of transborder water governance was the combination of my graduate experience and my work with Coast Salish communities. After completing my master's degree, I was invited to teach Environmental Studies courses at Northwest Indian College, a tribal college that serves more than one hundred tribes and bands across Canada and the United States. The majority of the students reside within Coast Salish territory, however, the students represent a diverse range of Indigenous communities throughout North America.

Northwest Indian College is located on Lummi Nation (between Bellingham, Washington, and Vancouver, British Columbia), and the traditional territory of the host tribe spans the Canada–U.S. border (part of the Coast Salish cultural group, which plays centrally in my work). I maintained my teaching position while in graduate school, thus grounding me in multiple boundaries. I lived in the U.S., worked in Lummi Nation, and went to school in Canada. I transected multiple boundaries in my daily practice, borders that also had distinct socio-economic and environmental ties.

Although my role as teacher and student (and later, mother) was at times exhausting, it provided me with a tremendous vantage point to keep my work grounded; it allowed me to bear witness to the ongoing legacies of colonial oppression, land disposition, cultural oppression, and the abuses and travesties that continue to haunt generation after generation of Indigenous people. Northwest Indian College is an inspirational place. It is a place where students of all ages (my youngest student was 15, my oldest student was 87) come to better themselves and their community.

Through researching and writing my dissertation and working at the tribal college, my questions of transborder water governance became increasingly linked to issues of environmental and social justice and decolonization. The concepts of environmental degradation, extraterritorial pollution, and externally created rules, regulations and standards were present in the stories of my students (many of whom are fisherpeople). Meanwhile, my studies at the University of British Columbia gave me the conceptual and analytical tools to link these issues to wider academic conversations.

My tenure at Northwest Indian College also exposed me to signs of hope, self-determination, and improved governance. I saw the hard work and dedication of Indigenous leaders and scholars such as Tom Sampson, Billy Frank Jr., Cheryl Crazybull, Greg Cajete, LeRoy LittleBear, David Wilkins, and Winona Laduke, who successfully walk between worlds and provide inspiration to link the work of decolonization with self-determination and environmental protection.

I was also exposed to the work of groups such as the Yukon River Inter-Tribal Watershed Council and the Coast Salish Gathering whose work linked efforts of environmental protection with wider goals of decolonization and self-determination. I became aware of the ongoing fight to harvest shellfish for the Semiahmoo community north of the international boundary.

The stories of my students, my colleagues, and my mentors, together with my exposure to a department full of inspiring critical scholars, imprinted on me this journey that unfolds in the pages that follow. It also prepared me for a brief interlude, which took my family and I away from the Salish Sea to gain perspective in a different region – the Freshwater Nation/Ojibwa Territory of the Great Lakes. As a faculty member at Michigan Technological University, working with the new Great Lakes Research Center and the Environmental and Energy Policy Program, I saw similar trends in the Great Lakes. The issues facing the Great Lakes mirror many of the issues facing the coastal Pacific. The stories of pollutants, boundaries, and self-determination, governance and justice fill the pages that follow. However, as I write this, my family and I have returned to the Salish Sea Basin – a place that has become our true home.

Considering the personal nature of these issues, I felt it important to situate myself within the pages of this text. Together with the stories that I present to you, I wanted to share with you my parable of discovery.

The themes explored in the parable of discovery help to inform the overarching question: how does one make a good upstream neighbor?, by providing more nuance to conceptualizations of governance, borders, power, and justice.

Conclusion

For water – the giver of life – figuring out how to "get along with your neighbor" is of utmost importance. It becomes tied to issues of justice and equitability. And as situations change, so do the relationships. There is constant negotiation and renegotiation, like canoeing in a turbulent river; you need to adjust your steering as you head into the next bend. Just like cooperating with neighbors, it is often difficult to predict what issues will come next, but if you are prepared (in mind and body), the chances of addressing those issues gracefully, successfully, and peacefully are much greater. For water governance, "mind and body" equate to "political will", "institutional frameworks", and "capacity". The next bend in the river includes global climate change, persistent organic pollutants, and endocrine disrupting chemicals – things that were not part of the equation when the original binational treaties were created.

This book allows its readers to bear witness to these powerful cases and see how they both individually and collectively are contributing to transboundary water governance. In a time when it is easy to become overwhelmed with negative stories of environmental and social ills, it is my hope that these cases will provide a ray of hope. The stories show how not only in the face of adversity, but perhaps because of adversity, people are banding together to fight for the health and well-being of their communities. Thus, this story is not just about transnational environmental governance and Indigenous communities, it also provides a parable of how communities can draw strength from hardship.

The book also challenges those in dominant governance frameworks to become more sensitized to the power dynamics associated with governing environmental resources. Even framing water as a "resource", for example, assumes it is something divisible, countable, fragmentable. For many communities, water is a "gift from the Creator", to be treated with great reverence. The chapters that follow help provide examples of how to address the issues of transboundary water governance given different frameworks, histories, and worldviews.

As the conceptualization of the modern nation-state as a "fixed" border is under increased scrutiny, yet fiercely protected in some circles, this is an important time to rethink how we approach transboundary waters. Thus, this work is about strengthening community, individual growth, and reconnections of people to places and their environment. It is also about transboundary water justice, which is intricately tied to scalar politics and the water–justice–power nexus.

The book highlights new water governance frameworks, yet flags important areas requiring further consideration. The cases presented in the pages that follow are not just about how Indigenous communities are working to address environmental issues. Rather, the cases highlight how the acts of addressing environmental issues are leading to wider goals of self-determination. Fighting for culturally significant resources is, in fact, leading to cultural revitalization. This is occurring in interesting and, at times, surprising ways.

Notes

1 Throughout this book, I use the term "Indigenous" as a way to denote people who have a deep and sustained connection to their land and water. As international legal scholar, S. James Anaya, writes:

> [T]he term Indigenous refers broadly to the living descendants of preinvasion inhabitants of lands now dominated by others. . . . They are Indigenous because their ancestral roots are embedded in the lands in which they live, or would like to live, much more deeply than the roots of more powerful sectors of society living on the same lands or in close proximity. Furthermore, they are peoples to the extent they comprise distinct communities with a continuity of existence and identity that links them to the communities, tribes, or nations of their ancestral past.

2 Wolf, 1999; Blatter *et al.*, 2001; Kliot *et al.*, 2001; Yoffe *et al.*, 2003.

3 Molle, 2006, 2009; Sneddon and Fox, 2006; Berry *et al.*, 2012; Vogel, 2012.

4 Biswas, 2004; Mitchell, 2004; Warner and Johnson, 2007.

5 Schmeier, 2013.

6 See, for example: Smith, 1992, 1993, 2000; Delaney and Leitner, 1997; Howitt, 1988, 2002; Brenner, 1997, 2001, 2004; Swyngedouw, 1997, 2004; Marston *et al.*, 2005; Sayre, 2005, 2009; Jonas, 2006; Leitner and Miller, 2007; Kaiser and Nikiforova, 2008; Manson, 2008; Harris and Alatout, 2010; MacKinnon, 2011. For a full review of this literature, see Norman *et al.*, 2012.

7 See, for example: Gibbs and Jonas, 2001; Perreault, 2003, 2005, 2008; Liverman, 2004; Brown and Purcell, 2005; Bulkeley, 2005; Fall, 2005, 2010; Loftus, 2007; Budds, 2008; Loftus and Lumsden, 2008; Molle, 2009; Norman and Bakker, 2009; Bakker, 2010; Dore and Lebel, 2010; Harris and Alatout, 2010; Linton, 2010, Cohen and Davidson, 2011; Vogel, 2012; Jepson and Brown, 2014; Jepson, 2013; Norman *et al.*, 2014.

8 Note: I use the term "upstream" to indicate an aquatic neighbor; it is inclusive of riparian, coastal, groundwater, and watershed neighbors.

9 Rose suggests three orders to analysis: "that of the archive itself; the visual and spatial resources of its contents (the actual pictures); and the desires and imperatives of the researcher" (Crang *et al.*, 2004, p. 416).

10 Thing in itself (German).

11 The survey helped to identify distinct trends of rescaling, the results of which were published in *Annals of Association of American Geographers* (Norman and Bakker, 2009).

12 I draw on Gilbert and Tompkins' (1996, p. 2) definition of postcolonialism as an "engagement with and contestation of colonialism's discourses, power structures, and social hierarchies", which contributes to the political agenda to "dismantle the hegemonic boundaries and the determinants that create unequal relations of power based on binary oppositions".

Part One

Rescaling transboundary water governance

2 Mobilizing theory

"Environmental degradation and social injustice are two sides of the same coin"
—Agarwal, 1982

In this book, I suggest that much is to be gained by analyzing how political and legal regimes of resource management are operationalized on the ground and how these regimes impact historically connected communities in different ways. Unpacking the tensions between the fixity of modern political borders, the fluidity of natural resources (and pollution inputs), and the socio-political implications of governing within these systems (such as "counting" and "dividing" ecosystems) provides more nuance to the practicalities of governing resources in a b/ordered landscape.

For Indigenous communities, the nation-state framework rarely coincides with the traditional territory of their ancestry (Barman, 1999; Harmon, 2000; Simpson, 2000, 2007; Carlson, 2001; McManus, 2005; Miller, 2006).[1] The fragmentation of communities due to the application of the nation-state system has ongoing consequences and power geometries and these consequences are both complex and reflexive (Clayton, 2000; Gregory, 2004; Raibmon, 2005; Harris and Hazen, 2006; Kennedy, 2007; Harris and Millerd, 2010; White *et al.*, 2012). The articulations between mobility, territoriality, and power are central to this understanding (Gregory, 2004; Steinberg, 2009). In addition, the narratives of contact continue to shape contemporary discourse and framings of colonial settlement and the re-fashioning of native space (in the Pacific coastal region of North America, see Boxberger, 1989; Clayton, 2000, Harris and Millerd, 2010). These narratives continue to influence access to and protection of water sources.

The issues surrounding the cases in this book are complicated by extraterritorial pollution inputs, compromised ecosystem health, the policies of respective governments responding differently to the pollution inputs, as well as the framing of issues as "countable" (as in Chapter 5) or "manageable" (as in Chapter 6 and Chapter 9).

Thus, this book focuses both on the historical and contemporary impacts of "colonial bounding" for Indigenous communities, as well as the counter-narratives that are contributing to decolonization, self-determination, self-governance, and environmental protection. This book engages with the cultural and political aspects of transnational water governance by highlighting the counter-hegemonic activities that are emerging throughout Indigenous communities. In the sections below, I outline key literature that helps inform the central questions of this volume.

Drawing on literature from postcolonial theory, Indigenous studies, border studies, environmental governance, and the politics of scale help to usefully inform discussions of the cultural and political aspects of transboundary water governance. Thus, in the volume, I propose three original and key conceptual claims.

First, I suggest that looking at *the colonial legacies of border-making* can help refine critical assessments of transboundary water governance. Specifically, I suggest that all borders (even seemingly "natural" ones) are part of cultural construction and wider politics of power that help define and redefine the landscape. Pursuant to this, I argue that studying transboundary water governance at the *site* of the border helps to move discussions beyond a nation-state framework, challenging what Agnew (1994, 2010) famously refers to as the territorial trap. Agnew suggests that the territorial trap is how "conventional thinking relies on three geographical assumptions: states as fixed units of sovereign space, the domestic/foreign polarity, and states as 'containers' of societies" (1994, p. 53). This is important given the nation-state focus of a significant proportion of the literature on environmental governance, an obvious oversight considering the tendency of flow issues such as water to transcend national borders.

Second, I argue that the application of the *hydrohegemonic framework* usefully being employed by scholars to understand the underlying power dynamics and social and political constructions of water governance – particularly in the Global South (Harris *et al.*, 2013) and the Middle East (Zeitoun and Warner, 2006; Zeitoun and Allan, 2008; Abukhatar, 2013) can be applied to North America. These discussions are particularly poignant for Indigenous communities whose traditional territory spans and pre-dates the colonial constructions of the nation-state.

Third, I explore how *discursive strategies (counter-narratives)* are currently being used to untrench these colonial borders through performative techniques and cartographic strategies. These strategies, thus, contribute to a rescaling of water governance, which contributes to wider goals of decolonization and self-determination. Understanding transboundary governance of water, in other words, requires close attention to the cultural politics of the border.

Whose border? The colonial legacies of b/ordering in water governance

A critical investigation of "the border" and an inquiry into border politics is fundamental, yet rarely applied, to inquiries into transboundary environmental governance. At first brush, this might seem a redundant exercise. How can one talk of *transborder* issues without talking of the border? Observations in the field and through literature reviews reveal that, in fact, it is quite common to omit discussions of *the border*, border politics, or the process of b/ordering in discussions of transboundary environmental governance. In fact, the naturalization of borders as *a priori* containers of State power is pervasive throughout the governance literature and continues to guide conventional thinking (Newman, 2002, 2006; Agnew, 2010, 2012; Fall, 2010; Popescu, 2012).

However, political borders are not passive, unproblematic backdrops that neatly bound national identities and peoples (Sack, 1986; Anderson, 1991; Ó Tuathail, 1996; Newman, 2002, 2006; Paasi, 2009). Rather, contemporary political borders are active sites, which provide great insight into political processes and power relations. As Knight (1982, p. 517) eloquently reflects: "Territory is not; it becomes, for territory itself is passive, and it is human belief and actions that give territory meaning". The acts of nation-building or entrenching borders, however, are discursive acts that occur beyond the site of the border (Balibar, 2004). Nation-building occurs in classrooms when children pledge allegiance to their flag, in sports games when people sing national anthems, during national holidays when people are reminded of their country's greatness, as well as in everyday practices such as obtaining driver's licenses. These national identities, in turn, impact the management of natural resource regimes.

As borders are closely linked to issues of power and identity, investigating the border helps to unpack the social projects that are inscribed upon them (Fall, 2005, 2010) as well as to open up wider questions regarding identity, citizenship, and nationalism (Anderson, 1996).

In recent years, border studies have moved away from the predominantly International Relations model, which privileges the nation-state as the sole site of analysis, to a more nuanced understanding of borders as negotiated, reflexive, and wrought with power dynamics (Balibar, 2004; Kostovicova, 2005; Agnew, 2007; Fall, 2010; Furlong, 2006; Norman and Bakker, 2009). Works in postcolonial studies have helped to articulate power-dynamics associated with the ongoing legacies of colonial boundary-setting (Balibar, 2004; Sundberg, 2004, 2008).

The ongoing legacies of these colonial constructions – including both national borders and Indigenous reserve/reservation borders – continue to influence daily practice (Braun, 2002; Harris, 2002; Evenden, 2004; Holifield, 2010, 2012; Norman, 2013). Projects such as identifying "hydrohegemony" and "transboundary water justice" have also brought these discussions more into focus (Zeitoun *et al.*, 2013).

Furthermore, although the geographic literature provides avenues to explore power dynamics related to borders (or the act of "b/ordering" as van Houtum *et al.*, 2005 suggest), many of these ideas have yet to be translated to the administrative practices of environmental management that transgress neatly bound jurisdictions.

Sovereignty, the State, and the citizen

Within a modern state system, sovereignty is often considered the foundation of State power. Clearly defined and well-protected borders are considered a key component in rationalizing and upholding state sovereignty (Brown and Purcell, 1995; Gilbert, 2007). However, the power relationships are more complex than just maintaining a sovereign state. As Mitchell Dean explores – drawing on

Foucault's work – three lineages of power, sovereignty-discipline-government, describe the modern forms of state authority, which are exemplified by the geopolitical form of the State (Dean, 1999; Gilbert, 2007). Disciplining citizens to uphold and protect the welfare of the State through individual actions is central to "bounding" nation-state borders and "securing".

As Michel Foucault explains, through his work on governmentality, the mechanisms for protecting a population are no longer just the sovereign protecting territorial peripheries. Rather, a shift occurs in eighteenth-century Europe, from a "form of power targeted on a territory to a form of power bearing on a population" (Donzelot, 1997, p. 3). Or, as explained in the *History of sexuality Vol. 1*, and the beginning of his work on biopower, the population is governed from the "right of death" to the "power over life" (Foucault, 1979). The idea of the sovereign protecting itself from the outside and the inside (from external threats *and* by educating its population to uphold and protect the state) diversifies the methods by which the State is protected. As Donzelot (1997, p. 5) explains,

> In place of the necessity to compel obedience in order to ensure the safety of his territory, the sovereign opts for the proper use of freedom in order to maximise the security of the population.

This follows Paasi's (1999) observation that the creation of a border is simultaneously discursive and material, a vehicle for the internalization of state power and nation-building, in which national identity is simultaneously materially bounded and discursively self-policed. The federal practice of tightening borders serves as a way to demarcate the "us" and "them" – or, where the "we" starts and "them" begins (Brady, 2000, p. 173). These practices reify dichotomous worldviews, which are tightly bound within the political demarcations of a nation-state framework. In turn, citizens internalize (or metabolize) these boundaries and reproduce them throughout the whole nation (not just at the ports of entry). This idea of decolonizing the mind, that Indigenous scholars advance (for example Smith, 2002; Wilson, 2008; Absolon, 2011), is a fundamental component of building robust governance models. This work bucks the dominant frameworks and encourages people to see fully the power dynamics associated with governance systems, particularly transboundary governance models.

Where the border begins – Treaty of Westphalia

Although it is difficult to pinpoint a time in history when a boundary became conflated with citizenship and nationhood, many scholars of international relations point to the Peace of Westphalia (1648) as that very defining moment (Jackson and Owens, 2005). What has come to be known as the Westphalian system marks a transition away from city-states and towards governments of larger territorial units, in which the nation comprises the territory and the people inhabiting the land. Thus, it is only in relatively recent history that territorial power and sovereignty have been conflated into distinct territorial units that can be determined by abstract concepts such as latitudinal lines (e.g. the 45th and 49th parallel) that have little or no reference to major water sources. For those interested in water governance, this transition is of importance as it places the resources (including water) *inside* the purview of these boundaries and requires negotiations with "foreign neighbors" to determine water rights and uses.

For the Canada–U.S. border, the demarcation of the border consists of a patchwork of treaties and agreements that roll out through various wars and negotiations, which I briefly outline in Textbox 2.1. Although the short history of "how the international border came to be" may seem like an interesting series of events that passively occurred over time, something largely unconsidered in the transboundary water governance literature is that this series of events paved the way for Western expansionism and ultimately carved the landscape into two nations, which has had everlasting – and often devastating – impacts on the original inhabitants of the region. Even with mechanisms such as The Treaty of Amity, Commerce, and Navigation, Between His Britannic Majesty and the United States of America, 1794 (or the "Jay Treaty"), which included a mechanism to assure Indigenous communities "free movement and free trade between nations", history tells us otherwise. Article 3 of the Treaty states:

> It is agreed, that it shall at all times be free to His Majesty's subjects, and to the citizens of the United States, and also to the Indians dwelling on either side of the said boundary line, freely to pass and repass, by land or inland navigation into the respective territories and countries of the two parties on the continent of America, (the country within the limits of the Hudson Bay company only excepted).

Because of the Treaty, the U.S. Embassy is guided under the premise that: "Native Indians born in Canada are therefore entitled to enter the United States for the purpose of employment, study, retirement, investing, and/or immigration". And Hele (2005) deftly reflects that this clause is responsible for most of the Indian claims. Despite this powerful Treaty, experiences show that the impacts of colonization (and b/ordering) run deep. As this book explores, this b/ordering, in turn, impacts how water and marine resources are governed.

What is water?

A fundamental question, as it relates to worldviews, is "what is water?" For environmental governance, this question is multilayered and includes the material itself – is water a resource? Is it measurable and divisible among people? Is it a human right? Is it a responsibility? Or is it a gift from the Creator? A starting point in this conversation may very well be in the question that geographer Jamie Linton asks in his thought-provoking book, *What is water: the history of a modern abstraction* (2010). Linton examines the social construction of water and how humans' relationship to water has changed over time. The application of this question, for the purpose of this book, is how has water changed from a *natural right* or *gift* to a *resource*. The extension of abstracting water into a resource poses the risk of commodification – a journey that political ecologists and critical geographers such as Bakker (2005, 2013) consider a slippery slope. Similarly, for Indigenous peoples, the abstraction of water into a commodity is fundamentally counter to the spiritual elements of water as a lifesource (Phare, 2009).

Water governance

Broadly, water governance debates address the mechanisms and institutional frameworks through which decisions about water are made. It is important to emphasize here the distinction between government and governance, as the decision-making frameworks discussed here (and elsewhere) extend far beyond the reaches of conventional government mechanisms. Indeed, the differences between government and governance hold significant implications for organizational structure and participating actors, particularly, but not solely, for Indigenous communities. One way to distinguish between the two is that "government" often refers to a branch or authority of a political authority (such as a nation, state, or municipality) taken as representing a whole, whereas "governance" is the *process* in which multiple actors, including civil servants and stakeholder groups, participate in the decision-making process (Bakker, 2010; Norman *et al.*, 2013). It is important to note here that the procedural dimensions of governance are as much about the processes of decision-making as they are about its outcomes (Norman *et al.*, 2015).

Indeed, procedural differences are, in large part, how governance is defined. Zimmer and Sakdapolrak (2012) categorize a variety of definitions of "governance" into two groups: the descriptive and the analytic. Descriptive characterizations see governance as focusing on "identifying, characterizing and explaining changes in ways of steering and reformulates classical concerns of political science" (Zimmer and Sakdapolrak, 2012, p. 327). This approach explores the emergence of new actors, modes of communication, and organizational structures (i.e. Swyngedouw, 2005), as well as the inclusiveness of non-state actors (Biermann *et al.*, 2009; Norman and Bakker, 2009). As Chandhoke (2003, p. 2959) reflects: "we have witnessed a shift from hierarchical and rigid government to flexible forms of governance in which the state is but one actor among several cooperating entities". In other words, a descriptive characterization of governance highlights the multiplicity of actors involved in the governance process.

The second approach uses governance as an analytical concept. Scholars employing this approach explore the *processes* that societies undertake to steer themselves and how negotiating between actors informs this process (see for example Schmidt, 2007; Harris and Alatout, 2010; Vogel, 2012). This approach examines where and how governance takes place; from this vantage point, "there has been no transition from government to governance; rather we have witnessed a change in governance modes" (Zimmer and Sakdapolrak, 2012, p. 327). For example, as Budds (2009) shows, governance occurs in daily interactions and in multiple, non-contiguous spaces. In this approach governance occurs within and beyond the formal negotiations that occur between fixed groups such as stakeholder groups, government agencies, and business groups (Zimmer and Sakdapolrak, 2012).

The distinction between government and governance matters because the chapters in this book are concerned both with the processes used to make decisions about water, as well as the relationships between Indigenous communities, governmental and extra-governmental actors in the decision-making processes. In earlier work, I explored the ways in which subnational and extra-governmental actors are increasing involved in decision-making processes with respect to transboundary waters – a domain over which national governments have had almost exclusive control since the colonial imposition of the boundary itself (Norman and Bakker, 2009). Moreover, the tensions between water as a fluid, boundary-crossing substance, and the fixed jurisdictional scale for management, necessitates close attention to the politics of scale (see Norman *et al.*, 2015). Thus, decisions about water are *necessarily* (if often implicitly) decisions about what actions are to be taken at what scale.

Governance models that follow State regimes tend to treat nation-state systems unproblematically, or naturalized and abstracted as a bounded demarcation of political power (Brenner *et al.*, 2003). For example, as explored in Chapter 9, when Luna/*Tsu-xiit* "the lost whale" transgressed from U.S. waters to Canadian waters, a slew of agencies and personnel were required to handle this "international/ multijurisdictional incident". In this complex case, I suggest that questioning how managers are able to transcend b/ordered spaces when they are fixed to national standards, protocols, and rules – let alone transcend boundaries of human–animal transmogrification – provides an impetus to re-evaluate the fixity of these systems.

Transcending these nested boundaries relates to postsovereign framing of border studies and posthumanist thinking for animal geography. In both cases, the need remains to (re)locate power dynamics within the "naturalized system".

Governance systems and worldviews

As the chapters in this book will demonstrate, governance systems, themselves, are not politically neutral. Rather, belief systems are embedded within the production of science, and carried out within governance practices. The notion that Western science and policy is based on fundamentally different ideas of nature and science than those outside a Western European tradition is well documented (Berkes, 1999; La Duke, 1999; Cajete, 2000; Little Bear, 2000; Wildcat, 2004). The idea that these systems are "dependent on the culture/worldview/paradigm of the definer" (Little Bear 2000, p. ix) is also explored in science studies, more generally (e.g. Latour, 1999; Whatmore, 1999, 2002).

Some scholars engaging in topics of Indigenous studies articulate the components of traditional ecological knowledge (TEK) as a combination of knowledge systems, systems of practice, and belief systems (Gadgil *et al.*, 1993; Berkes, 1999). Reo

(2011) stresses that these systems are both interconnected and inseparable (see also Nadasdy, 1999, 2006; Menzies and Butler, 2006).

Literature within Native Science identifies that one of the fundamental differences between Western and non-Western views of nature is the placement of humans within or outside nature. As Cajete (2000, pp. 26–27) explains, "Western science and society perpetuate the illusion of 'objective' detachment and psychological disassociation" whereas Indigenous Knowledge or "Native Science continually relates to and speaks of the world as full of *active* entities with which people engage". Thus, the Western tradition of Science often places humans *outside* of the "natural" system looking down; conversely, in many Indigenous traditions, nature and culture are not separate entities, rather relationships are both reflexive and collapsible – where human and animal forms are easily interchanged.

These sometimes conflicting worldviews of nature–human relationships are complicated under the task of environmental management. Nadasdy (2004) expertly describes the complications related to co-management in the Yukon Territory in his book, *Hunters and bureaucrats*. In this study, Nadasdy (2004) shows how embedded belief systems frame the relationship between land and people – and people tasked to "co-manage" are asked to operate in a foreign framework. Practices such as enumeration of resources have built-in power dynamics, which the burgeoning politics of calculation literature links directly to colonial forces (Mitchell, 1991; Elden, 2007).

Thus, when the differences between the foundational belief systems go unrecognized or unarticulated, complications occur. For example as Reo (2011) articulates:

> Many initiatives that engage tribes and their TEK holders only seek tribal input, such as biological data, that is most easily integrated into existing management structures. Increasing attention on tribal belief systems would provide a more holistic understanding that could benefit TEK-related initiatives. Such a shift could reduce misunderstandings about tribal natural resource perspectives and lead to insights valuable for society at large.

The Case of Luna/*Tsu-xiit* explored in Chapter 9 exemplifies the issues of miscommunication related to science and governance that Nadasdy (2004) articulates so well. The lack of basic understanding of the fundamental belief systems of Indigenous peoples is at the root of the majority of the governance failures between environmental managers and Indigenous peoples (Awuah-Nyamekye and Sarfo-Mensah, 2011; Reo, 2011; Sarma and Barpujari, 2011). This is seen the world over: Awuah-Nyamekye and Sarfo-Mensah (2011) show how the dichotomy of policy versus Indigenous spirituality has had grave impacts on contemporary distribution of land in Ghana. Sarma and Barpujari (2011) examine how, in India, culture, particularly the cosmologies and religious beliefs of Indigenous communities, have implications for the conservation of natural resources.

A foundational difference between TEK and other models of knowing is the importance of place in the creation of developing frameworks – where the humans and animals mutually evolve through reflexive relationships with the surrounding environment. This place-based model is reflected in contemporary ideologies and governance frameworks. Stumpff (2010) explores this concept with the connection between tribal systems and environmental management in the context of the Bison for Confederated Salish and Kootenai tribes in Western North America. Stumpff (2010, p. 9) writes:

> Tribal systems of land values and landscape-level management differed from private and public land management as it developed within the framework of the U.S. Government. The relationship between people, time and the land was understood through different principles. An important traditional principle was that the relationships within an ecosystem came from a concept of mutual evolution – the idea that peoples, species and processes adapted together in the most useful and efficient ways.

This concept of mutual evolution holds true for many of the Indigenous communities discussed in this book, including the Mowachaht/Muchalaht First Peoples and the Coast Salish First Peoples – where complex dynamics and histories exist between humans and animals, particularly orcas (Drucker, 1951).

Politics of scale

A growing body of literature supports the argument that a scalar perspective is crucial for understanding water governance (Swyngedouw, 1999; Harris, 2002; Sneddon and Fox, 2006; Perreault, 2008; Feitelson and Fischhendler, 2009; Harris and Alatout, 2010; Norman *et al.*, 2013). Harris and Alatout (2010) suggest that more explicitly linking the literature on state and nation-building to water governance and scale would help strengthen our understanding of the complex dynamics characterizing the relationship between nature and society (see also Kaiser and Nikiforova, 2008; Kuus and Agnew, 2008). Further, they insist that attention to the "iterative process and practices" that seemingly fix scales is critical (Harris and Alatout, 2010, p. 149). To this end, the geographic literature has begun documenting how performative acts and social movements are facilitating territorial rescaling (Cohen and Harris, 2014). In this book, I explore how performative acts are helping to produce discursive acts of decolonization for the Indigenous groups in the Salish Sea Basin, Yuquot Basin, Yukon River Basin, and the Great Lakes Basin.

Seeing scales as constructed and fluid rather than pre-defined and fixed opens up conceptual space to frame scale as a *process*. Towards that goal, MacKinnon (2011, p. 22) has suggested replacing the established concept of *politics of scale* with *scalar politics*, arguing, "it is often not scale per se that is the prime object of contention, but rather specific processes and institutionalized practices that are themselves differentially scaled". Although the focus on process is not necessarily a new idea (see Jonas, 2006), the need to remain mindful of scalar politics is salient particularly in management and policy realms where lexicons are often less precise (see, for example, McCarthy, 2005; Cohen and Davidson, 2011, Cohen, 2012; Cohen and McCarthy, 2014). Cohen (2012) for example, shows that the watershed scale remains undertheorized and that the conflation between governance tools and governance units has muddied the waters for analysis.

Counter-hegemonic tools for change

Strategic essentialism

Strategic essentialism is a concept that is often used in postcolonial studies to theorize citizen group unification. The term was coined by Spivak (1987) to describe a strategy that nationalities and ethnic and minority groups can use to present themselves as unified. Although significant differences may exist between individual members of these groups, the process of "essentializing" the group members to represent a singular (and simplified) group identity has proved to be a successful technique to achieve goals (Spivak, 1987, 1988, 1996; Guha and Spivak, 1988). The Indigenous communities, such as the Coast Salish and Ojibwa Nations, discussed throughout the volume, provide examples of how cultural groups whose membership represents a diverse range of bands, tribes, and family recognize the benefits of strengthening the connections (based on a common language and traditional networks) both to support the cultural revitalization of individual tribes and bands and to help negotiate without external agencies.

Performativity

Similarly, techniques such as performance theory (Mountz, 2010) and counter-mapping (Harris and Hazen, 2006; Sparke, 1998, 2006) are documented strategies for activists to re-imagine and recreate new space. "Performance theory" is an analytic to help describe and understand the production of scales and scalar hierarchies (Mountz, 2010). The concept of performativity was conceived through the work of critical gender theorist Judith Butler (1997) and has been taken up by scholars in a range of disciplines, particularly feminist theory, cultural studies, and philosophy. Her work is also very influential with critical geographic scholars engaged in issues of environmental governance (see, for example, Sundberg, 2004, 2011; Harris, 2006). Performance theory helps us understand how discourses and practice can help create (or recreate) new geopolitical scales (Brown and Purcell, 2005; Kaiser and Nikiforova, 2008; Harris and Alatout, 2010; Cohen and Harris, 2014).

Counter-mapping, social media, and virtual rescaling

In addition, cartographic tools such as "counter-mapping" can be used to present physical spaces as unified. Increasingly, Indigenous activists' movements have successfully employed tools of counter-mapping to assert rights over land (see Wainwright and Bryan (2009) for examples in South America). In the Salish region, this occurred as a visualization of the Salish Sea (see Rose-Redwood, 2011), which was used for 20 years by environmental groups and Indigenous communities, prior to the official naming of the Salish Sea in the records of Canada and the United States (Tucker, 2013; Norman, 2013). Counter-mapping was also used for the creation of the British Columbia Treaty groups mentioned above (Sparke, 1998; Thom, 2010) and is integral to the processes of creating – and sustaining – the Coast Salish Gatherings.

Social media is another tool used in the counter-mapping project to virtually rescale regions. Digital platforms help share information, unify voices, and build momentum for collective causes. This is noteworthy particularly for the younger generation who are able to navigate sophisticated technologies, while promoting shared causes – most notably, language revitalization and environmental causes.

In several cases presented in this book, Indigenous communities – particularly in the Salish Sea, the Great Lakes, and the Yukon River – employ digital media and shared platforms to aid in environmental protection activities. Digital platforms afford the opportunities for Indigenous communities to advance their goals through participation in virtual platforms that are not bound by nation-state frameworks. Rather the "boundlessness" of digital platforms contributes to a virtual rescaling, which is likely to contribute to goals of self-determination and empowerment. The use of collaborative media platforms can also be very empowering for those in rural, remote, and isolated communities where a sense of "connectedness" to the outside world has in times past led to feelings of desperation and isolation. In communities where many of the ills that are facing them are from outside sources (extraterritorial pollution, poverty due to limited opportunities, global climate change) it is quite easy to be overwhelmed with helplessness. However, being connected – even virtually – can contribute to a sense of being. This "virtual rescaling" can be powerful, as it transcends a nation-state framework (and in essence is counter-hegemonic).

Conclusions and reflections

In this chapter, I have introduced some of the key concepts that ground and influence this work. I suggest that looking at the colonial legacies of border-making can help refine critical assessment of transboundary water governance. In particular, I suggest that bringing together works in border studies, environmental governance, and the politics of scale helps to understand the underlying power dynamics and social and political constructions of water governance. Lastly, I suggest that looking at discursive strategies (such as creating counter-narrative) helps to untrench the daily influences of colonial boundaries that are often unseen by the uncritical eye. Insights from postcolonial theory and feminist geography and the application of performance theory, critical cartography, and counter-mapping can help with these decolonizing practices. Ultimately, this chapter provides a rationale for closer attention to the cultural politics of the border and how these politics influence transboundary water governance practices and policies.

Throughout the chapters that follow, I engage with literature related to the politics of scale, border studies, and water governance to help understand the cultural politics of transboundary water governance, particularly for Indigenous communities in a postcolonial context. I explore how water governance can link to decolonization and self-empowerment. I also show how performative and discursive techniques help to actively rescale a region, challenge colonial boundaries, and also work towards goals of self-governance.

The examples provided in this volume continue to challenge implicit assumptions about the fixity of territorial scale, by analyzing the creation of social constructions of virtual spaces through digital platforms. This is empowering particularly for Indigenous communities whose goals of self-determination, self-governance, environmental protection, and cultural revitalization often necessitate a reframing or rescaling of fixed colonial boundaries to more traditional boundaries.

Box 2.1 Drawing the lines, treaty by treaty

The first treaty that helped define what is now known as the Canada–U.S. international border was the Treaty of Paris. The 1783 Treaty marked the end of the war between Great Britain and the separating colonies from the United States. Under this Treaty, the 45th parallel established the border between Lower Canada (Quebec) and New York State (including Vermont), while the St. Lawrence River and the Great Lakes became the boundary between Upper Canada and the United States. For many years, this delineation remained vague – and largely theoretical – due to the rugged and forested territory and no clear boundary lines. However, the Jay Treaty of 1794 helped articulate the boundary as a clear line, through the creation of the International Boundary Commission. The Commission, which still exists today, was tasked to survey and demarcate the 45th parallel – a task that proved more difficult than expected due to rugged terrain, inclement weather, and basic survey methods (Savelle, 1940; Barber, 1983).

It was not long after the Jay Treaty that the westward expansion of newcomers led to the creation of a new treaty. The Convention of 1818 articulated the boundary along the 49th parallel between Lake of the Woods (in what is now Minnesota) and the Rocky Mountains (then known as the "Stony Mountains"). However, to the west of the Rocky Mountains the 1818 Treaty was more ambiguous, calling for "co-custody" of the territory that was referred to as "Oregon Country" to the American settlers and "Columbia Department" or "Columbia District" to the Hudson's Bay Company. During the period of co-custody, settlers could claim land on behalf of American or British interests (Savelle, 1940).

Not surprisingly, the co-custody arrangement proved a difficult proposition. Negotiations – and posturing – between interested parties occurred until U.S. President Polk and the British Prime Minister ultimately agreed to demarcate British interests to the north of the 49th parallel and American interests to the south.

During the years of co-custody, the U.S. had made overtures of expanding its claim to the territory upwards to the 54th parallel (U.S. President Polk running on the campaign promise: "Fifty-four forty or fight!"). However, the U.S.–Mexico War tempered the appetite for expansion and the two parties eventually settled their claims through the signing of the 1846 Oregon Treaty (Price, 1967).

The land south of the 49th parallel became known as the "Oregon Territory" with "Washington Territory" being formed in 1853. The land north of the 49th parallel remained unorganized until 1858 when the Colony of British Columbia was formed, which was motivated in large part by the Fraser Canyon Gold Rush and the subsequent fears of renewed American expansionism. In 1866, the two British colonies of Vancouver Island and British Columbia amalgamated when the Colony of British Columbia joined Canada in 1871. Thus, the 49th parallel and marine boundaries established by the Oregon Treaty became the Canadian–U.S. border.

The negotiations for the northern boundary along Alaska, the Yukon Territory, and the province of British Columbia had a long history of dispute, dating back from the Anglo-Russian convention of 1825. The United States inherited the disputed territory with the Alaska Purchase in 1867. The line was finally agreed upon by the federal governments through arbitration in 1903 with the Hay-Herbert Treaty, which, although settling the dispute between Russia and the U.S., did not address issues of Indigenous claims to the land.

Although the Oregon Treaty provided, in theory, a clear boundary line along the 49th parallel, minus Vancouver Island, which was preserved for British interests, ambiguity still existed as to *where* that line actually was. It was not until the Northwest Boundary Survey (1857–1861) that the land boundary was defined, and it was not until 1872 that the water boundary was defined between the Gulf Island and the San Juan Islands (which was predicated by a pig being shot on San Juan Island, leading to the aptly named Pig War of 1859) (Vouri, 2008; Neering, 2011).

Through the 1850s the western part of North America began to feel the impacts of the policy of Manifest Destiny. This, in conjunction with the Donation Land Act of 1850 – which led into the general homestead policy – facilitated an increased population with the arrival of promised land in the Oregon Territory, including Washington (Evenden and Tuberville, 2006).

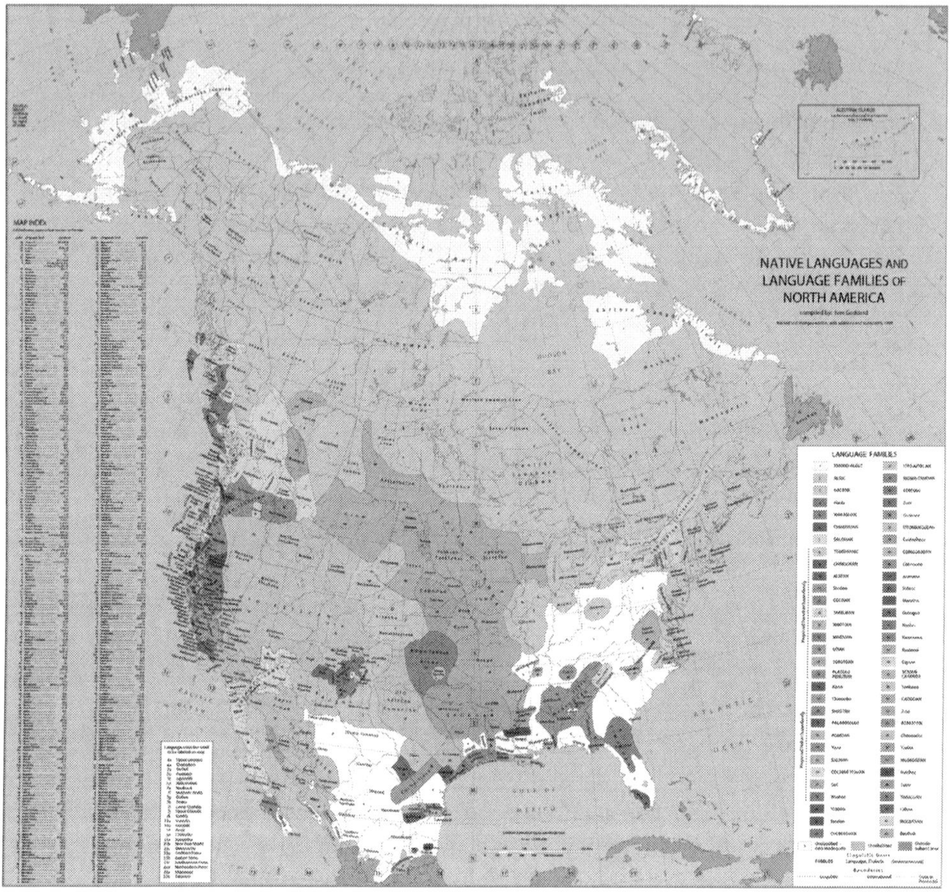
NATIVE LANGUAGES AND
LANGUAGE FAMILIES OF
NORTH AMERICA
LANGUAGE FAMILIES
MAP INDEX

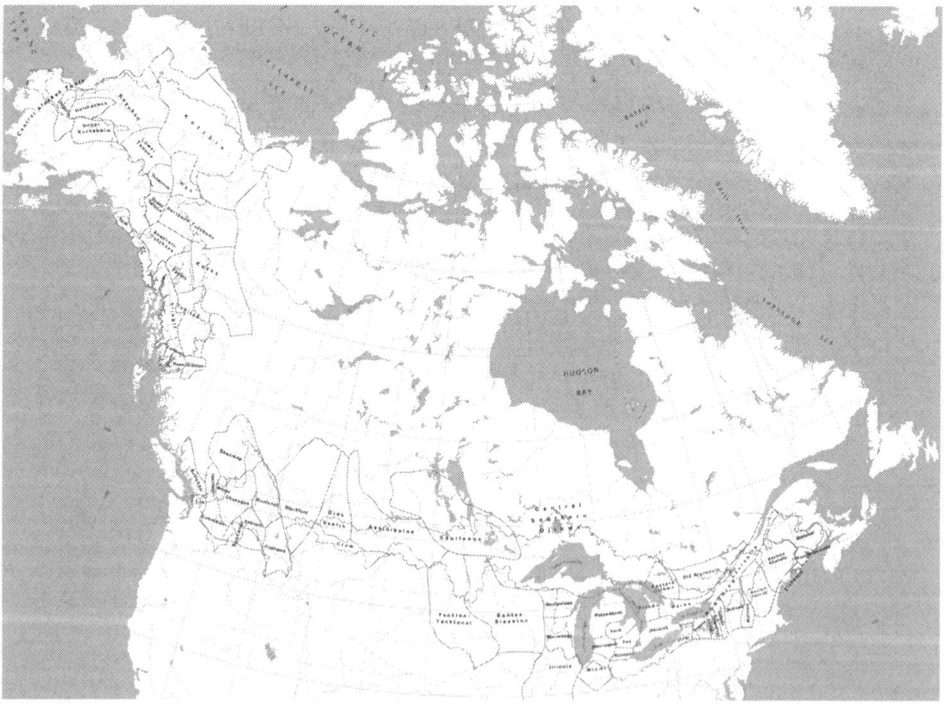
HUDSON
BAY

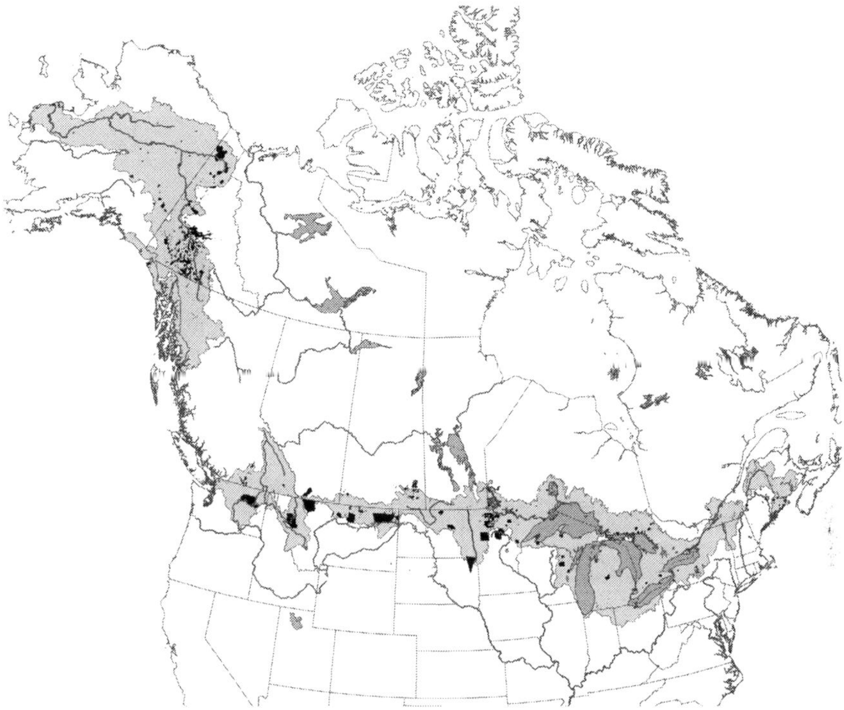

Figure 2.3 Map of Indigenous reserves/reservations within the international watersheds spanning Canada and the United States.

Source: Cartographer: Dan Cole, Smithsonian Institution.

FACING PAGE

Figure 2.1 *(Top)* Map of Indigenous languages and language groups in North America (Goddard, 1997).

Source: Originally published in the Languages volume of the *Handbook of North American Indians* (Goddard, 1997). Reproduced with permission from Smithsonian Institution, Department of Anthropology.

Figure 2.2 *(Foot)* Map of Indigenous language groups spanning the Canada–U.S. Border (based on Goddard's 1997 map).

Source: Cartographer: Dan Cole, Smithsonian Institution.

Box 2.2 Maliseet Nation/Wolastoqiyik (Maine, New Brunswick, and Quebec)

> "Indian Nations had always been considered as distinct, independent political communities, retaining their original natural rights, as the undisputed possessors of the soil . . . The very term 'nation,' so generally applied to them, means 'a people distinct from others.'"
>
> —John Marshall, 1832 Worcester v. Georgia, 31 U.S. (6 Pet.) 515, 561

Maliseet Nation – Houlton Band

The term Maliseet was derived from early contact between the Mi'kmaq peoples and the Early Europeans. The Mi'kmaq referred to their neighbors as "broken talkers" as their dialect was significantly different from their own language. The Maliseet referred to themselves as Wolastoqiyik – People of the Wolastook River (which in English is known as the St. John River). *Wolastoqiyik* means people of the "beautiful river".

The Maliseets are River People who have relied on the Wolastoqiyik basin for sustenance for thousands of years. The basin is one of the largest in the East Coast of North America, with approximately 21,000 square miles of drainage. The Maliseet Nation comprises dozens of bands and tribes in Maine, New Brunwick, and Quebec.

One of the bands in the United States is the Houlton Band of Maliseet Indians, which includes approximately 800 members, who were not officially recognized by the U.S. federal government until 1980 – 200 years after the international border was designated. The Houlton Band started the process of formal recognition in the early 1970s by forming the Association of Aroostook Indians, which included Maliseet members residing in northern Maine and other non-recognized Indigenous groups.

The Meduxnekeag – a tributary of the St. John River – is vital to the cultural and economic well-being of the Houlton Band of the Maliseets. It is a river known for its bountiful brook and brown trout. To ensure the preservation of tribal practices, traditions, and maintaining history, the Houlton Band has actively been purchasing land along the Meduxnekeag River, meaning "rocky at its mouth".

The St. John River and its many tributaries have been the focus of transboundary agreements through the binational organization, the International Joint Commission. Although the inclusion of Indigenous peoples in these processes has been historically limited, recent movements towards watershed boards have opened up the possibility for greater inclusion of Indigenous peoples in the discussions of transboundary waters.

The St. John River and Canada–U.S. transboundary water issues

The international nature of the St. John River has elicited federal attention for quite some time. As early as 1918, a report from the International Joint Commission indicated that the pollution – related to potato starch factories – "... exists on one side of the Boundary line which is an 'injury' within the meaning of the Boundary Waters Treaty of 1909 to health and property to the other". The pollution was referred to as: "transboundary in its effect and extension" (IJC, 1977).

In the early 1960s, Maine and New Brunswick, independently of each other, initiated detailed basin-wide planning studies to maximize resources and to minimize water quality issues. In 1969, Maine created the Northern Maine Regional Planning Commission, and New Brunswick, in 1970, created the St. John River Basin Board. Both agreements had a strong mandate of working cooperatively between countries.

Also during this time, the North Atlantic Treaty Organization (NATO) created the Committee on the Challenges of Modern Society (CCMS) as a way to expand its purview and to address economic, social, and technical issues incurred by its member countries. Inland water pollution was one of the issues the CCMS wished to address and, in 1972, Canada and the United States agreed to work together in a "demonstration of international cooperation in resolving pollution problems in international streams" (IJC, 1977, p. 11).[2] During this time, the two federal governments informed the International Joint Commission of their agreement to run a joint water quality study of the St. John River, to be carried out by the Canada–U.S. Committee.

The IJC study reported that water quality was compromised in the river due to potato starch, pulp mills, and municipal waste. As a result, the two federal governments agreed to undertake actions to mediate the pollution sources and to jointly monitor the water quality of the St. John River at the site of the river.

Several decades later, the neighboring St. Croix River, which also crosses between Maine and New Brunswick, became the first International Watershed Board, designed to "proactively assist the Commission in preventing and resolving disputes regarding the boundary waters of the St. Croix River" and seek to find "local solutions" for the international waterways. A key debate for this region is whether or not alewives should have free passage into the waterways, which, after heated debate, has just been supported by state, provincial, tribal, and federal entities.

Notes

1 Although some Indigenous communities lie within a single nation-state (for example, Aboriginal communities in Australia), the impacts of jurisdictional fragmentation continue to play out through placement onto reserves and inability to inhabit traditional territory.

2 IJC (1977), *Water Quality in the Saint John River Basin.*

3 From supranational to intertribal

Transboundary governance at different scales

Disputes over pollution, water quality, water rights, water diversions, and exports have played out along the Canada–U.S. border since the international border was first demarcated. In response, over the past 100 years, distinct types of transboundary institutions have emerged to address disagreements and facilitate exchange of information. This chapter provides an introductory overview and analysis of four transboundary institutions, operating at different scales, that govern water along the Canada–U.S. border: the International Joint Commission (IJC), the North American Free Trade Agreement's Commission for Environmental Cooperation (CEC), the British Columbia–Washington Environmental Cooperation Council (ECC), and the Yukon River Inter-Tribal Watershed Council. Analyzing these transboundary institutions provides insight into how governance processes operate at different scales, and through different frameworks, mechanisms, and guiding principles.

Analyzing the historical circumstances under which these governance mechanisms were created – including who led the charge and under what socio-political contexts – helps to identify the spatial politics of transboundary water governance, and the colonial legacies they either reify or reject. The historical context in which these institutions were conceived reflects the priorities of the time of development and has much to do with negotiated power dynamics. My aim of historicizing the creation of these institutions is to bring border politics (and colonial legacies) more directly into the discussions of transboundary water governance – something that is largely unconsidered in the environmental governance literature. This provides important context as we move into section two, where I discuss mechanisms that are contributing to the "decolonization" of transboundary water governance.

The chapter starts with a discussion of the signing of the Boundary Waters Treaty (BWT) of 1909 and the creation of the IJC. The second and third sections are more contemporary in focus, with brief overviews of the development of the supranational CEC (1994) and the subnational ECC. The IJC provides a binational perspective; the CEC provides a tri-national perspective; the ECC provides a regional, bilateral governance mechanism relatively autonomous from federal involvement; while the Yukon River Inter-Tribal Council example provides a multinational and intertribal example. This chapter provides an introduction to the IJC, but Chapter 4 goes into more depth about its expanding mechanisms through their International Watersheds Initiative. I chose these four institutions because they emerged under different socio-historical circumstances, they represent different jurisdictional scales, and they have different relationships with the state. Although I could identify other institutions to analyze (particularly the regional, sub-state, and intertribal contexts), these four provide good examples to discuss wider trends. In addition, I can speak to these organizations on a personal level, having either interviewed people who work in these organizations or participated in meetings and workshops hosted by these groups.

Engagement in the governance of transboundary water occurs at various jurisdictional and managerial scales throughout North America (see Table 3.1). These mechanisms also change over time, reflecting different priorities and socio-historical circumstances. Historicizing the development of these transboundary institutions helps to unpack the social projects that are inscribed upon them. This analysis also helps to open up wider questions regarding identity, citizenship, and nationalism.

Table 3.2, for example, identifies five distinct periods of water management specific to the Canada–U.S. border. These include: the Cooperative Development Era, the Comprehensive Management Era, the Sustainable Development Era, the Participatory Era, and a new category, which I refer to as "the Postcolonial Era". These eras reflect different priorities and different interpretations of the hydrological landscape. In addition, the changing patterns of communication between people and social networking have had significant impacts on how local communities are engaged and mobilized into global discussions. Identifying these distinct eras helps to highlight the reflexive relationship between institutional mechanisms and the changing hydrosocial context. Thus, as scholars such as Swyngedouw (2004, 2006), Budds (2009), and Bakker (2013) suggest, water issues are inseparable from the political, economic, and historical circumstances they inhabit. This chapter documents how different governing institutions are conceived – and re-conceived – in divergent spatial and temporal circumstances, and with different priorities in mind. Situating the mechanisms in the specific context where they were created helps to further explain the nuances of the changing patterns of water governance. This analysis is noteworthy particularly in a transboundary context, where different political systems, laws, and values converge.

It is important to note that the first three mechanisms follow state regimes and treat the Canada–U.S. border as a fixed, naturalized, and abstracted bounded demarcation of political power. The third, however, begins to reframe the governing entities to focus on subnational entities, while the last framework begins the analysis of Indigenous-led mechanisms that focus on intertribal water governance. All of the mechanisms are important components of transboundary water governance and reflect changing expectations of water governance (particularly an increase in citizen involvement in the decision-making process and greater consideration of ecosystems in the governance of water).

Table 3.1 Cooperation mechanisms for transboundary water governance

Governing mechanism	*Scale*	*Function*
International Joint Commission	– Binational – Federal – Canada–U.S.	– Quasi-judicial; reviews applications for projects and grants or withholds approval – Advisory role, non-binding – Operates through Reference process – "Prevent and resolve transboundary environmental and water-resource disputes . . . through processes that seek the common interest of both countries"
NAFTA Commission for Environmental Cooperation	– Tri-national – Federal – Canada–U.S.–Mexico	– Advisory role, non-binding – Helps prevent potential trade and environmental conflicts – Promotes the effective enforcement of environmental law, all as part of its mandate under the North American Agreement on Environmental Cooperation
Intertribal	– Multinational	– Ranges from non-binding to treaty-based – Culturally-based; wider interpretation of "water issues" to include human and ecosystem protection; cultural revitalization and decolonizing methodologies
Environmental Cooperation Councils	– Binational – State–provincial	– Advisory role, non-binding – "Help mitigate and address environmental issues of mutual concern"
ENGO/Citizen Groups	– Binational and domestic – Local – Watershed	– Participatory – Action-oriented – Non-binding, non-regulatory – "Consensus based negotiations, and implementation of policies through local voluntary efforts"

The Boundary Waters Treaty (1909): a success?

On 11 January 1910, in Washington, DC, the United States Secretary of State, Elihu Root, and the United Kingdom's (His Majesty's) Ambassador to the United States, James Bryce, signed the *Treaty between the United States and Great Britain relating to Boundary Waters, and Questions arising between the United States and Canada* – more commonly known as the Boundary Waters Treaty of 1909 (BWT). The BWT represents the culmination of years of diplomatic negotiations to ensure "friendly relations" between Canada and the United States and increased public pressure to address growing transboundary water issues.

The main water-related issues facing Canada and the United States during the Treaty's negotiation were: navigation, hydroelectric power generation, allocation of boundary waters for industrial and agricultural uses, and pollution. (It is important

Table 3.2 Eras of Canada–U.S. transboundary water management (1945–2007)

Transboundary water era/Time period	*Role*	*Example*
Cooperative Development		
1945–1965	– Projects of mutual benefit – Federal government encouraged hydroelectric development	– Columbia River Treaty – St. Lawrence Seaway and Hydropower Development – Niagara Treaty
Comprehensive Management		
1965–1985	– Issue-based – Comprehensive river basin planning and more "environmentally conscious" framework – Water expertise built up at federal level	– Great Lakes Water Quality Agreement
Sustainable Development		
1985–2005	– Linking economy and environment – Issues more integrative, anticipatory and preventive	– Great Lakes Annex
Participatory		
2000–current	– Increased citizen participation in established frameworks	– IJC International Watersheds Initiative
Postcolonial		
2000		– Coast Salish Gathering/ Yukon River Inter-Tribal Watershed Council

Source: Adapted from Norman and Bakker (2009).

to note, however, that the broad terms, "pollution" or "environment" were not mentioned in the BWT, rather they employed terms such as "domestic and sanitary uses". The lack of inclusion of these more broadly defined terms continue to play out in the interpretations and applications of the BWT.[1]) Recognizing the importance of these water-related issues, public pressure from individual citizens, lobby groups, and water resource technocrats provided the initial push to develop the BWT (Dreisziger, 1981).

Those advocating for the development of a shared water treaty argued that it would become increasingly difficult to negotiate a "fair" treaty given the growing asymmetry of power between the nations. In fact, representatives of the Canadian Department of Foreign Affairs and International Trade and the U.S. State Department suggested that there was only a brief time in the history of Canada–U.S. relations for the negotiation of a treaty such as the BWT – noting that "the Treaty simply could not be negotiated in today's political climate" (personal communication, 2008). These comments suggest that recent U.S. administrations and elected officials (i.e. senators) would not likely concede authority for the sake of equitable representation.

Like many international mechanisms, issues of state sovereignty are central to the negotiation of treaties. Finding approaches that are mutually beneficial to the signatory parties – but do not restrict sovereign rights to resources – is a delicate balance in international negotiations (Susskind, 1994; Rieu-Clarke, 2005; Schmeier, 2013). For the BWT, negotiating a treaty on a continental scale required Britain (on Canada's behalf) and the United States to agree on the relative authority and scope of its mechanisms.[2] It is important to note that, under this binational framing, the Boundary Waters Treaty did not consider Aboriginal or Treaty rights. Although the International Watersheds Initiative (discussed more in Chapter 4) attempts to widen its purview to include citizens of the basins (including Indigenous communities), they are still considered "stakeholders" rather than equal partners. The framing as "stakeholders" rather than "sovereign nations" with Treaty rights to specific land and water resources remains a significant issue in environmental governance (see von der Porten and de Loë, 2013a, 2013b). Thus, when I explore the guiding questions of this book related to changing governance mechanisms, social and environmental equity, and "good neighborliness", it is imperative to understand that the central mechanism for governing transboundary waters in Canada and the U.S. starts out with a narrow interpretation of the "legitimate actors". The "legitimate actors" problem can be challenged by the consultation process established through Section 35 of the Canadian Constitution Act of 1982, which aims to protect Aboriginal Treaty rights, as well as through key sections in land claim agreements that require First Nations to be consulted/involved in negotiations related to lands and waters. Similarly, Treaty tribes in the U.S. are asserting their inherent and negotiated rights to water through established Treaty rights. To reach the potential of these, however, often becomes an issue of limited capacity – in the both timely and expensive consultation and legal process. Thus, although the purview is widening slightly (through watershed boards as discussed in Chapter 4), the original framework remains very much focused on a federally controlled, top-down approach, and the issue of capacity for Indigenous communities to actively participate in the process requires additional attention.

Strength of the Boundary Waters Treaty

Another critical point in the negotiation of the Boundary Waters Treaty between Britain and the United States (which continues to be important today) was determining the strength of the proposed commission. The settlement of the Treaty was delayed as the governments debated whether to assign the commission "real arbitral power or merely to assign a more limited mandate to recommend courses of action, which the governments could accept or reject as they saw fit" (Carroll, 1981, p. 44). Canada preferred the "stronger" version (the Gibbons-Clinton draft), which allowed for a commission with authority over the final decision and the creation of a supranational court to adjudicate boundary water disputes. The United States opted for the "weaker" version that limited the arbitral powers of the proposed IJC. The U.S. position is unsurprising given that during the time of the Treaty negotiation, the Harmon Doctrine[3] – which maintains that a country is sovereign over the portion of an international watercourse within its borders – was at the forefront of American thinking (McCaffrey, 1996).

In the end, the "weaker version" of the Treaty was adopted. Although some considered the limited scope of the Treaty a major concession by Canada at the time, many water policy experts suggest that the limited arbitral capacity is actually a key contributor to the longevity of the BWT, ultimately suggesting that governments would likely shy away from the IJC if the mechanisms were too binding or authoritative. This follows the observations within international environmental governance literature that upholding State sovereignty limits international agreements (Adamson, 2005). But, again, a key point to remember in the context of Indigenous governance is that if you are not party to the agreement, you are unable to fully participate on a nation-to-nation basis.

Supporters of the Treaty often describe it as a "resilient document" with the flexibility to adapt to changing border demographics and new demands for water use. Part of this "success" follows Corti's (1997) observation that the commons is best looked after when an immediate and well-defined interest exists and the states are likely to incur costs with its neglect. The socio-economic and political costs associated with the numerous shared waterways suggest that perhaps the success of the BWT was a political inevitability.

Those more critical of the BWT suggest that despite its longevity and flexibility, the Treaty has yet to reach its full potential (Carroll, 1981; Dreisziger, 1981). In fact, many current water managers, particularly at the subnational level, argue that the limited authority of the Commission is a key reason why the BWT consistently fails to live up to its original mandate.

At the very least, the creators of the BWT recognized that conflict involving transboundary water was inevitable – especially in light of the extraordinary length of the border and the large number of water bodies between Canada and the United States (Holmes, 1981). Addressing this point, the BWT puts in place mechanisms to regulate, and if possible, resolve what they refer to as "endless and normal" transboundary disputes.[4] Most notably, Article X of the BWT specifies the creation of the International Joint Commission (IJC), an independent commission to regulate, review, and resolve issues relating to the boundary and transboundary waters of Canada and the United States. At the time of negotiation, two issues – St. Mary and Milk Rivers in the west and the Niagara hydro development in the east – were considered major irritants. Both of these issues were resolved peacefully through employing the BWT (although issues related to the equitability of the allocation of water through the St. Mary–Milk Rivers continues to be a source of consternation between actors (Bankes and Bourget, 2013). An ongoing legacy of the BWT is the establishment of the International Joint Commission, described below.

The International Joint Commission: an arm of both states

> *I do not anticipate that the time will ever come when this Commission will not be needed. I think that as the two countries along this tremendous boundary become more and more thickly settled the need for it will increase . . .*
>
> —Elihu Root, Secretary of State (1909)
> (quoted by Munton, 1981)

The primary purpose of the IJC is to help prevent and resolve disputes relating to the boundary and transboundary waters of Canada and the U.S. Under the BWT, the IJC has administrative, quasi-judicial, arbitral, and investigative responsibilities. The administration powers, detailed in Article VI, include activities such as directing and measuring boundary waters (e.g. the St. Mary and Milk Rivers in Alberta and Montana). The quasi-judicial powers found in Articles III, IV, and VII involve reviewing applications and granting (or withholding) permission for projects that would divert, use, or obstruct treaty waters (Willoughby, 1981, p. 24). Article X outlines the arbitral powers relative to questions arising between Canada and the U.S. However, it is important to note that these arbitral powers have never been employed in the entire history of the BWT and the IJC. Article IX deals with investigative powers affording the Commission the right to examine and make recommendations on water issues along the boundary.

Although the mandate of the IJC is large, the actual number of commissioners is modest. The IJC comprises six members, three appointed by the Governor in Council in Canada and three by the President of the United States and confirmed by the U.S. Senate. Administrative staff support the work of the Commission in offices in Ottawa, Ontario, and Washington, DC A third office in Windsor, Ontario was created by the governments when they signed the Great Lakes Water Quality Agreement (GLWQA) in 1972 and gave the IJC management responsibility. In addition, regional task forces and site-specific governing boards conduct much of the work (as detailed below). This model of governance is framed as a federal–federal model.

Understanding how the IJC inherently reinforces the nation-state is linked to the initial framing set out by the Boundary Waters Treaty. Historically, the IJC has addressed a small number of major disputes in a formal nation-to-nation setting. The scope of the IJC is determined, in part, by the underlying premise that the "authority over water in its own territory is absolute". Thus, to ensure that the IJC does not overstep its authority and become a form of "continental government," the IJC operates through a reference system (Holmes, 1981) – or formal request by each country. Under this system, the IJC becomes involved in an issue *only* at the request of both countries (the United States and Canada). The BWT does not specify or require that both countries must agree on a reference, but all references to date have been joint, and it is now generally accepted (for practical and procedural reasons) that future ones will be as well (Clamen, 2013).

The key issue associated with this, however, is that the interpretation of "nations" is binational and not multinational. If Indigenous nations want to make a reference, they are not considered legitimate requests by the letter of the law. In fact, such a case just occurred in relation to the Pebble Mine, where a consortium of forty ENGOs (environmental non-government organizations) and tribal governments requested the IJC to "examine and report on the water-related impacts from sulfide mining and exploration and development of the Rainy River and Lake Superior Basins". In the official response back, the IJC responded:

> You are correct in noting in your letter "The Boundary Waters Treaty of 1909 provides the principles and mechanisms to resolve and prevent disputes", but it is the government's Treaty. Consequently, the IJC cannot unilaterally undertake a study such as the one you request without approval from the Governments of Canada, and the United States would have to give the Commission a Reference and the associated funding for the Commission to undertake such a study.

Using the words "the government's Treaty" in their response reinforces this idea of the narrow interpretation of nationalism. Although the group was not granted a Reference for study, they were told that a study was underway to develop a Water Quality Plan of Study for the Rainy–Lake of the Woods Basin (which includes looking at sulfides). Operating and problem-solving through International Watersheds Boards (as discussed in the next chapter) may help widen the participation in the process.

Acting without a reference?

The possibility of "acting without a reference" is an important point to consider. At least some commentators have suggested that Canada should have sent a unilateral reference to the IJC on controversial issues such as the Devils Lake between North Dakota and Manitoba, but this did not occur (Brandson and Hearne, 2013). The need for IJC intervention may be obvious and needed, but unless both Canada and the U.S. agree and formally submit a request, the IJC does not intervene. While a solo reference is theoretically possible, it has never occurred – largely because a solo reference would mean that only one party would potentially bear the costs. In addition, the party not agreeing to a reference (either Canada or the U.S.) would likely not make data and information available, which would, in essence, destroy the principle of sound science and joint fact-finding, which is essential to an impartial process.[5]

The receipt of a reference leads to the IJC to establish a panel of experts, typically with an equal number of members from each country to study the issue and make non-biased recommendations. To ensure neutrality, the technical experts operate in their personal and professional capacity as experts in the field, rather than as representatives of a specific agency, or in the interests of their country of origin. The Lake of the Woods and Rainy River Task Force, established in 2010, is an example of a Reference designed to review and make recommendations regarding the binational management of the Lake of the Woods and Rainy River

Basin and the IJC's potential role in this management (Clamen, 2013). The responsibilities of the IJC are, therefore, primarily focused on investigations under references and long-term management of works pursuant to applications. For the reference system to work, the parties need to agree – in theory – to abide by the decision that the independent Commission finds after their investigation. The recommendations set forth by the IJC are non-binding, however, both governments typically do follow the recommendations of the IJC (although, in some cases, after many years have passed).

Important to this book – and the chapters that follow – is that the BWT (and the IJC) are based on *binational* rather than multinational or multilateral purviews. The premise that the BWT works to ensure sovereignty between *two* nations – Canada and the United States – and does not include mechanisms for inclusion of the numerous Indigenous nations inhabiting these spaces reifies governance structures that are based on colonial conceptions of space. In Chapter 1, I began to explore terms of "what makes a good upstream neighbor". In that early examination, an early consideration of "good neighborliness" was being party to the decision-making process. The BWT's initial considerations do not consider Indigenous communities in their framing, thus are not conceived as "neighbors" at all. The narratives that I present in this volume help to explore how these reframings and counter-narratives are occurring and the potential for better capacity for transboundary governance institutions.

Columbia River Treaty – widening the process

That said, this limited framework is under scrutiny. At the time of writing, the Columbia River Treaty (CRT) is under renegotiation. The Columbia River Treaty regulates the largest transboundary hydropower system in North America along the Columbia River, flowing from the western province of British Columbia, through the U.S. states of Washington, Idaho, and Oregon and through hundreds of Indigenous communities that have inhabited the basin continuously for at least the past 15,000 years. The Treaty has the potential to expire in 2024, if the signatories – Canada and the United States – give notice of termination after September 2014. Renegotiation of the Treaty has raised grievances related to lack of protection for the ecosystem (particularly the salmon habitat, which was decimated with the construction of the dams), inequitable cost-share between the parties, and lack of renegotiation of Indigenous rights.

The renegotiation process, to date, has proved to be far more inclusive than the original, narrowly defined Treaty of 1964. First Nations and Tribal governments have been at the table with the regional actors during discussions. The conversations have widened from the original narrow scope of power and flood control, to cultural and environmental considerations. Whether the federal governments agree with the recommendations forwarded on to them by the regional actors is yet to be seen, but the early signs suggest greater inclusion.

In addition, in the Columbia River Basin, a team of regional actors led by the NGO Columbia Basin Trust has actively been working to solicit input from people impacted by the terms of the Columbia River Treaty, in particular, First Nations and Tribes whose social, economic, and cultural fabric is largely disrupted by the constructions of dams, and the decimation of the salmon habitat. The discussions in 2013 showed significantly more inclusion of First Nations and Tribes, as well as inclusion of environmental considerations (both of which were excluded during the original Treaty of 1962). How this participation translates to change, however, is yet to be seen.

Regardless of the outcome of the Columbia River Treaty's renegotiation, the signatories for both the BWT and the CRT do not include the Indigenous nations that inhabit the lands. This exclusion has led to a series of accords and treaties signed by Indigenous governments across the borderland. For example, the Tribal and First Nations Treaty Accord, signed 23 November 2004 at Sault St. Marie, Michigan "demands that the rights and sovereignty of the Tribes and First Nations of the Great Lakes be respected and that any governmental effort to protect and preserve the Waters of the Great Lakes Basin include full participation by Tribes and First Nations." They also pledge, "that we share the interests and concerns about the future of the Great Lakes Waters, further pledging to work together with each other and with the other governments in the Great Lakes Basin to secure a healthy future for Great Lakes". (See Appendix A for full wording of the Accord.[6]) As a way to address these issues and to insert themselves into the conversation of transboundary water governance, a number of formal mechanisms, treaties, and

Figure 3.1 The first meeting of the International Joint Commission, 1912.

Source: IJC, Ottawa (used with permission).

accords have, thus, been put forth by Indigenous communities and coalition builders.

Boards

Boards appointed by the IJC facilitate the majority of the IJC's work, engaging in responsibilities around a diverse range of issues (from water allocation to water pollution) within specific transboundary watercourses, and more recently, transboundary watersheds. Board members have a wide range of responsibilities, including: preparing technical studies, reports and plans, monitoring various data networks, and regulating water levels and flows. The Great Lakes Water Quality Board, established in 1978 pursuant to the Great Lakes Water Quality Act, is an example of a long-standing board designed to advise the IJC on Great Lakes' water quality issues. The technical experts are charged to act outside of their national interest and in their "personal and professional capacity".

When conceived in 1913, the boards dealt with issues of water quality and quantity as separate entities. However, concomitant with wider trends in environmental governance that materialized during the Comprehensive Management Era and Sustainable Development Era (see Table 3.2), the IJC proposed a more inclusive and integrative approach to water governance in the late nineties, namely through their proposal to extend the scope of their mandate to include not only boundary *waters*, but boundary *watersheds*. This more integrated approach has been adopted, albeit initially in a form that focuses on the integration of water quality and water quantity rather than on the watershed as a whole. These new watershed boards hold the promise of greater stakeholder and citizen involvement – with the premise that sustained communication will foster cooperative practice. The approach adopts a preventive – rather than a reactive – approach to water governance (Clamen, 2013). However, the watershed approach should not be conflated with equitable participation of actors and decision-making capacity – a common conflation in the governance literature (Norman and Bakker, 2009; Cohen and Davidson, 2011). This is particularly germane for Indigenous communities who hold different priorities within the watershed and different conceptions of transboundary water governance. In short, the *politics* of participation should be closely monitored in the design and implementation of these boards, and the creation of these spaces of governance does not automatically level the playing field for all actors, particularly if the framework reifies established, dominant historical legacies.

Adapting to socio-political change: declining role of references

Trends of governmental devolution and increased local participation consistent with the Participatory Era (see Table 3.2) have influenced the main instruments – the references and applications – used to enable the Commission, which, over the past several decades, have experienced notable decline (Figure 3.2). The declining references and overall changes in the IJC governance structure are indicative of wider trends in environmental governance (Norman and Bakker, 2009).

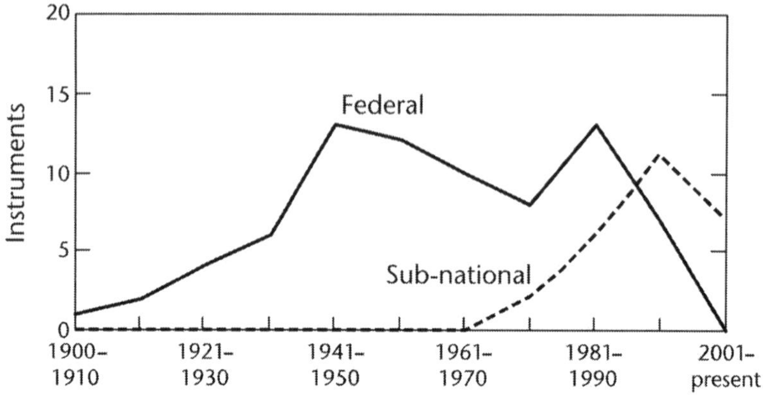

Figure 3.2 Number of International Joint Commission applications and references over time.

Source: Canadian Section of the IJC (2007), presented at a Department of Foreign Affairs, Canadian Conference, Ottawa (Norman and Bakker, 2009).

There are three main theories regarding the decline in IJC references. One is that the increased agency of subnational actors may limit the number of references. As states and provinces become increasingly involved in transboundary governance, the motivation to invite supranational representatives to assist in regional issues can decline. A second reason for the declining references is the lack of government funding (and a lack of political will) to support the boards. A third reason for the decline in IJC references could be related to an increase in the complexity of issues that accompany watershed and ecosystem approaches, which are significantly more complex than the relatively straightforward water quality and water quantity issues. Similarly, the complexity of political diplomacy increases in correlation with greater integration (particularly in relation to greater inclusion of Indigenous peoples and local actors).

Change over time: water-related issues and "glocalization"

In this time of transition, the IJC is attempting to carve out a new future (as explored in greater depth in Chapter 4). Whether the IJC is able to translate its strengths into this new governance model is yet to be determined. One of the main differences in contemporary water issues compared with the early 1900s is the shift in concern from water quantity to water quality. During the early years of the IJC, water quantity issues such as water levels, flow, and allocation were the main areas of focus for references and negotiations, although it is important to note that water pollution of the Great Lakes and other watersheds was also a concern. Towards the latter part of the century, public attention to water quality issues prompted a more comprehensive approach to the governance of water. This shift included a wider interpretation of environmental issues that more generally included ecosystem and sustainable development considerations. As part of this shift, the IJC began to consider water quality and water quantity projects together (rather than as separate entities). During this time, the IJC also attempted to diversify their pool of experts, who until the mid-eighties largely represented senior water resource engineers and managers. Today the experts, IJC staff, and committee members represent a wider range of disciplines (including social scientists, environmental specialists, resource economists and, in some instances, dedicated citizens with on-the-ground expertise and knowledge), and include a number of subnational experts, which reflects the trend of increasing delegation and decentralization more generally. The IJC, however, could be more diverse in its representation. For example, to date, there has never been an IJC Commissioner with Indigenous heritage – an inclusion that would undoubtedly enrich the Commission and contribute to a new vantage point from which to address shared water issues. As federal governments appoint the Commissioners (and not the IJC themselves), it is important to advocate for greater diversity during the nomination process. The IJC has, however, appointed board and task force members with Indigenous heritage, which is encouraging.

Going around the IJC? Provincial–state water agreements

Subnational participation in transboundary governance of water has become increasingly common throughout North America and beyond (Alper and Monahan, 1986; Alper, 1996; Norman and Bakker, 2009). This increased presence of subnational actors is part of a wider trend in environmental governance. In the Global South, for example, integrated watershed management techniques, which rely on the watershed scale as the primary locus of power, have become increasingly prevalent in water-related projects (Lautz and Giordano, 2005; Shah and van Koppen, 2007). Similarly, in Europe, the creation of the Water Framework Directive mandates a watershed approach to all rivers within the European Union, over 50 percent of which are transboundary (European Commission, 2000).

This section addresses transboundary water governance exercised at the provincial–state scale, that is, the relevant states and provinces dealing directly with one another rather than through the federal governments, or the IJC. North American examples include the Gulf of Maine Council, the Council of Great Lakes Governors and Premiers, and the British Columbia–Washington Environmental Cooperation Council. The last example is explored in greater detail below. The enactment of binational governance mechanisms at a subnational level marks a new era in transboundary governance of water.

The British Columbia–Washington Environmental Cooperation Council

It is perhaps unsurprising that one of the most developed province–state transboundary water agreements was developed far from Ottawa and Washington, DC, in a part of the continent with a reputation for environmental concern. Driven by a handful of events (not least of which was the 1988 Grays Harbor oil spill in

Washington, followed by the infamous 1989 Exxon Valdez spill in Alaska), the British Columbia–Washington Environmental Cooperation Council (ECC) was created in 1992 to address the myriad issues shared between British Columbia and Washington.

The ECC provides a forum where officials, mostly representing regional or state/provincial governments, can bring initiatives forward and share information. It also provides a process for formally established task forces, work groups, and committees to address identified priority areas.

The rescaling of environmental governance is not necessarily a linear process; rather, it is a process of informal diffusion of responsibility in which different scales can reassert authority at critical moments. Both strong leadership and the presence of crisis are likely agents of change. In the British Columbia and Washington example, strong leaders play an important part in shaping transboundary governance, regardless of scale (Alper, 1997). Key leaders, from the governor and premier to local mayors and NGO (non-governmental organization) directors, provide critical roles in shaping transboundary environmental governance agendas (Van Rooy, 1997, 2004; Norman and Melious, 2008). This is true also in the Indigenous-led mechanisms for change, where sustained relationships between Tribal and First Nation leaders helped establish intertribal Councils.

The friendship and shared commitment to environmental issues of then-governor Booth Gardner and then-premier Mike Harcourt was instrumental for the creation of the ECC (Jolly, 1998). Harcourt himself reflected in an interview that the political similarities between himself and Gardner were instrumental in moving the idea from conception to reality (personal communication with Harcourt, 2007). Thus, in many ways, their political will and shared vision drove the conception of a binational institution – an example of how informal governance mechanisms beget mechanisms that are more formal.

Like strong leadership and existing relationships, crisis consistently serves as an impetus for political change. Kaika (2003), for example, shows how the naturalization of water as a "scarce resource" drove political change in the 1989–1991 Athens drought. Similarly, Nevarez (1996) shows how an "environmental crisis" – a drought in Santa Barbara, California – helped to streamline political agendas. In the case of the British Columbia–Washington Environmental Cooperation Council, a crisis served to transition dialogue into action. The leaders of the day conceived the ECC; however, in order for the vision of transnational environmental governance to transition into action a concrete impetus was required.

Genesis of the British Columbia–Washington Environmental Cooperation Council: a story of oil and water

On 22 December 1988, 230,000 gallons of high-grade gasoline oil spilled into the ocean near Grays Harbor, Washington. The spill affected more than 110 miles of scenic coastline on the Olympic Peninsula and the coast of Vancouver Island (Jolly, 1998). The thick oil covered the wings and feathers of wintering shorebirds such as the black-bellied plover and the western sandpiper. Scores of volunteers and wildlife biologists convened at the beaches in an attempt to clean the grounded birds and the surrounding environment (Larsen and Richardson, 1990).

The international scale of the spill – coupled with the lack of plans to deal with such a disaster – prompted officials in Washington and British Columbia to put in motion a series of actions to coordinate transboundary water issues. The Director of the Washington State Department of Ecology at the time, Christine Gregoire, considered the Grays Harbor spill a key event for the development of regional governance of shared resources. At a keynote address to participants of the Georgia Basin–Puget Sound conference in Seattle, Washington (2005), Gregoire (who then held the post of Governor of Washington) reflected:

> As the oil spread from the Washington coast into the waters of British Columbia, I thought to myself . . . 'OK. What next? Who do I call? What actions do I take? This is now bigger than the State of Washington.' This frightening experience led me to think critically about how we coordinate these types of issues. Ultimately, it led us to develop new systems for managing binational resources.

In response to the Grays Harbor spill, state and provincial officials created the British Columbia–Washington Oil Spill Task Force to investigate the prevention of future oil spills, to coordinate emergency responses to future spills, and assess methods for expediting compensation claims. However, an even bigger spill led to the creation of a more expansive binational governance system in the Pacific region.

On 24 March 1989, the *Exxon Valdez* ran aground in Prince William Sound, Alaska. Ironically, the British Columbia–Washington Oil Spill Task Force held its first meeting just one day before the *Valdez* spill. The timing of this event, and the high-profile media coverage of the *Valdez* spill, helped create a swell of momentum for the creation of a more comprehensive governance mechanism to address multijurisdictional governance issues surrounding oil spills and water quality. The original task force grew to include Oregon, California, Alaska, and later Hawaii in what is now called the British Columbia/States Oil Spill Task Force (Jolly, 1998) – a mechanism that remains active today.

Environmental Cooperation Agreement/Environmental Cooperation Council

The success of the Oil Spill Task Force and the momentum gained through the concern for future environmental crises helped provide the impetus for British Columbia and Washington to expand their efforts into general environmental areas of shared concern (Jolly, 1998). The political climate and leadership of British Columbia and Washington also aided the expansion at the time.

Governor Booth Gardner and Premier Michael Harcourt formalized this relationship in May 1992 with the signing of the British Columbia–Washington Environmental Cooperation Agreement (ECA). This agreement committed the two jurisdictions to "promote and coordinate mutual efforts to ensure the protection, preservation and enhancement of our shared environment for the benefit of current and future generations" (ECC, 2013). It also committed the governments to develop, and implement, a governance instrument to address environmental issues of mutual concern.

As a result, the British Columbia–Washington Environmental Cooperation Council (ECC) was established. The ECC provides a forum where officials, mostly representing regional or state/provincial governments, can bring initiatives forward and share information. It also provides a process for formally established task forces, work groups, and committees to address identified priority areas. Five areas of concern outlined the original ECC structure: Georgia Basin/Puget Sound water quality, Columbia River/Lake Roosevelt water quality, flooding of the Nooksack River in Northwestern Washington, regional air quality, and groundwater management in the Abbotsford, British Columbia, and Sumas, Washington, area. A task force represents each of these priority areas.

Structure of the Environmental Cooperation Council

The structure of the ECC reflects the priority of maintaining a strong state–provincial relationship within a binational context. The council has four members: two co-chairs and two members. The co-chairs represent agencies at the provincial–state level, including the Department of Ecology and Ministry of Environment. The two members represent regional offices of federal agencies, including the U.S. Environmental Protection Agency (region 10) and Fisheries and Oceans Canada (Pacific region). This structure aims to provide a balanced perspective between the countries at both a federal and subnational scale.

The ECC conducts the majority of its work through task forces and committees. The members of the task forces represent multiple scales of government and non-governmental actors including: federal (within the regional offices), state–provincial, city, county and district, as well as citizen and industry groups. Each task force has two co-chairs, with representatives from British Columbia and Washington. Interestingly, the ECC members represent their appointing governments, unlike the IJC process, which adheres to "personal and professional" roles (rather than speaking on behalf of the government).

The ECC and its task force committee chairs met every 6 months between 1992 and 2009 (with venues alternating between British Columbia and Washington) to report the status of their projects. Budget cuts, staff reductions, and different political priorities limited the meetings between 2009 and 2013. This 5-year hiatus represents issues common in transboundary governance that are linked to government agencies. Changing governmental regimes and fiscal priorities can immobilize groups and stunt actions. It is encouraging that the meetings resumed under new leadership in 2013 (Davidson, 2013). However, without safety nets in place to ensure sustained support from governmental offices, it is important to look for non-State solutions for transboundary issues.

In terms of the structure of the ECC, the committees report to the council, and the council reports directly to the Premier of British Columbia and the

Governor of Washington. The governance processes aim to be transparent, with agendas and meeting minutes publicly available through websites and meetings open to the public.

Two "lead agencies" deal with the day-to-day operations of the ECC: the British Columbia Ministry of Environment, Lands and Parks (Ministry) and the Washington Department of Ecology (Ecology). These agencies are responsible for the implementation of the goals outlined in the Environmental Cooperation Agreement signed by British Columbia Premier Harcourt and Washington State Governor Gardner. They provide the necessary institutional support and staffing to manage the council and coordinate the international task forces. They also engaged in other activities promoting transboundary environmental governance, such as coordinating. This sub-governance structure, where subnational actors take a more prominent role than federal actors, is indicative of rescaling processes found throughout North America. What is interesting, however, is that while the documentation of rescaling of environmental governance mechanisms is pervasive within a domestic setting,[7] few studies look specifically at rescaling in a transboundary setting.[8]

Memorandum of Understanding and Agreements

The Environmental Cooperation Agreement provides the general framework for binational cooperation and the creation of its council. In 1996, the lead agencies developed a Memorandum of Understanding (MOU) to detail further their specific roles in binational governance. The MOU serves as a framework to assist in the implementation of the ECA and to serve as a link between specific agreements. Specifically, the provincial/state agencies agree to:

- designate lead liaisons for cross-border communications who serve as primary contacts on issues related to the ECA;
- establish communications among staff members (upon request by the other jurisdictions);
- enable open information-sharing and awareness of processes for public review;
- comment on environmental issues with cross-border impacts;
- refer appropriate agencies within the state and province when an issue needing resolution does not fall within the responsibilities of the lead agency; and
- create working relationships with regional representatives of federal agencies to assist with transboundary cooperation.

Furthermore, the state and province agree to support the implementation mechanisms prepared by the lead agencies:

- exchange draft permits on proposed major projects that could have cross-border impacts;
- include the regional office of the other jurisdiction in the distribution of environmental assessments for major projects within a close radius to the border;

- develop early notification procedures to identify problems or sources of controversy to residents or government agencies in the border region;
- establish procedures to cooperatively respond to emergencies that could cause environmental harm or damage; and
- cooperate in the development of environmental information, including education, training, and technical support.

The ECA between British Columbia and Washington outlines the operations necessary to address the numerous transboundary environmental issues. It serves to guide the International Task Forces – or lead agencies if no task forces exist – in their work. One telling component of the MOU is the commitment to resolve disputes or conflicts at the lowest possible staff level. The ground-up approach attempts to "ensure the rapid resolution of disagreements before negative impacts on the environment or economy occur" (ECC, 2013). If the issue is not resolved at this lower level, however, a plan is in place for the involvement of senior management to achieve resolution. This initial deferment of responsibility to subnational scales of governance is indicative of broader trends of devolution found throughout the region.

Nearly a decade after the enactment of the British Columbia–Washington ECC, the Pacific region saw the creation of two other state–provincial agreements: the British Columbia–Montana agreement and British Columbia–Idaho agreement. These provincial–state agreements, solidified in 2002 when Premier Campbell signed agreements with the respective governors of Idaho (Kempthorne) and Montana (Martz), are part of the growing trend of subnational governance of transboundary water resources. However, the success of these agreements varies from issue to region (see, for example, Locke and McKinney 2013 for a discussion on the Flathead MOU). To date, there is no binational environmental agreement between Alaska and British Columbia – a noticeable absence, given the presence of emerging environmental concerns related to potential mining activity in the Taku River Watershed (see Rivers without Borders, 2013).

The regional allegiances have "scaled up" in recent years to form the Pacific Coast Collaborative, which includes the states of California, Oregon, Washington, Alaska, and the province of British Columbia. This Collaborative, signed in June 2008 by governmental leaders of the five jurisdictions, is:

> [T]he first agreement that brings together the Pacific leaders as a common front to set a cooperative direction into the Pacific Century. Out of this agreement was born the Pacific Coast Collaborative – a formal basis for cooperative action, a forum for leadership and information sharing, and a common voice on issues facing Pacific North America.
>
> (Pacific Coast Collaborative, 2013)

The Pacific Coast Collaborative aims to tackle issues ranging from Global Climate Change, Ocean Acidification, Green Energy, Regional Transportation (such as Green Highways, Green Ports, Rail), to Sustainable Regional Economies. The

Table 3.3 Agreements and MOUs for the British Columbia–Washington Environmental Cooperation Council

Agreement title/Date	*Signatories/parties*	*Aim/scope*
Environmental Cooperation Agreement		
1992	– Premier, Province of British Columbia – Governor, State of Washington	General environmental agreement between British Columbia and Washington. Main purpose is to ensure coordinated action and information-sharing on environmental matters of mutual concern. Outlines support mechanisms and provides procedures
Inter-agency Agreement – Air Quality		
1994	– Director, Air Sources Branch, BC Ministry of Environment (MOE) – Manager, Air Quality and Source Control, Greater Vancouver Regional District (GVRD) – Air Quality Program Manager, Washington Department of Ecology (DOE) – Air Pollution Control Officer, Washington Northwest Air Pollution Authority	Pledges British Columbia and Washington to control air pollution that flows across the international boundary; defines the respective roles and responsibilities of signatories; specifies procedures and schedules and appropriate contacts within each agency; facilitates timely information-sharing; consults in advance concerning activities that might cause significant transboundary air pollution as well as taking steps to avoid or mitigate the effects of air pollution; establishes shared Airshed Task Force
Inter-agency Memorandum of Understanding (MOU) – Columbia River		
1995	– Regional Director, Kootenay Region, BC MOE – Regional Director, Eastern Region, WA DOE	Aim is to "assure continued coordination and cooperation relative to major environmental issues within the international portion of the Columbia River drainage." Specifically, prior notification of waste discharges, opportunity for comment on planning documents with transboundary impacts, and timely notification of spills
MOU on Environmental Cooperation		
1996	– Deputy Minister, BC MOE – Director, WA DOE	Outlines responsibilities to support Environmental Cooperation Agreement
MOU of Referral of Water Right Applications		
1996	– Deputy Minister, BC MOE – Director, WA DOE	Details requirements for information-sharing and coordination of water-related activities and water right applications between the MOE and DOE

Table 3.3 continued

Agreement title/Date	*Signatories/parties*	*Aim/scope*
MOU on Environmental Assessment		
2001	– Deputy Minister, BC Environmental Assessment Office – Director, WA DOE	Inter-jurisdictional cooperation (and information-sharing) regarding the practice of environmental assessment and environmental review. Parties agree to give prior notification and information-exchange related to major project proposals in the vicinity of the other jurisdiction
Implementing the MOU on Environmental Assessment		
2001	– Deputy Minister, BC Environmental Assessment Office – Director, WA DOE	Background document for clarification of MOU. Facilitates information-sharing and mutual understanding of the Environmental Assessment and Environmental Review laws, policies, and processes of each jurisdiction; facilitates notification and information-exchange regarding major project proposals in the vicinity of the other jurisdiction. Aims to promote strong communication between WA and BC regarding major project proposals, complements existing bilateral notification arrangements between BC and WA agencies

initiative has prioritized global climate change as an area of concern, and, in October 2013, British Columbia, Washington, Oregon, and California signed the Pacific Coast Action Plan on Climate and Energy, "a comprehensive and far-reaching strategic alignment to combat climate change and promote clean energy" (Pacific Coast Collaborative, 2013). The State of Alaska, however, did not participate in this agreement.

Supranational governance: Commission for Environmental Cooperation (CEC)

During the same period that regional participation in international environmental governance was increasing in North America, supranational governance also began to emerge. This shift in governance downwards to the local, and upwards to the supranational – commonly referred to as "glocalization" (Swyngedouw, 1997) – was present throughout North America in the late eighties and early nineties. The creation of the North American Free Trade Agreement (NAFTA) in 1992 (enacted in 1994) and its subsequent "green side agreement" exemplifies this shift in governance.

North American Free Trade Agreement

NAFTA seeks to create a continental free trade market by eliminating the majority of tariffs on products traded between Mexico, the United States, and Canada. North America became the largest trade bloc in the world – in terms of combined gross domestic product of its members – when the members signed the agreement in 1992. Although the agreement primarily deals with trade disputes, a provision – Article 2004 – also provides for disputes dealing with environmental issues.

The provision aimed to ensure that each member country knew about, and agreed to, the potential environmental hazards associated with trade issues. Specifically, the provisions allowed for the creation of panels of environmental experts, the submission of scientific advice, and the inclusion of public commentary (Marchak, 1998, p. 142). In the pre-9/11 discourse on globalization and the disappearance of borders – exemplified by entrepreneurs such as Ohmae (1995) – it was perhaps easier to imagine (and enact) a tri-national environmental agreement.

North American Agreement on Environmental Cooperation

NAFTA was the first major international trade agreement to include a separate accord for environmental protection. The North American Agreement on Environmental Cooperation (NAAEC) – NAFTA's side agreement – aims to help prevent potential trade and environmental conflicts and promote effective enforcement of environmental law (CEC, 2013). Subsequently, NAAEC created the tri-national Commission for Environmental Cooperation (CEC) and two binational organizations focusing on the Mexico–U.S. border: the North American Development Bank (NADBank) and the Border Environmental Cooperation Commission (BECC) (Diaz-Bautista *et al.*, 2008). The Montreal-based CEC is one of the primary governance mechanisms to address transboundary environmental issues under NAFTA. The CEC was established "to investigate allegations of non-enforcement of national environmental laws and for monitoring the adverse environmental impacts of the NAFTA trade system" (Mumme, 1999, p. 2) and to "address regional environmental concerns, help prevent potential trade and environmental conflicts, and to promote the effective enforcement of environmental law" (CEC, 2013).

Structure of NAFTA's Commission for Environmental Cooperation

The CEC complements NAFTA by incorporating provisions relating to the resolution of environmental concerns arising from free trade (Marchak, 1998; Norman and Melious, 2008; Healy *et al.*, 2014). The formal obligations of the countries include "periodic publication of reports, education, scientific research, and assessment of environmental effects and promotion of environmental goals" (Marchak, 1998, p. 144).

The CEC comprises the Council, the Joint Public Advisory Committee (JPAC), and the Secretariat. The Council is the CEC's main governing body, which includes the federal environmental ministers (or equivalent) of the member countries. The JPAC is a 15-member, independent volunteer body that provides public input and advice to the Council on issues within the scope of NAAEC. The Secretariat comprises professional staff who provide technical and operational support to the CEC, the Council, and its committees. The Secretariat is responsible for conducting research pertaining to the North American environment, environmental law and standards, and environment/trade issues; implementing CEC initiatives; and processing citizen submissions on enforcement matters (CEC, 2013).

Public process

Through the JPAC, the CEC provides a mechanism for the public to play an active whistle-blower role. The Citizens Submissions on Enforcement Matters provides a process for the public to submit a claim to the CEC for review when a member-country's compliance to their environmental policies is under question. Following the review, the CEC may then choose to investigate the matter further and report on its findings, subject to the Commission's approval (CEC, 2013).

Another method for engaging civil society in this process is through a publicly available digital database. The CEC has catalogued approximately 350 transboundary environmental issues along the Mexico–U.S. and Canada–U.S. borders. Users can search the database by subject, agreement name, or by parties to the agreements. A list of 200 environmentally related North American agreements is also available. The database provides digital links to the full text of the agreements, as well as to other Internet sites that provide related information. The CEC also developed an interactive *Google Earth* mapping tool, which creates a picture of industrial pollutant data across North America. This tool allows any user "whether in Manitoba, Mississippi, or Michoacán" to access the pollution profile of participating industries throughout North America.

Critiques of the Commission for Environmental Cooperation

Despite the inclusion of sustainable development terminology in the preamble of NAFTA and the creation of the environmental side accord, the relative "greenness" of NAFTA is highly contested (Johnson and Beaulieu, 1996; Audley, 1997; DiMento and Doughman, 1998; Spalding, 1999). Many criticize the environmental side accord for lacking political teeth. The process relies on individual countries to adhere to domestic environmental laws, rather than raising international standards or instilling enforcement mechanisms. Thus, the CEC's effectiveness is only potentially as strong as each country's environmental policies. This limitation reinforces the critiques about environmental regimes and nation sovereignty outlined in Chapter 2.

Another issue associated with CEC capacity is that the Council and JPAC members are political appointees. The members, therefore, are subject to swings in the political climate and may reflect the current administration's view on the environment, rather than serve as advocates for the environment. In the U.S., for example, appointees from the Bush Administration represented organizations such as the U.S. Army, General Electric, and the western cattle/sheep ranchers' association. It should be noted, though, that the political appointees are to represent "the North American public", not their country. Although this is not always achieved, it certainly was the case more in the early years of JPAC. The mechanisms for representation of the "North American public" is through a National Advisory Board and Governmental Advisory Council, which are supposed to represent each country's internal and public views. Another promising aspect of JPAC is that there have been numerous Indigenous representatives on JPAC and it has held several distinct meetings on Indigenous issues (Phare, 2014).

Under the right political climate, the public nature of the accord can also act as a lever to "shame leaders into action" (Malkin, 2000). This has been successful in certain high profile cases – particularly along the Mexico–U.S. border (Mumme, 1999). The gap between the CEC and the public, however, has provided limited engagement with civil society despite efforts to engage the public in hearings and meetings (Personal interview with CEC representative, 2008).

Despite these weaknesses, many accept the contributions of the CEC "as a useful monitor of environmental trends in the region and as an important advocate of tri-national environmental solutions that advance regional sustainable development" (Mumme, 1999, p. 3). In particular, the CEC's work on establishing a tri-national agreement regarding transboundary environmental impact assessment is a milestone in regional environmental cooperation. Their work on "green building" has also provided a framework for North American businesses to participate in conservation activities relevant to their industries.

Another important contribution to transboundary water governance was the CEC's granting agency, which provided hundreds of grants for binational environmental projects, several of which were grant recipients in the western Pacific regions of Canada and the U.S. However, as of June 2007, the CEC ceased accepting grant applications with no expectation of reopening. Budget cuts and the increased costs of border security were seen as primary causes for the program's closure (Personal interview with CEC representative, 2008). The closure marked a significant loss for many environmental groups dealing with transboundary issues at a regional level. The Bertrand Creek Watershed Group, spanning British Columbia and Washington, is an example of a "local" citizen group who received funds from the tri-national organization to enhance goals of habitat restoration. This is an example of scale-jumping, where local citizens were engaging with a project at an international level (and funded by a tri-national organization). Those who had received previous CEC funding, such as the Bertrand Creek Group, reported a significant decline in ability to continue local, binational projects.

Transboundary, intertribal governance

Concomitant with the rise of subnational organizations involved in transboundary governance is the rise of intertribal, transboundary governance mechanisms. The section below highlights the work of one such organization, the Yukon River

Inter-Tribal Watershed Council (YRITWC) – spanning the U.S. State of Alaska and the Canadian Yukon Territory. Other intertribal governance mechanisms between Canada and the U.S. include the Coast Salish Gathering, discussed in Chapter 6. There are also a great number of tribes and bands that work between state and provincial borders, such as the Northwest Indian Fisheries Commission in Washington State and Treaty groups in Minnesota, Wisconsin, and Michigan, such as the Great Lakes Indian Fish and Wildlife Commission. In addition, there is increased work on providing a foundation for international dialogue between Indigenous groups (such as the Arctic Indigenous Knowledge Exchange and Indigenous Climate Change groups run through the United Nations).

The rise of these intertribal governance mechanisms is attributable to a number of causes, including the ongoing need to address extraterritorial pollution, and the increased political will among Indigenous communities to work together as a coalition to address these issues in a unified voice (representing a "scaling up"). But what is an important component of the development of these mechanisms (which I explore in this book) is the intentional way in which the structures are designed. Great effort is made by the intertribal organizations to reinforce and honor traditional governance structures and models, building on traditional structures and protocols. As Coast Salish leader Tom Sampson summarizes, "we protect the water for our people, by our people". Further, taking charge of the directives and direction of the environmental groups is interwoven with acts of decolonization – rebuilding capacity, learning to trust each other again, transitioning away from dependency, and operating outside of a dominant framework. Thus, for many of these groups, environmental protection is the guiding principle that brings them together and rationalizes the institution, but the purview is much wider than *just* environmental protection. Rather, the intertribal groups' mission is wrapped up with intergenerational healing, cultural revitalization, decolonization, and preparing the next generation of leaders. In order to accomplish this, the groups often take on a performative approach (such as the Canoe Journey) to meet interconnected goals of reconnecting people to their environment while amplifying their efforts known to the wider world. These efforts, then, are both about environmental protection (from the ground up and through building allies) as well as cultural revitalization. This work also takes on the responsibility of training the youth to become leaders in their community. The leaders understand the need to have the next generation capable of "walking between worlds". To stay rooted in the cultural traditions of their ancestors, yet be fluent in the ways of the dominant culture, is seen as an important component to address the multifaceted issues facing their communities, including environmental degradation and continued economic hardships. These wider purviews are represented in the governance structures. These wider goals of cultural revitalization and education are distinct from the other transboundary mechanisms discussed in this chapter, but are more prevalent in the second part of this book. The intertribal governance mechanisms can be seen as counter-hegemonic activities that strengthen and empower the communities to address hardships within their own terms. As seen throughout this volume, addressing environmental issues for Indigenous communities is often a twinned goal of ecosystem protection and counter-hegemonic activities. This occurs through action, education, and performative means, such as canoe journeys, water walks, protests, and teach-ins.

A key component of the YRITWC – which sets it apart from the IJC, CEC, and ECC examples that I cite earlier in this chapter – is that its governance approach is at its foundation more integrative. In addition, the tribal focus of the YRITWC makes its purview substantially different from the ones mentioned in the previous sections, particularly in relation to aligning goals of wellness and sovereignty to water governance. A difficulty, of course, is that the enforcement capacity ones apply to First Nations lands.

Yukon River Inter-Tribal Watershed Council

The Yukon River Inter-Tribal Watershed Council (YRITWC, or the Council) is a leading example in North America of an Indigenous grassroots organization whose purview spans multiple borders (Canada, U.S. provincial, state, and Indigenous nations). Similar to its contemporary, the Coast Salish Gathering, the YRITWC is designed by Indigenous leaders to protect and restore aquatic ecosystems with the aim of protecting and maintaining the cultural, economic, and environmental health of their communities. The scope of the river is staggering, with a length of 3,185 kilometers from its headwaters in the Yukon Territory, flowing west through Alaska and into the Pacific Ocean. The river's basin is even more striking with 850,000 square kilometers.

The Yukon River has long impressed people by its size and length (see Figure 3.3). Known as the "Great River" – the *Yu-kun-ah (Yukonah)* by the Gwitch'in peoples of its inner watershed, and the "large stream" – *Kwiguik* for the Yupik people who reside in the river's delta (Coates, 2013). This river provides a unifying source of livelihood, economy, and sense of place for those that live up and down its banks. The extraordinary size of the river, diverse range of ecosystems, multiple political jurisdictions, and the number of communities that rely on it for their livelihood, makes communication and information-exchange between member tribes a key goal of the Yukon River Inter-Tribal Council.

The YRITWC represents a collective initiative of seventy First Nations and Tribes that reside within the massive watershed. The aim of the Council is to improve the health and well-being of the watershed and the people who live within it. Simply put, the Council's vision is "to be able to drink water directly from the Yukon River" (YRITWC, 2013). The mission lays out its mandate:

> We, the Indigenous Tribes/First Nations from the headwaters to the mouth of the Yukon River, having been placed here by our Creator, do hereby agree to initiate and continue the clean up and preservation of the Yukon River for the protection of our own and future generations of our Tribes/First Nations and for the continuation of our traditional Native way of life.

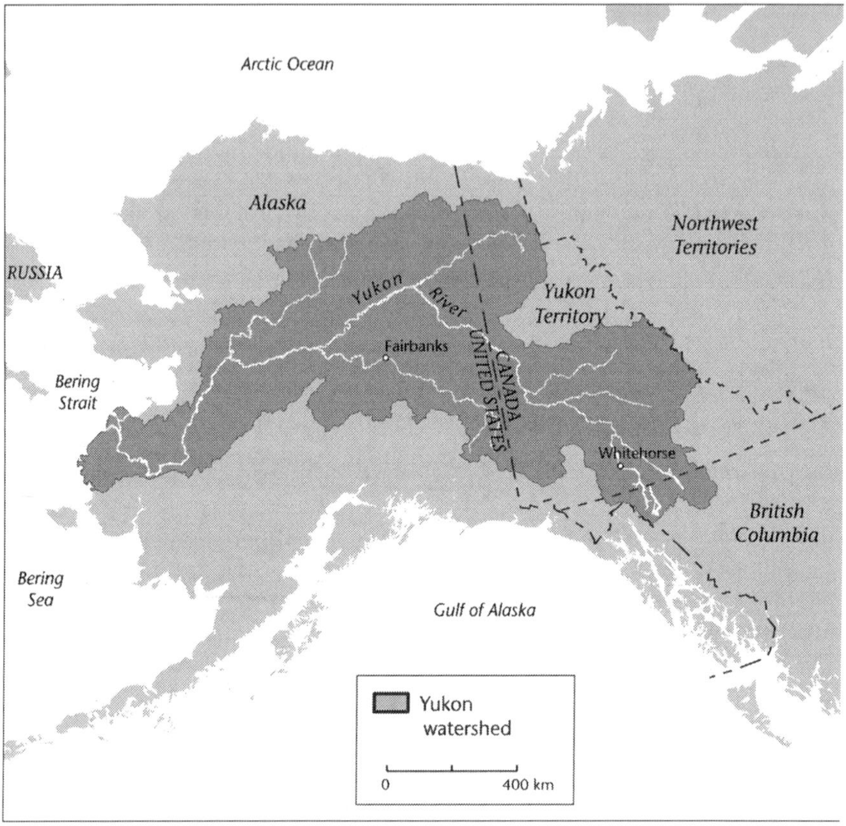

Figure 3.3 Map of the Yukon River watershed.

Source: Original map. Cartography by Eric Leinberger, University of British Columbia.

To accomplish this, the group is very deliberate about their approach. They understand the need to move forward with the modern technological advances available to them, but are also committed to cultural preservation and grounding in tradition. As John Waterhouse (2009), director of the YRITWC, noted in a phone interview, it is important to "attach your culture to the technology". This is particularly important for preparing the youth to serve as the next generation of leaders, of stewards of the Yukon; multigenerational education is a priority for the YRITWC. As Waterhouse noted, "you have to prepare them [the youth] to have the right tools and the right mindset for the future".

Governing the Yukon River is no small feat. The size of the watershed requires a dedicated effort by staff, volunteers, and partner agencies to continue to work towards their goals. With offices in Anchorage, Fairbanks, and Whitehorse the organization plays a leading role in advocating for the river (both regionally and internationally) and communicating between its upstream and downstream member tribes. This commitment is seen by the YRITWC's leading role in developing a basin-wide water management plan – one that crosses jurisdictions of all kinds. The Watershed Plan is the first of its kind. It incorporates years of discussions and dialogues between member tribes and First Nations.

The YRITWC lives between worlds. It can arguably be seen as a "glocal" river, which appeals to a global community, yet is grounded in local practice. The extra-basin outreach is seen as instrumental to meeting the YRITWC mission, as it helps secure funds for ongoing projects and helps build allies. Waterhouse considers campaigning for the river to be central to his mission. Travelling the world, Waterhouse highlights the need to keep the Yukon wild, to protect the river for the Tribes and First Nations that rely on it.

The media outreach has even been aired on prime-time television, such as Super Bowl advertisements in the United States – with upwards of 111 million viewers on game day. The YRITWC has also been highlighted in award-winning documentaries that have aired on the Public Broadcasting Service, adding to the awareness-building campaign. Playing on the romantic notions of the river, as "one of the last 'untouched' rivers in the world", is making the Yukon River accessible to those who will likely never see it in person.

Even though the campaign takes a global stand, the foundation of the organization is very much based on the people that live along its banks, grounded in traditional practice and committed to consensus-based governance.

The Yukon's reputation of being one of the last "wild" rivers in the world holds some water. Along its entire length, it only has four bridges that cross its water, the last of which is the Patton Bridge on the Dalton Highway, which was completed in 1975 as part of the Trans-Alaska Pipelines project. It remains the only bridge crossing the Yukon River in Alaska. Until 1957, the river was also free of dams. The only dam is above the town of Whitehorse, providing power for its town by flooding Whitehorse canyon and creating Lake Schwatka (Coates, 2013).

Although in comparison with other international rivers, the Yukon is relatively "untouched", the river's ecosystem is threatened by activities such as commercial fishing, pollution resulting from resource extraction, deforestation along its banks, and environmental issues such as global climate change impacts upon its ecosystems.

The multijurisdictional (and transboundary) nature of the watershed, in years past, had complicated the governance of the watershed. While agencies at the federal, state, and/or territorial level had some regulatory responsibility for the watershed, no single group existed to manage the watershed in its entirety. Recognizing that need, the Council was established in 1997 as a treaty-based organization of Indigenous governments dedicated to preserve and protect the environmental quality of the Yukon River for the health of their communities and the continuation of a traditional way of life for generations to come.

The YRITWC is both innovative and highly collaborative – the first of its kind dedicated solely to promoting the responsible management, use, protection, and enhancement of the massive watershed. The Council achieves these goals through a variety of methods, including educational programs, water quality monitoring, stewardship, and land-management practices. Central to its mission, the Council serves as a vehicle to involve the First Nations and Tribal communities in direct decision-making related to the governance of the watershed and to provide a forum where member villages, tribes, and nations collectively can express their needs (YRITWC, 2013). The YRITWC is a registered non-profit organization, which allows it to apply for grant funding and partner with agencies. The Coast Salish Gathering, on the other hand, has chosen not to register as non-profit and continues to do its work within the context of its member tribes and bands. The benefit of this is maintaining control over the activities. The downside, of course, is limited capacity.

The YRITWC continues to develop new programs with a focus of five main tenets:

1. Understanding: Getting to know the Watershed through monitoring, measuring, and researching, and using this knowledge to clean, enhance, and preserve life along the river.
2. Education: Promoting environmental and traditional education for the Indigenous peoples of the watershed through educational programs, scholarships, internships, volunteer opportunities, and incentive programs.
3. Stewardship: Honoring the traditional heritage through good stewards of the watershed and its tributaries, and restoring and preserving its health for the benefit of future generations.
4. Enforcement: Developing and enforcing strong state, federal, territorial, and provincial environmental standards to preserve the long-term health of the watershed.
5. Organization: Providing greater organizational strength to the Indigenous peoples of the Yukon River Watershed, both by assisting and improving Indigenous governments and by being a model of organization built on collaboration and mutual respect.

(YRITWC, 2013)

Structure of the Yukon River Inter-Tribal Watershed Council

The YRITWC's governance structure represents a commitment to inter-basin cooperation; consensus-based decision-making, and integrated resource governance. To carry out its mission, as of 2014, the YRITWC has a dedicated staff of fourteen individuals, and an Executive Committee that is selected through a process of consensus at the biennial summits. The members of the Executive Committee represent the geographic area of those governments, rather than the First Nation or Tribes themselves, including: Yukon Flats, Tanana River, Innoko Confluence, Middle Yukon, Innoko Confluence, Dahka Tlingit, Vuntut Gwich'in/Tr'ondek Hwech'in, Northern Tutchone, Kaska, and Southern Tutchone. The representatives provide steering for the staff and volunteers to meet its mission – they are also instrumental in communicating the work of the Council back to its constituents.

Biennial summits

A central part of the YRITWC's governance structure is to host biennial summits that represent the signatory Tribes and First Nation governments. The summit is a place to reinvigorate its members and allies and to (re)align them to goals and missions of the YRITWC. The summit also provides an opportunity to exchange information about activities, voice concerns, celebrate successes, realign priorities, and strengthen allies. The summit provides the intellectual and administrative space to reflect on the YRITWC program activities (as executed through the five departments). It also provides the staff and director with an opportunity to prioritize project areas, which will influence what grants and partnerships to pursue.

The summit is also a place where people can reconnect with the river and learn about the diverse ecosystem. As the summit location changes sites every year, the participants are able to see the river from different vantage points. The 2013 summit – hosted by the *Na-Cho Nyak Dun* (Big River People) – was held in Mayo, Yukon Territory. The 2011 summit was held downriver in Ruby, Alaska. Another way the YRITWC connects people to the river is through the annual Healing Journey.

Healing Canoe Journey

Since 2007, the YRITWC has coordinated an annual Healing Journey to help connect people in "heart" and "mind" to the Yukon River. The Council describes the twinned goals as a way for people to know, feel, observe, and experience the river. Connecting the river comes in many forms and is different for each paddler. The participants bear witness to and experience the health of the river through personal observation. They also carry on stories and oral histories along the way, making it a "living river". The YRITWC Director, John Waterhouse, sees it as part of the mission to visit with elders along the river and carry on the oral history tradition of the river. This blend of environmental protection, cultural preservation, and adventure has captured the attention of a range of agencies, organizations, and retailers. The National Geographic Society hosts a blogsite on their website, where Waterhouse – a National Geographic Society Fellow – documents the Journey. The outdoor outfitter Recreational Equipment, Inc. (REI) provides sponsorship with supplies and financial support for the Journeys, and the governmental agency United States Geological Survey (USGS) has helped with the scientific assessment of the water quality.

Similar to the Coast Salish Intertribal Canoe Journey discussed in Chapter 7, the YRITWC has partnered with USGS to conduct ongoing, real-time water quality data collection during the journey. The YRITWC describes the relationship on their website:

> As we paddle, one canoe tows a multi probe data sonde which collects and stores readings on 11 water quality parameters every two minutes. In analysis of this data profile, we can complement patterns and anomalies with the stories

> of the people. Across the YRITWC science efforts, we realize that the fusion of both modern science and Traditional Ecological Knowledge is fundamental in protecting and preserving the Yukon River for future generations.

The Healing Journey becomes a way to promote the river and build allies, while reconnecting the Indigenous communities with its waters.

Departments

To carry out its mission, the Council is organized into five distinct, but complementary, departments including: Sustainable Lands, Solid Waste, Science, Circuit Rider, and Energy.

The Sustainable Lands department's central responsibility is to coordinate the Brownfields Tribal Response Program. Cleaning and redeveloping contaminated sites containing hazard substances and pollutants or contaminants is a huge issue in rural Alaska, where waste disposal is incredibly expensive due to the terrain and lack of infrastructure to move bulky items. Rural communities in Alaska and the Yukon are particularly vulnerable to contaminated lands because of their extreme poverty (in some areas with the highest poverty rates per capita in North America), coupled with growing political influence of resource extractive industries (whose wealth does not tend to empower the local communities).

Contaminated sites are of particular concern for under-represented and marginalized communities, including First Nations and Native Americans. The link between poverty and contamination is well documented through environmental justice literature (Boyd, 2012). Originally, the environmental justice movement tended to focus on links between urban poverty and industrialization, but increasingly scholars are documenting the links between Indigenous communities and environmental justice (Westra, 2008; Holifield, 2012).

The YRITWC (2013) identifies the following examples of Brownfields within the Yukon Watershed:

- old or illegal dumps;
- petroleum spills;
- abandoned or idle structures with lead paint, asbestos, or other hazardous materials;
- old fuel storage areas or former gas stations;
- mine-scarred lands.

The disposal of solid waste is also a key area of concern within the Yukon Watershed. The frozen tundra environment and the remote nature of much of the watershed with limited transportation makes removal of waste very expensive and the health and environmental concerns of leached contaminants high. To address these issues the YRITWC started a Backhaul Program in 2004 to address solid waste issues in the watershed, including removing materials that are possible soil, air, and water contaminants. Between 2004 and 2008, the program removed and processed more than 10 million pounds of solid waste material. The Backhaul Program is an example where grant funding (mostly from the U.S. EPA (Environmental Protection Agency and the State of Alaska) and public and private partnerships have helped with the efforts of waste removal that directly impact the wellness of Indigenous communities.

The YRITWC also has a Science Department, which adopts an observation-based program referred to as "traditional science". "Traditional science" as defined by the YRITWC is guided by "long-term observations of Traditional Ecological Knowledge (TEK) into particular focus areas" (YRITWC, 2013). For example, they apply what Indigenous scholar Shawn Wilson (2008) refers to as the "Indigenous Research Paradigm". They further describe this focus as using:

> TEK to guide focus areas, form strong relationships within communities, train technicians, and build local capacity for Indigenous Peoples to execute their natural liberty as sovereign people. We live in the moment, striving towards a goal that is not solely defined by measurements and calculations, but rather enhanced by their combination with traditional knowledge. Our survival is intimately linked to the condition of the natural world and we believe in living respectfully with the life around us.
>
> (YRITWC, 2013)

These approaches are similar to those seen in Salish Sea Basin, the Great Lakes Basin, and the Yuquot Territory (explored in Part Two).

The fourth department focuses on capacity-building and support for individual communities. The Circuit Rider program is a U.S. Environmental Protection Agency funded program, which provides support to tribal communities. The YRITWC (2013) identifies the following as services:

- Grant Writing Management and Grant Writing Assistance in group training and/or one-on-one local intensive training. These training sessions will/may include grant writing approaches, grant reporting requirements, grant tracking approaches, assurance of timely grant reporting, how to submit grant revisions, and we will provide assistance in grant extensions.
- Tribal Council/Board training, which may cover Council responsibilities, administrative oversight, financial oversight, fiscal responsibility and reporting, in addition to ongoing planning.
- Bookkeeping and accounting support services to tribes in need of intensive support. Support services will include review of software being utilized for recording, audit preparation needs, internal bookkeeping systems, checks and balances, and reading budget vs. actual and profit and loss statements.
- Facilitation of tribal government strategic planning sessions when possible. These sessions will produce visual strategic plans focusing on administrative and financial needs. Planning will involve: Council members, Tribal Administrators, Environmental Directors, and Bookkeepers.

As of 2014, twenty-five communities are enrolled in the Circuit Rider program. This program provides opportunities for capacity-building within tribes to be competitive for EPA-funded grants and to maintain funding. This service is an example of YRITWC's commitment to working with external agencies to meet shared goals. They are cognizant of the need to generate external funds (and to be successful, you need to work within the framework of the funding agencies). The trick is to be able to "walk between worlds" without losing sight of the core, guiding values of the community. The Boundary Bay example, discussed in Chapter 5, explores the issues associated with the politics of calculation and working in a "foreign defined network". This framework can be seen as a neocolonial framework, in which those that hold power (in this case, funding) define the framework. However, as the pages in this text reveal, every situation needs to be assessed and recalibrated to fit what is best for the community. In the YRITWC's case, the mission is operationalized through a suite of approaches, which bring in outside help, yet maintain a firm goal of maintaining control over the process. Scale is an important factor in this approach as well. YRITWC is an example of a large-scale watershed, which is designed to operate with external funds. What this means is that an element of control will likely be lost in the process. However, it does mean that larger-scale projects will be possible. The YRITWC has taken the position that, with others, more is possible, and the guiding principles will be reinforced through the biennial Summits and also through ongoing communication between tribes and bands.

The projects under the Energy Department also reflect this philosophy of collaboration with partner organizations. The department hosts Solar Energy Training for tribes. The vision of the Energy Department articulates the need for technological advancement and training to meet a goal of sustainability, which they describe thus:

> We see a future where not only the electricity but also the heating and transportation needs of the Yukon watershed are met by harnessing the natural energy of the area, namely the water, wind, sun, geothermal, and biomass.

They accomplish this through a five-step process:

- Promote and implement energy efficiency and conservation measures to reduce waste.
- Explore alternative energy options throughout the watershed to identify the best "fit" between available resources, location, community, environment, and economic and technical feasibility.
- Educate and train Tribal staff to work on energy issues in watershed communities, aiming to save people money, reduce pollution, and spread energy awareness.
- Develop partnerships with Tribal communities and energy professionals to meet local needs.

One example of the positive benefits of the partnership approach is the ability to tap into some very innovative projects. For example, in Ruby, Alaska, the YRITWC partnered with the local tribe, city, and local utility to install the first hydrokinetic river turbine in the United States. The benefit of the turbine is that it produces energy with no dams or water diversions. One year later, the YRITWC was awarded almost $450,000 from the Alaska Renewable Energy Fund to expand the project.

Awards and recognitions

The YRITWC has been recognized for its work. The Council received the Alaska Governor's Pollution Prevention Award in 2000 and has been recognized by Harvard University for its innovations in governance. In 2003, it was named as a semi-finalist in the Harvard Project on American Indian Economic Development; and in 2005, it received High Honors. In 2008, it received the Harvard IBM Innovations in Governance Award. Harvard describes this as a model of self-determination, governance, and collaboration, with high achievements in three main areas: the initiation of the YRITWC, the development of a complex and high-quality operational system, and the impact and reach of the Council on the health of Native peoples along the Yukon River and beyond (Harvard University, 2005).

In 2011, the Council received another prestigious honor when Clarence Lee Alexander from Fort Yukon, Alaska, received the Presidential Citizens Medal. Alexander was among thirteen people who received this prestigious award that recognizes people who have dedicated their lives to bettering others and who provide opportunities for others to lead a life of service (see Figure 3.4). Alexander was recognized for his commitment to the environmental protection of the Yukon River. His efforts have helped close numerous open-burning dumps and remove or recycle millions of pounds of waste along the Yukon River. As U.S. President Barak Obama (2009) reflected in the ceremony, "We don't always get to choose the challenges that we face. But how we respond is entirely up to us". Alexander has provided leadership in the Sustainable Lands department of the YRITWC and has provided inspiration for other regions to follow suit. His work encapsulates empowerment and action.

The recognition of its successes is also clear when looking at the successful grant records – securing millions of dollars from a diverse range of funding agencies (both public and private).

Conclusions

The International Joint Commission, the North American Free Trade Agreement's Commission for Environmental Cooperation, the British Columbia–Washington Environmental Cooperation Council, and the Yukon River Inter-Tribal Watershed Council are examples of four transboundary institutions existing along the Canada–U.S. border, operating at different jurisdictional scales. Although a different

Figure 3.4 Photo of Yukon River Inter-Tribal Watershed Council co-founder, Clarence Lee Alexander, Fort Yukon, Alaska, receiving the Presidential Citizens Medal during a ceremony in the East Room of the White House in Washington.

Source: Used with permission from Associated Press: Photo by Haraz N. Ghanbari.

set of political–historical circumstances created each of these institutions – and they differ in scope and purview – all share the overarching aim of providing tools for coordinating environmental issues across borders.

The enactment of the Boundary Waters Treaty of 1909 marked the beginning of formal binational cooperation of water issues between Canada and the United States. Although the BWT remains a central document for the governance of transboundary waters, there is a growing call to widen the purview of the long-standing Treaty institution, the International Joint Commission, particularly in relation to greater participation of citizen groups and Indigenous communities. Partly in response to this call, the Commission developed the International Watershed Boards concept and then subsequently initiated the International Watersheds Initiative to help implement it, which I discuss in the next chapter.

NAFTA was the first major international trade agreement to include a separate accord for environmental protection. The creation of the CEC marks a significant shift in transboundary environmental governance, with the creation of a public arm to help monitor the potential adverse environmental impacts of the NAFTA trade system. NAFTA's CEC, however, has been criticized for its lack of enforcement ability, as well as its inability to move beyond the individual countries' environmental standards. As the process relies on individual countries to adhere to domestic environmental law, its utility is limited. Critics suggest that for the CEC to be effective it would require raising international standards, instilling enforcement mechanisms, and reinstating the small grants program.

The British Columbia–Washington Environmental Cooperation Council provides an example of a regional approach to transboundary governance of water. The ECC is part of a growing cohort of provincial–state organizations designed to address transboundary environmental issues at a regional scale. The ECC and its contemporaries aim to deal with shared environmental issues with relative autonomy from the federal governments. The increased presence of subnational actors in transboundary governance, however, does not suggest necessarily increased institutional capacity. Furthermore, the capacity for continuous governance is largely at the whim of the provincial and state governments, which, for the British Columbia–Washington ECC, meant a 5-year hiatus from their activities.

Lastly, the Yukon River Inter-Tribal Watershed Council provides an example of an Indigenous-led grassroots environmental organization whose purview spans the Canada–U.S. border and Indigenous Nations. With seventy member tribes and First Nations as signatories to the initial Treaty, the Council provides an example of a watershed approach that strives for representation up and down the river. The mandate is also linked to ecosystem health (protection of water quality) as it provides a framework for cultural preservation. Similar to the Coast Salish Gathering, the YRITWC prioritizes equitable representation and consensus-based decision-making. The newly conceived Yukon River Watershed Plan, which is being considered for adoption both in Alaska and the Yukon Territory, reflects this ongoing commitment to collaborative, Indigenous-led governance.

Each of these mechanisms provides windows to understand how governance mechanisms develop and operate. It is important to recognize that the first three mechanisms are conceived through a binational framing, whereas the last mechanism is multinational framing. The YRITWC has made great progress in conceiving transboundary water governance in a postcolonial context, which continues to be explored in Part Two with the stories of water bodies and governance activities intermixed with the themes of water, governance, borders, and power. In the next chapter, I continue to explore the tensions and opportunities of the IJC's International Watersheds Initiative in operating in a postcolonial governance framework.

Notes

1 Specifically, four main issues that influenced the BWT negotiations were the transportation of the St. Lawrence Sea Way Project, water allocation of the St. Mary and Milk Rivers, Niagara River hydro development, and pollution in the Chicago Drainage Canal.

2 Although the British were one of the signatories and designers of the Treaty, they ultimately had no part in one of its main developments. Despite their lack of direct governance within the IJC, the power relations between the UK, Canada, and the U.S. had a significant impact on the negotiation of the Treaty and the boundaries of the Commission. At the time of Treaty negotiation, there was a delicate balance between the UK and America. Other foreign events such as the negotiation for Alaska Territory also shaped the final version of the Treaty.

3 U.S. Attorney General Judson Harmon, in response to Mexican protests, noted that "the fundamental principle of international law is the absolute sovereignty of every nation, as against all others, within its own Territory" 21 Op. Attorney General. 281–282 (1895). For a review of the impacts of the Harmon Doctrine on Canada–United States relations, see McCaffrey (1996).

4 Within the Treaty, the Boundary Waters define the waters from main shore to main shore of the rivers, lakes, and other waterways along which the international boundary passes.

5 The reference process, however, continues to evolve as the IWI evolves. As Clamen notes (2014) the IJC is now initiating projects with Watershed Boards that up to now might have been references.

6 Also available at: www.greatlakescommons.org/wp-content/uploads/2013/04/Tribal-and-First-Nations-Great-Lakes-Water-Accord.pdf.

7 Kliot *et al.*, 2001; Giordano *et al.*, 2002; Yoffe *et al.*, 2003; Dinar, 2004; Espey and Towfique, 2004.

8 See Fischhendler and Feitelson, 2005 and Norman and Bakker, 2009 for an exception.

4 Rescaling water governance

From federal–federal to international watersheds

In the early 1880s, John Wesley Powell – a North American scientist, geographer, and explorer – made a daring suggestion to define the Western U.S. states through watershed boundaries, rather than Cartesian borders. Having spent decades exploring and documenting the physical and cultural geography of the American West, he came to understand the intricate link between water and human organization. Notably, his respect for, and knowledge of, Indigenous communities and cultures influenced his interpretation of human–environment relationships in a way that was far more nuanced than many of his contemporaries. Powell's dedication to both hydrogeology and ethnology is present throughout his work, particularly in relation to advocating for a "watershed approach" to governance. As Powell described, a watershed is "that area of land, a bounded hydrologic system, within which all living things are inextricably linked by their common water course and where, as humans settled, simple logic demanded that they become part of a community".

Powell's vision of aligning political boundaries with watershed basins, as shown in Figure 4.1, aimed to minimize conflict related to "out of basin demands". The watershed approach was, in essence, a call to live within one's hydrologic means, both spatially and temporally. That is, not to take from your neighbor's basin *or* from future generations. The rationale that Powell outlined in the 1880s for a watershed framework – and, ultimately, the consequences of not doing so – is hauntingly prophetic, particularly in relation to out-of-basin withdrawals.

Of course, reading today's political maps we know that Powell's watershed approach was not adopted. In the end, the delineation of U.S. state borders was decided by political elites and big business interests such as railroad magnates, whose interest in having "straight rail lines" was incommensurate with watershed borders.

Although Powell's vision did not come to fruition, the desire to rethink a watershed approach to governance is still alive in many people's imaginations and is actively being constructed by environmental organizations, and tribal, state, provincial and even federal agencies. A key issue with this restructuring, however, is aligning political management structures with hydrologic basin borders. These difficulties are compounded when the watershed spans international boundaries – adding a level of political complexity when federal governments are required for negotiations.

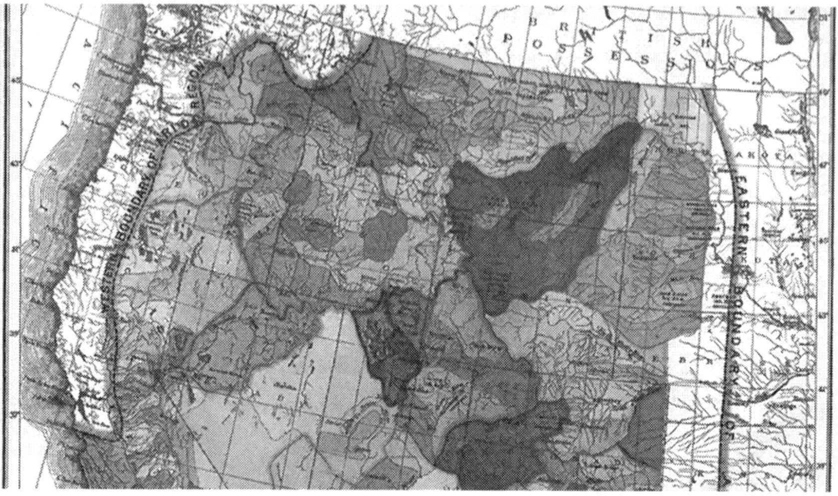

Figure 4.1 Map of John Wesley Powell's proposed watershed states in the American West.

Thus, the conception of the International Joint Commission's International Watersheds Initiative is an important movement to consider. On the one hand, the initiative reflects an attempt to reframe governance models to represent hydrologic borders, with representation from actors living within its basin. On the other hand, the initiative is intrinsically bound by a nation-state framework, which at its very foundation reifies (rather than erases) international borders, and is exclusionary of sub-state actors.

Thus, in this chapter, I look at both the opportunities and challenges of the IJC's International Watersheds Initiative (IWI). This discussion is important particularly for Indigenous communities, as the IWI may provide an entry point for greater engagement in governance processes and open up the opportunity for "nation-to-nation" dialogues.

The watershed approach and rescaling IJC

The (re)emergence of the "watershed approach" is, in some ways, a response to a changing socio-political climate, which has come to value and expect ecological protection and citizen participation in decision-making processes. The International Watersheds Initiative reflects these changing expectations. The development of an international watershed approach is significant as it serves to rescale the governance of transboundary waters from a federal-to-federal to watershed scale; and it aims to provide a model for non-state actors, including Indigenous peoples, citizen groups, non-governmental organizations, and industry.

Although discussions within the environmental governance literature largely champion the watershed approach as a beneficial way to address environmental issues at a "manageable scale"[1] studies suggest that, in an international setting, the realities of the political borders may impede such approaches. Fischhendler and Feitelson (2005) make an interesting case that reducing the scope of transboundary management of water to include *just* the border waters, rather than encompassing the whole river basin, is more effective because it minimizes external players and lowers political costs. The recent data harmonization project coordinated by the United States Geological Survey (USGS), the International Joint Commission, and Environment Canada exemplifies this "border focus" approach (Figure 4.2). The IJC describes the importance of the data harmonization project on their website:

> When data stewards are able to "sing from the same songbook" they can paint a seamless portrait of what we know on the landscape. Having different data protocols and standards in the US and Canada made the reaching the potential of applying GIS to local transboundary watersheds especially challenging. Not only do the two countries use different data collection methods, they use different measurement standards – like "feet" instead of "metres" – and may also use different names for the same rivers.

A strategic priority for the IWI, IJC's Transboundary Data Harmonization (TDH) Task Force, has worked with federal, provincial, state, and local agencies to

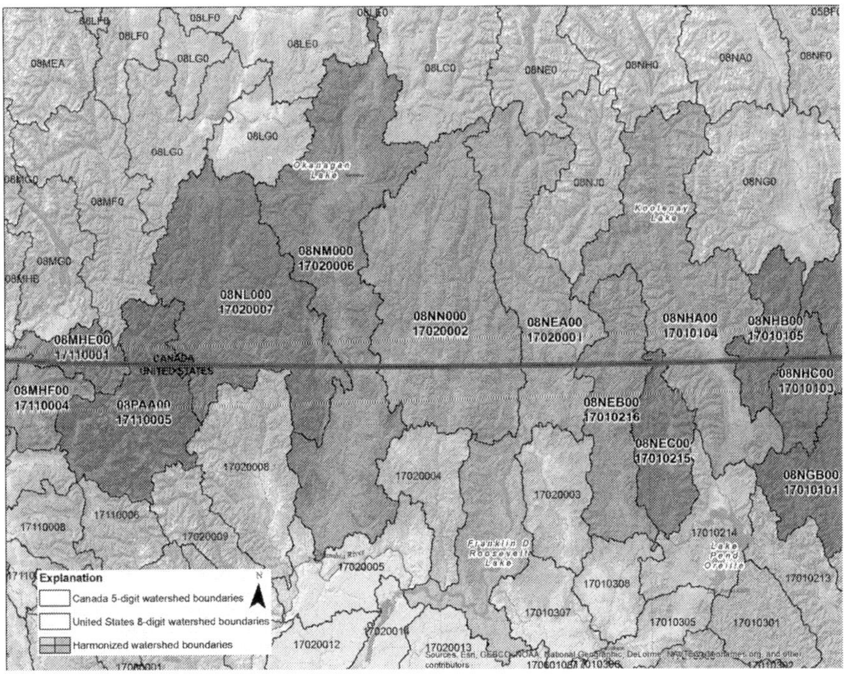

Figure 4.2 Map of Canada–U.S. Transboundary Hydrographic Data Harmonization project.

Source: IJC, used with permission.

overcome barriers and to integrate data sources since 2008. Hydrographic data is now being standardized along the 5,000-mile (8,000-kilometer) U.S.–Canada border. The TDH Task Force has developed a standardized suite of hydrographic interpretations that are now being used by agencies in the U.S. and Canada (IJC, 2014).

This accomplishment, as depicted in Figures 4.2 and 4.3, represents a shift in the culture of *binational* water governance. The lack of synched data sources has consistently been reported as a major barrier for effective governance of transboundary waters (Norman and Bakker, 2009). The harmonization project, which was driven by both advances in GIS capabilities and the political will to prioritize coordinating governance, is perhaps an early sign of a new, postcolonial era of IJC governance.

Despite these gains, it is important to remain cognizant of the politics of *participation* in watershed governance. As Cohen and Davidson (2011) caution, a watershed approach should not be privileged as a naturalized scale for water governance. After all, the governing bodies are still highly political and the managing bodies are still steeped in national politics. Thus, although a watershed scale may seem more "natural" than political boundaries and more "inclusive" than political boundaries, it is important to remember that watershed boundaries are also socially constructed and politically mobilized (Fall, 2010).

For the International Watersheds Initiative, the governance structures are, at their very foundation, framed by the IJC – whose power is located in the federal capitals of Ottawa and Washington, DC. After all, the basis of the IJC is the Boundary Waters Treaty whose formal signatories only recognize Canadian and

Figure 4.3 Image of watersheds along the Canada–U.S. border from Space.

Source: IJC, used with permission.

U.S. governments, and which gives no attention to Indigenous rights in its original mandate. This framing continues to temper the ability to "connect" and "unify" international watersheds, politically. However, the IWI has made great progress in asserting the need to think *proactively*, rather than *reactively* – a fundamental departure from the BWT's original mandate and a key element in becoming a good upstream neighbor. In addition, the latest International Watershed Board – the Rainy–Lake of the Woods Watershed Board – has made significant progress in reframing its governance body to *explicitly* include Indigenous representatives, something that the previous boards have not done. This board is the first to have designated membership for Indigenous Peoples (First Nations, Metis, and Tribal members) as well as an equal number of governmental and non-government members. In addition, the board emphasizes the need to have the majority of its members "living within or connected closely to the basin" (IJC, 2014). If the other established boards follow suit, this would represent a widening of the IWI purview to be more inclusive and work towards actualizing a postcolonial framework of transboundary governance. Understanding the context in which the IWI was developed helps to understand the challenges and opportunities that lie ahead.

Responding to a Reference – the development of Watershed Boards

In 1997 – 100 years after Powell's watershed proposal – the governments of Canada and the United States asked the International Joint Commission (through a Reference) to explore how to meet the environmental challenges of the upcoming century. The Reference asked the IJC to conduct a "self-study" to "examine its important mission in the light of relevant agreements and references, and to provide . . . proposals on how the Commission might best assist the parties to meet environmental challenges in the 21st century within the framework of their treaty responsibilities". As a result of this study, the IJC suggested the formation of International Watershed Boards in its landmark 1997 report (*The IJC and the 21st Century*). As Murray Clamen (2013) – a career IJC employee – explains, a central aim of the International Watershed Boards is to coordinate with citizen groups and include stakeholder representatives familiar with the particulars of the geographic region. The subsequent initiation of the International Watersheds Initiative by the IJC is, in part, an attempt to more seriously implement the International Watershed Boards concept and to shift the thinking from *reacting to* an issue, to *preparing for* an issue.

This request provided the opportunity for the Commissioners to reflect on the strengths and weaknesses of the long-standing Commission. The responsibility for designing a new approach fell on the IJC staff members, who worked with the Commissioners to design a forward-thinking, long-term plan for the next generation of water issues and users. As one senior IJC staff member reflected:

> Basically, I think they were saying, "Well, okay, it's been a great 90 years. You've done lots of wonderful things, but all the dams are built . . . so, what

> do you think you might be able to do for us in the future?". . . And we thought, well, you know, this kind of a [watershed] approach might actually be very helpful because we now have many more State people on our boards, some non-governmental folks. We see these relationships developing. We thought, "This might work. We think we might have a role to play as well." That was part of our *21st Century Report*, the Watershed Board Initiative.

In this quote, you see that the conceptualization of the IWI was both about keeping the IJC relevant (i.e. the "dams are already built") and also including more directly sub-state actors. The conceptualization of a "politically neutral space" was mentioned as a goal and continues to be run through affiliations that are bound by either "Canadian" or "American" identities. Another IJC staffer stated:

> Our Commissioners were thinking about, well, what really could we offer our governments – other than just being available to solve problems when asked? And some of our Commissioners were reflecting on our experience and they said, "We think this is really a neat idea, and we think this could be the wave of the future". . . Our report, *The IJC in the 21st Century*, [shows that] we're not talking about this week, or next week, we're talking about the next century and something that would evolve over time . . . It was really building on our own experience, with our own Boards.

The broad reference to study "the water-related issues of the 21st century" provided an opportunity within the IJC to outline a new governance model that would meet the needs of a changing socio-political-environmental climate, while remaining true to the original purpose of the BWT. The Reference did not specify the designation of a watershed approach. Rather, as the quotes above indicate, the Commissioners and staff found the timing right to launch a governance model with greater public participation, which operated at a regional watershed scale. This design was consistent with what one IJC official called a "growing expectation that the public would be generally involved in the work of government". A key understanding for this project is the long-term thinking in this change. Although they were not explicit about adopting a "postcolonial framework", in essence the framing of the IWI can be considered an attempt to create a "politically neutral" space in which jurisdictional hierarchies are flattened. Whether this is possible, however, is another matter, and a central question of this book. Can organizations that are inherently grounded in a nation-state framework transition to a "borderless" framework with room for equality in participation? Looking at the history of the organization might help in understanding its potential and inherent limitations. Understanding these limitations may, then, help locate priority areas for greater inclusion of diverse worldviews in the governance of shared water.

The IJC and the 21st Century report

This International Watersheds Initiative was officially unveiled on 21 October 1997, with the report, *The IJC and the 21st Century*. The report responded to the governments' Reference by identifying a series of environmental and social concerns that the countries would likely encounter in the coming years. The report also addressed the institutional challenges associated with managing dynamic environmental issues as well as challenges associated with governmental downsizing and jurisdictional fragmentation.

The report suggested that International Watershed Boards would "provide much improved mechanisms for avoiding and resolving transboundary disputes by building a capacity at the watershed level to anticipate and respond to the range of water-related and other environmental changes" (IJC, 1997, p. 30). This approach differs from earlier IJC governance models as it attempts to view borders as hydrological rather than political; it includes subnational players, and it adopts a "proactive" rather than "reactive" approach.

Resistance to Watershed Boards

Despite the efforts to have a "ground up" watershed approach, the IJC's IWI originally received a tremendous amount of resistance across sectors, many querying, "Why fix something that isn't broken?"[2] The slow acceptance of the watershed approach led the IJC to defend the watershed concept and clarify its position with two additional reports after the *21st Century Report*, one on Transboundary Watersheds (2000) and a discussion paper on the International Watersheds Initiative (2005). In these ancillary documents, the IJC stressed that the watershed approach was "in addition to", rather than "in place of", the reference system (IJC, 2000, 2005). Despite these clarifications, the watershed approach remains relatively narrowly applied.

The resistance to the Watersheds Initiative is particularly salient considering the larger issues surrounding the "local trap", which tends to inflate the capacity of local actors in environmental governance. As discussed in Chapter 2, the disconnection between institutional capacity and expectations of local actors remain an under-assessed, yet highly relevant, issue for transboundary water governance. Furthermore, resistance to the Watersheds Initiative questions the efficacy of the multijurisdictional model, which, as seen in the increasingly popular Integrated Water Management Approach, largely receives uncritical acceptance in the governance literature.

To explore this tension between a broadly reported social demand for "local participation" in environmental governance and the rejection of the Watersheds Initiative, I first outline the proposed role of the Watershed Boards and then detail the changing circumstances within the IJC that led to its inception. I then query the Watershed Boards' future role within the IJC and transboundary governance in general, specifically exploring the benefits (and detriments) of situating a regional watershed model within a federal framework.

Role of the International Watershed Boards

Originally, the IJC designed the Watershed Boards to assume a multidisciplinary, integrative approach to water governance, which engages both governmental and non-governmental actors at a watershed scale. Practically, the design of the Boards aimed to coordinate activities with the IJC while maintaining a strong regional presence. To facilitate the development of the Boards, the IJC provided a general guideline for their development and general structure. Generally, the IJC proposed the following roles for the Boards:

- coordinate with existing institutions and agencies within the watershed;
- report on the state of the watershed to the IJC;
- serve as liaison between the community and the IJC; develop monitoring indicators; run water-related studies (as directed by the IJC);
- facilitate the prevention of disputes; foster the development of an "informed transboundary community" regarding watershed management;
- field comments and complaints regarding the watershed; interface between different jurisdictional and ecological systems (i.e. freshwater, terrestrial and marine).

(IJC, 1997, p. 30)

Additionally, the IWI Boards were designed to work with the already established IJC boards – in particular, the control boards in the specific watershed – when appropriate. However, for those regions that have not had a reference (including British Columbia and Alaska), the prospect for creating a new Board is low.

A guiding framework for the IWI Boards is to move beyond government-to-government discussions to embrace greater public participation. The premise behind this approach is that local people – as delineated at a watershed scale – often remain in the best position to resolve difficult transboundary environmental situations. As one Senior IJC staff member commented:

> The original Boards were not set up well to handle public participation. It can't just be two federal representatives making decisions, imposing them and telling us, "Well, trust us. It's good for you." This [the Watersheds Initiative] is the right decision for us.

The original Boards were directed to have at least one meeting annually with the public to receive comments and answer questions. In some cases this was a satisfactory approach, however, overall it represents a minimalist approach to public involvement and participation. The IJC attempted to broaden their jurisdictional scope by including "all the various levels of government and non-governmental actors" (IJC official) into their watershed model. This enhanced multijurisdictional approach places greater emphasis on engaging local actors in the governance structure.

The current (and proposed) IWI Boards highlighted in Figure 4.4 show the potential for coverage along the Canada–U.S. border. Following IJC protocol, in order for the Watershed Boards to become initially established, political support from both countries and subnational stakeholders is necessary. In 2005, the Commission identified three existing boards to apply the IWI concept: the St. Croix

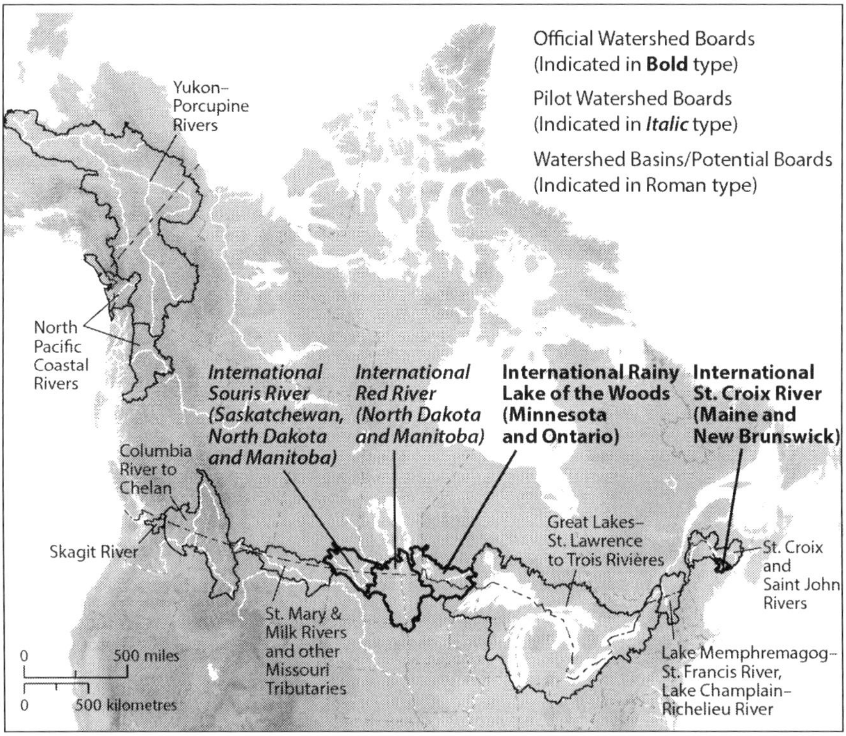

Figure 4.4 Map of official and proposed International Watershed Boards.

Source: Original map. Content based on IJC Watershed Report (IJC, 2014). Cartographer: Eric Leinberger, Department of Geography, UBC.

River (New Brunswick, Maine), the Red River (Minnesota, North Dakota, and Manitoba), and Rainy River (Minnesota and Ontario). In 2007, the Commission added a fourth pilot international board: the Souris River (Saskatchewan, Manitoba, and North Dakota). In 2007, the International St. Croix River Watershed Board became the first "official" International Watershed Board and, in 2013, the International Rainy–Lake of the Woods Watershed Board became the second official Board. The International Red River and the International Souris River Board remain pilot IWI boards. To date, International Watershed Boards have only occurred where IJC boards had existed – it is unclear if this will remain as an informal prerequisite for participation in the IWI.

New role of the Boards: Water Quality and Quantity Boards

Although Boards have long been part of the IJC's governing process, the International Watersheds Initiative marks a departure from the previous IJC governance model. The watershed role moves away from the legal and engineering framework, which dominated the Commission during its first 50 years, to embrace a broader governance approach. During the earlier years of the IJC, the governance structure had a narrower scope and, subsequently, operated with much less infrastructure. In fact, the original BWT calls for only two secretaries, and engineers "as required". Subsequently, support staff to perform operational duties did not appear at the IJC until the second half of the century. As one former Commissioner explained:

> We dealt with dams and other things, so you needed somebody who was an engineer. And because you dealt with legal issues, you had a treaty and governance issues, you needed some law experience.

This governance structure, he continued, "fostered a quasi-judicial and technical body". In the 1970s, however, additional staff were brought in to reflect a more multidisciplinary approach to water management and the need for broader expertise to assess reports and deliberate on references and applications. This broader approach exists to this day.

The Water Quantity/Quality Boards have served their (narrowly defined) purpose relatively well. However, as discussed in Chapter 3, the original boards were largely fragmented and had limited capacity. Rather than dealing with water issues holistically, the IJC addressed quantity and quality issues as separate entities. As one senior IJC staff member noted on the Watershed Boards' attempt to remedy this division:

> [The Watershed Boards reflect] a growing recognition of integration. You can't just sort of separate and say, "Okay, well this group will deal with water quality, and that group's going to deal with water quantity" because they're related. And then, after all of that, trying to weave that into a structure and approach that makes sense without stepping on everybody else's toes.

The earlier compartmentalized style largely reflects the type of governance approach at the time of creation (see Table 3.1). The first move to address water quality on a large scale was with the Great Lakes Water Quality Agreement in 1972. Similarly, the first "local actors" made their way into the IJC structure around this time. An IJC career employee from Washington, DC reflected on the first engagement of local actors:

> One of the first examples of "local" players becoming involved in IJC issues was on the Point Roberts project – [a] Professor at Western Washington University, was on a study board. That was sort of my first introduction to actually having somebody that wasn't a government person.

The Point Roberts Reference exemplifies the beginning of a multidisciplinary and multijurisdictional approach to water governance within the IJC.

Some motivation exists within the IJC to try to merge these boards (at least theoretically), as described below by two different IJC staff members:

> We noted that water quality and water quantity functions were handled separately, and they were also handled not only by different groups, but with different reporting structures. [We] had a board that handled water quantity issues, and . . . a water quality group, [that] reported directly to governments. So, you had different groups exchanging diplomatic notes, and directing all of their functions to the IJC . . . we are in the process of working with those groups to basically bring the issues together, and then we'll see how that progresses. But again, it's a slow process.

And:

> So maybe if the Commission were to push harder and merge the boards, it might work. That's a little bit of a push and a pull with what makes sense to the people that live there, so that's sort of the situation there. Again, the boards, I think, are working well together as a group. They hold their meetings jointly. They do give us our report jointly. So, they're acting [together], but they are not one.

The attempted convergence of water quality and quantity issues under the umbrella of the Watersheds Initiative marks a widening of governance for the IJC consistent with the new Participatory Era of water governance (Pentland and Hurley, 2007).

IWI and Indigenous communities

To move towards a Postcolonial Era of governance, the IJC will need to continue its efforts for greater inclusion of non-State actors and to actively include First Nations and Tribal governments as equal partners in the governance process. The designated membership of First Nations, Metis, and Tribal members in the Rainy–Lake of the Woods Board is certainly promising. Whether the other boards will follow suit, however, is yet to be seen. In addition, in previous years, Indigenous governments have been invited to the table as "stakeholders", on equal footing with other citizen groups. This approach, at its foundation, is flawed, as Indigenous communities have unique sovereign status, which needs to be addressed through formal government-to-government relationships (Ranco *et al.*, 2011; Von der Porten and de Loë, 2013a, 2013b). As Ranco *et al.* (2011, p. 221) note, in the context of Indigenous communities in the U.S.:

> Environmental justice in the tribal context cannot be contemplated apart from a recognition of American Indian tribes' unique historical, political, and legal circumstances. American Indian tribes are sovereign governments, with inherent powers of self-government over their citizens and their territories.

> Their status as sovereign entities predates contact with European settlers. This separate status, nonetheless, was affirmed by the United States early on and is enshrined in the U.S. Constitution. Tribes today continue to exist as distinct sovereigns within the boundaries of the United States.

The notion of sovereignty, of course, is complicated in the transboundary context, where Indigenous communities in Canada have a different status and relationship with their federal government (Harris and Millerd, 2010; Thom, 2009, 2010). I explore the implications of this asymmetry in greater detail in the next chapter (Chapter 5), and then turn to Indigenous-led governance mechanisms throughout Part Two.

Building on the IJC's strengths

The IJC developed the International Watersheds Initiative to adapt to changing environmental and political conditions. In particular, the IWI was a response to growing public expectations of local participation in the environmental governance process. It also reflects one strand of water governance literature that asserts the need for a "watershed approach" (Montgomery *et al.*, 1995; McGinnis, 1999) for effectively substituting hydrological boundaries for political borders.

The IWI attempts to capture some of the strengths of the previously established mechanisms such as the Water Quantity/Quality Boards, and the reference and fact-finding capabilities. In fact, the Commissioners who initially proposed the IWI concept modeled it after the Great Lakes Water Quality Agreement, which was making great strides at including water quality and quantity issues throughout the Great Lakes Basin (Clamen, 2014). Although the IJC is receiving fewer requests for references (as shown in Chapter 3), the governance model has several positive attributes, which could be incorporated into the new Watershed Board model. Similarly, it is prudent for the IJC to pay close attention to the successes and failures of the Water Quality and Quantity Boards as they develop the new Watersheds Initiative.

Lessons from the reference process

Beyond the practical matter of "obtaining facts" and "studying issues", the reference and fact-finding process has demonstrated an ability to create a model (governance community) for effective transboundary governance. As the IJC establishes the task forces and study boards, the members engage in a series of intensive meetings to investigate issues of shared concern. This face-to-face cooperation and collaboration creates an environment conducive to effective transboundary governance, such as trust and relationships. The attribute of clear communication, which contributes to qualities of "good upstream neighbors" is consistent across venues and platforms. For example, participants of the IJC Study Board, indicated to me that the board provides a "neutral" platform to discuss issues of shared concern. As one senior water manager reflected:

> I've found, over the years, a really important role of the IJC basically is that they're able to bring people together, experts from many different agencies. Experts from agencies that don't work very well together, but when they're working for something like the IJC, they work well together. That's a very important role that they play. They don't have enough money to do that, but if they had money, they'd play that role perfectly.

Thus, facilitating binational fora and providing logistical support for binational collaboration is a clear value-added benefit of the IJC.

The benefits of the traditional governance models of the IJC, however, often do not translate to the wider public. Because the governance process remains closed to the public until the final review stages, when public comments are solicited in open sessions, the benefits of consensus-building have – in years past – rarely translated to wider civil society. However, in more recent years, the IJC has attempted to provide more opportunities for public involvement (Clamen, 2014).

As exhibited in the chapters that follow, this continuity and face-to-face collaboration is an essential component for effective transboundary governance. The hope is that the Watersheds Initiative's greater local involvement will allow these strengths to translate to the wider watershed community.

Beyond the reference role: benefits of the Boards

Although a reference is not needed to create an International Watershed Board, to date, the existing Watershed Boards have all had previous IJC references or applications. The creation of International Watershed Boards certainly requires political support both regionally and from the federal government. However, once a Board is established, it may take on regional projects and studies without seeking additional references. Interestingly, if governments send the IJC a new reference the IJC could use an existing Watershed Board. Although some level of coordination with the IJC is expected – as outlined in the general guidelines of the Watershed Board – the day-to-day operations may operate largely at the discretion of the regional actors; independent from the Commission.

There are several advantages to this new model. For one, it allows each IWI to create a place-based governance structure that caters to the regional nuances of the watershed community. For example, the needs of the relatively water-abundant (and marine-focused) Pacific region will clearly be different from those of the more water-scarce (and irrigation-focused) prairie regions. Another advantage to this new model is the ability to respond quickly to issues. Rather than waiting for a reference in order to address a problem, the IJC designed the new boards to sustain relationships and govern water in times of non-conflict or crisis. When an issue does arise, however, the established relationships and knowledge of the watershed system should, theoretically, help the board members identify a solution in a timely manner. The design of this more "proactive approach" to water governance aims to foster binational relationships at a watershed level, deter conflict, and encourage long-term cooperation.

Cooperation in time of non-crisis?

One consideration for this model, however, is the question of whether State-run transboundary governance organizations *are* able to maintain continuity in times of non-crisis. After all, in my field research, federal, state, and provincial water managers consistently revealed that the presence of a *specific issue* is a central driver for cooperation. These issues give focus to discussions, whereas "water approaches often diffuse focus, making it more difficult to ascribe plans". As one state water manager reflected, "Without an issue, you have no transboundary environmental cooperation. Issues are everything". What, then, is the motivation to convene in times of non-crisis? Study Boards and information-sharing help provide a focus (and meaning) for the Boards, but will this be enough to sustain momentum? That is, how will the Boards ensure that this "relationship-building" actually occurs? This is also a consideration as institutions transition from reactive systems (such as the reference system) to proactive systems (such as the watershed and ecosystem-based systems). In addition, as explored in Part Two, for Indigenous-led transboundary institutions, the twinned goals of ecosystem protection and processes of self-determination and self-governance provide added impetus to participate in times of "non-crisis".

Answers to this question may also lie in pragmatic questions, such as: will the IJC be able to provide greater financial support for the IWI? How often will they meet? Will the IWI truly achieve diverse representation? In particular, will the IWI succeed in having meaningful inclusion of representatives of Indigenous heritage? Will the benefits of meeting outweigh the costs of attending? This latter point is especially pertinent in light of increased border wait-times post-9/11 (Davidson, 2013).

These questions are particularly salient for the local, non-governmental actors who may be representing themselves or a small interest/environmental group as well as Indigenous communities who are already facing capacity issues in relation to water governance. Local actors often disproportionately carry the burden of attending transboundary meetings (Norman, 2014). The governmental employees, although often over-committed and over-worked, are at least able to build these meetings into their job responsibilities. The local actors face greater challenges as the likelihood for financial compensation for their time is less likely than for their governmental counterparts.

Capacity-building and multijurisdictional integration

As mentioned above, relationship-building and creating neutral platforms for shared governance is likely to emerge as a main contribution of the International Watersheds Initiative. Likewise, providing infrastructure and institutional support will likely be another main contribution of the Initiative. However, for this to occur, local groups need to trust that working with (or under) the IJC will demonstrate clear benefits. In particular, the added value of the IJC partnership needs to surpass the requirements (or perceived burdens) of a more "formal" governance structure. For First Nations and Tribes, this benefit is less clearly defined.

Integration

The Watershed Boards under the IWI hold the potential to level the playing field for the actors involved in transboundary governance. This is particularly important for the local actors and Indigenous communities, who may have an interest in, and valuable knowledge of, the watershed, but may have difficulty accessing traditionally conceived international governance mechanisms.

For example, several local ENGO members working in binational watersheds reported the benefits of access to federal-level actors – in essence "scale jumping". For example, local stakeholders reported that regular contact with federal employees helped find a "voice" for their concerns. This relationship also provided access to, and knowledge of, institutional and grant funds. For the governmental actors, the opportunity to dialogue in this multijurisdictional format created space for integration of ideas among actors, which helped counter the "silo effect" where committee members make decisions largely without the consultation of local actors. As one senior water analyst reflected:

> Having been there at the creation, the idea would be, you get local people involved. You don't know as much as they know about it, but you help them understand the scientific and the technical issues that are involved. And then, you lead them to make the right decisions. And, the only thing that's left out of all of this is the big "I", and that's interest groups and the subset of that's lobbying, that special interests are not as well represented, nor should they be, in a very interesting participatory decision process.

The IJC has attempted to foster multijurisdictional relationships from already established connections and largely views their efforts as a long-term investment. This investment, according to those within the IJC, has started to pay off:

> And I think we've made a lot of progress [working with regional groups]. Our Board had always worked closely with the St. Croix Waterway Commission. They have a fabulous executive director, and I think we've actually come a fair way in terms of working, not only with them, but also with the state, with the province, so that there's a common understanding of where we are and where we're trying to go. Perhaps, not unrelated to that, we have managed to bring some small dollars to the table to get some things done that might not have been done otherwise.

The presence of strong leadership and regional interest in transboundary issues helps solidify these multijurisdictional partnerships. Subsequently, in April 2007, the IJC designated the St. Croix Watershed Board as the first "full-fledged International Watershed Board" (Brooks, 2007). This is an interesting example of a watershed where initial antagonism to the IWI eventually turned to strong support.

Drawing on the strengths of an integrated governance structure – where the IJC joins established regional groups – could prove mutually beneficial. Connecting with existing binational organizations has proved to be a positive first step for the creation of Watershed Boards. Although this has occurred informally – the four International Watershed Boards had a strong foundation for binational cooperation – the IJC is currently exploring the possibility of formally adopting this approach:

> And what the Commission is looking at is whether it could perhaps, and the decision's not made for sure one way or the other, but whether it could work with other organizations, to at least provide an initial forum and then see whether there was someone that appropriately would take on the issue. Whether that, for example, might be the Washington–British Columbia Environmental Cooperation Council, whether that might be some group, but right now, the issue seems to be swirling without the organizational structure in place to take it, and it's trying to attach itself to a review of the orders that we are doing.
>
> (Personal interview with IJC staff member, 2007, Washington, DC)

However, if the IJC is joining an already established group, it begs the question, is the IWI truly adding value or is it unnecessarily redundant?

Value added?

Integrating subnational and federal efforts for governing transboundary water presents several institutional challenges. One key question that consistently emerged during interviews and facilitated discussions with water practitioners involved in transboundary water governance in the IWI was "what is the 'value-added' component of the IJC International Watersheds Initiative?" The regional water managers, in particular, expressed skepticism that the IJC could provide anything substantially different from the already established regional organizations. A main argument from regional stakeholders and water managers was, if momentum already existed for binational cooperation at a regional scale, the organization would function with or without the involvement of the IJC. Examples of value-added components in working with a Treaty-based organization, though, are access to additional funding; a governance structure that, once created, is less likely to succumb to political maneuvering without IJC involvement; and a century-long engagement in transboundary management.

The acceptance of, or resistance to, the IJC is, however, regionally dependent. In the Pacific region, for example, there is a long history of resistance to federal involvement in governance, in particular the IJC (Alper, 1996). Respondents substantiated this finding at the transboundary workshop in Vancouver, British Columbia, where regional water managers largely dismissed increased IJC involvement at the watershed-scale as impractical. Many noted that the IJC role should remain operational (i.e. monitoring water levels of the Columbia River system) rather than attempting to broaden its role.

The IJC knows of this regional preference for their involvement. As one senior staff member reflected:

> When we talk about Watershed Boards, it's really more of a recognition that these kinds of relationships are evolving, and we think we have something to add to this whole thing, so, when we talk about watershed boards, it sounds like they're going to be *our* things – that, it's going to be different. In some basins, we're going to be the *big* deal. In other basins, we may be an observer – it's going to run the gamut. Although we've been at this for a long time, we could probably sit down across the border and predict each one wrong – that is just how it's going to turn out.

The quote above helps to explain how those involved with the IJC understand how the engagement will be different, depending on the specific watersheds and communities involved.

This resistance to a strong IJC presence in the Pacific region was particularly noteworthy for those involved in the British Columbia–Washington Environmental Cooperation Council (ECC). In the ECC, where provincial and state actors have created several regionally based binational committees centered around transboundary water issues (such as the Abbotsford-Sumas Aquifer; Flooding of the Nooksack River; Georgia Basin–Puget Sound) and Indigenous groups have created strong coordinated transboundary governance mechanisms (such as the Coast Salish Gathering), some consider the IJC's involvement as co-opting their efforts. The difficulty for the IJC, then, is to find a way for the Watershed Boards that adds to (not undermines) the already established binational organizations, or, as noted by a member of the IJC, the trick is "to add value without stepping on toes".

Conversely, for those geographic regions that do not have an established (or strong) subnational transboundary environmental organization, reasons for the absence were usually quite apparent. For example, a sparse population-base at the border may temper the local interest in transborder water issues, as seen in the prairie regions of Alberta-Montana. A long-standing distrust of the neighboring province or state may also deter the creation of a transboundary organization at a watershed scale, as seen in British Columbia–Montana. These issues require attention (and buy-in) from governments on both sides of the border for the Watershed Boards to expand beyond the four current boards. For some regions, this is no small task. For example, the Flathead Basin in British Columbia and Montana and the Devils Lake diversion controversy in Manitoba and North Dakota are examples of deep-rooted transboundary issues in which different national, state, and provincial priorities have made it consistently difficult for the parties "across the line" to see eye-to-eye (Brandson and Hearne, 2013; Locke and McKinney, 2013).

Institutional support and funding

One potential role of the IJC is the contribution of institutional support and financial assistance for existing transboundary watershed groups. This suggestion captures support from a wide range of people involved in water management, including state, provincial, municipal, and ENGO representatives. The IJC also heard this directly through their community workshops. As one IJC staff member reflected:

> [O]ne issue that definitely was on the table [at the workshops] was, "Well, are you bringing money?" because if you're bringing money, you're bringing advantages that would not exist within the region. And if you're not bringing money, we're not quite sure that you're bringing advantages, and perhaps, we can cover the ground ourselves.

Similarly, a member from the Gulf of Maine Council noted in an interview that consistent funding could be a key role for the IJC at the watershed level. She also commented, however, that their binational organization agreed early on that lack of funds would not ruin their relationship:

> When we entered this agreement, we treated it like a marriage . . . we agreed to cooperate regardless of the ability of the other countries' ability to bring equal funds to the table.

For the Gulf of Maine Council, this clear understanding proved prudent; considering that the contributions of funds are strikingly asymmetrical, with American counterparts who contribute approximately 80 percent of the funds to the organization. Despite this imbalance, the Council has operated with noted success for more than two decades. How (and if) the IJC involvement in the transboundary region will help level the playing field, and enhance the institutional capacity of the watershed group, is yet to be seen.

Although respondents listed financial support as a key asset that the Watersheds Initiative could provide for local groups, the IJC staff report that they have not received adequate institutional/financial support to meet their goals. As one senior staff member reflected:

> We don't have much money, so we don't really know quite how this is all going to work out. Our instinct is that this is the wave of the future. These different levels of organizations, often organized around the watershed because there's a lot of issues that you're just forced to deal with being in the watershed, but we don't really know how it's going to work. Some of it is instinctual, and we can't really prove that it is working, or it's going anywhere. That's sort of our gut. We're trying to figure out where we play, where we fit in.

Despite the financial hurdles, the IJC staff remain optimistic that the Watersheds Initiative is the right role for their organization.

The right change?

Not all, however, believe that the IJC should expand its role beyond their traditional fact-finding and reference roles. For example, LeMarquand (1993, p. 61) maintains that:

> Although there are demands for the Commission to take on existing new challenges . . . the IJC operates best within a fairly narrow range of issues, including boundary water project supervision, fact finding, and evaluation. Going beyond this range would likely result in failure.

Similarly, LeMarquand suggests that the IJC's "much needed reform" should focus on what it already does well. That is, expand its role as a third-party advisor (fact finder and technical mediator), as well as a neutral mediator and program evaluator. LeMarquand (1993, p. 60) aptly queries, "What are we looking for in good transboundary resource management apart from nondegradation of shared resources and maintenance of good bilateral relations?" He proposes that ideally the "artificial line dividing the countries should not hinder achievement of outcomes that could be attained within a single jurisdiction". To achieve this lofty goal, the IJC would need to undergo significant reform. Notably, he suggests that the IJC needs to focus on *equity* between scales of governance, respond to public concerns and interests, increase political accountability, and develop good information and information-sharing techniques. Interestingly, many of these proposals are goals of the Watershed Council model, which he rejects.

Another suggestion for reform of transboundary water governance was with small refinements, rather than in relation to the major issues. As one State water manager noted, "when an issue becomes elevated, it really needs to be handled within an established binational structure". Here, the manager views the federal capacity of the IJC as an asset, but suggests small refinements to increase its capacity. For example, the manager reflected that she personally, "would like to see the governing mechanism to be more progressive". Rather than having a solely issue-driven process, she would like to see more sustained conversations that focus on preventative, pre-emptive measures. This, she surmised, "would be a good role for the transboundary watershed councils". Here, the State representative saw upholding a strong nation-to-nation governance structure as instrumental for dealing with transboundary issues; however, she also saw many opportunities to refine the IJC to engage in activities that are more "preventive". Another career governmental water specialist suggested that the best role for the IJC would be facilitative:

> I mean, the IJC is not going to go away, it's still going to have a role, but if it wants to be really relevant in this Participatory Period, it has to find a niche for itself. I'm not sure if they [the IJC] think of it that way, but that's where the watershed approach would take them. I think they would play a facilitating role in this top down, bottom up situation.

Others, however, are less optimistic over the future role of the IJC, questioning whether the new Initiative is "too little, too late". Or, put another way: does the Watersheds Initiative do enough to keep the IJC "relevant" in this changing political environment? Several interviewees commented that if the IJC sincerely wanted the Initiative to succeed, they needed to act swiftly. One senior water analyst warned:

> It may be too late. There was a window of opportunity where there was a lot of momentum and interest in the program. But, this energy has largely diminished.

I also found this sense of diminishing enthusiasm at the local scale. One regional water manager with more than two decades of professional experience in transboundary issues expressed doubts about the IJC's future role in multi-jurisdictional governance. During an interview, he reflected on his involvement with the IJC's Watersheds Initiative:

> They started out with a lot of energy. Brought us all in to launch the program, had a lot of promises of excellence. It all sounded good, but in the end we asked, how is this different from what we are already doing?

Ultimately, this may prove to be a central question for the IJC to address as they attempt to reinvent themselves in the twenty-first century.

When asking the IJC staff about their changing roles, the responses were generally optimistic, despite their uncertain future:

> I think we have to realize that and accept that we don't know what the future's going to hold, but we think it's moving in this direction. We think we can contribute, and we think we can help the governments achieve their purpose in the Boundary Waters Treaty, which was to resolve and avoid disputes. That's sort of the principal goal here, how do we contribute, how do we help the governments do that. I think that's basically where we are. But then we're people too, so then we want to be – want to get some recognition.
>
> (IJC staff member)

Transboundary watershed – transcending borders?

The previous sections have largely focused on the role of the Watersheds Initiative as a tool to increase local/regional involvement in the governance process. However, a central question remains. Does the Watersheds Initiative's emphasis on hydrological borders transcend or "soften" political borders? Or, does the initial federal–federal framing of the IJC (through the Boundary Waters Treaty) continue to reify nation-state boundaries, despite its new watershed approach? I turn to this question below.

As noted in the previous chapter, the development of the IJC occurred under the political climate of strong national sovereignty. During the time of treaty negotiation, the Harmon Doctrine – which maintains that a country is sovereign over the portion of an international watercourse within its borders (McCaffrey, 1996) – was at the forefront of American thinking. Mexican protests against diversions from the Rio Grande led to the development of the Doctrine, which, arguably, colored the governance structure of the IJC. Under this climate, the U.S.

rejected the original Clinton draft of the BWT, which gave the IJC greater authority, in favor of the current model, which limits the arbitral powers of the IJC and clearly upholds nation-state boundaries.

One could argue that the Watersheds Initiative attempts to subvert the Harmon Doctrine's original influence over the IJC by de-emphasizing political borders and prioritizing hydrological borders. However, it is unclear whether this shift in governance fosters a change in identity for those living within the binational watershed community. As discussed previously, increased security at the border post-9/11 – and a general discourse of fear – has had notable impacts on communities attempting to create a transnational watershed identity.

Even before the hardening of borders post-9/11, projects of creating "transnational identities" had limited success. One such example of attempting to redefine a physical space in people's geographic imagination is the two-decade-long attempt to create a binational "Cascadia" identity that spans the border between British Columbia and Washington. However, despite sustained efforts through educational campaigns and propaganda (including scores of maps and pamphlets), the concept of a binational Cascadia community remains unrealized. Both the environmental and business-led Cascadia projects remain largely in the imaginations of those directly involved in the projects and have not translated to the wider community (Alper, 1996; Blatter *et al.*, 2001; Sparke, 2006). That said, as explored in Part Two, the 'Salish Sea' has increasingly captured the geographic imagination of its residents.

At a smaller scale within the Cascadia region, several community actors have joined forces to address transboundary water pollution of the Abbotsford-Sumas aquifer, spanning British Columbia and Washington. Promoting a general understanding of watersheds and an appreciation that their border communities share water issues is central to the transboundary committee. However, despite a decade-long coordination, and numerous grants to connect projects, the area remains largely bound within a nation-state framework. The majority of the people, although clearly cognizant that they live in a "border-town", do not connect (ecologically, hydrologically, or socially) to the communities on the "other" side of the border (Norman and Melious, 2008). In both of these regional cases, the very real impacts of a hardened border – increased security post-9/11 – may have dampened State-led efforts to create transboundary identities.

However, Part Two of this book provides counter-examples to this "hardened" border. Here I highlight how Indigenous communities have made great strides in redefining their geographic spaces, (re)connecting their community to traditional territories and promoting practices of self-determination and self-governance. These cases are different, however, as the community members have historic ties to the wider geographic region; the separation of the land into two countries is a relatively recent phenomenon.

In the case of the IJC's International Watersheds Initiative, it is useful to question the role of federal involvement in these regional projects when analyzing the general absence of imagined (or real) transnational watershed identities. Some argue –

particularly those within the IJC – that federal involvement in the watershed council helps to create a transborder watershed community by providing infrastructure and increased capacity to work at an international scale. Conversely, others suggest that the federal involvement may actually *subvert* attempts to create a regional watershed identity by reifying or "hardening" borders by their presence.

Whether the creation (and support) of a binational watershed council fosters a new (borderless) geographic imagination for the council members or, more broadly, "softens the border" to the wider watershed community is unknown. Although it may be too early to predict the impacts of the IJC International Watersheds Initiative on the transboundary watershed communities, reflecting on the previous case studies may offer some insight.

Social construction of hydrological borders?

An essential consideration of the possibilities of "softening" or "blurring" the nation-state borders is the actors' drive for coordination. This follows the earlier discussion that political borders are not passive, unproblematic backdrops that neatly bound national identities and peoples (Paasi, 1999; Anderson, 1996; Newman, 2006). Rather, viewing contemporary political borders as active sites provides great insight into political processes and power relations and helps open up wider questions regarding identity, citizenship, and nationalism (Anderson, 1996; Fall, 2005).

For the Coast Salish communities discussed in Chapters 5 and 6, the Great Lakes Ojibwa communities discussed in Chapter 7, and the Yukon River Inter-Tribal Council discussed in Chapter 3, the drive for (transborder) coordination runs deep. I argue that enactment of the Coast Salish Gathering and the Yukon River Inter-Tribal Council serve as counter-narratives to bordered geographies by emphasizing the *connectedness* of the Indigenous communities rather than reifying divisions through entrenched national identities. Not only are the Council members compelled to address growing environmental issues facing their community, they also attempt to reconnect a cultural continuum that spans and pre-dates the Canada–U.S. border. Creating a fully-functioning (transboundary) governance structure that helps rectify a degraded physical environment will, in turn, help preserve a traditional way of life, not only in terms of stewardship of marine ecosystems, but by re-establishing – and celebrating – the cultural connections of their communities. Here, the Councils' establishment not only serve as instruments to foster binational exchange of information, but also as a way to reconnect with ancestors and families. Thus, creating a binational governance structure is part of a wider goal of reconnecting communities and traditions. Because of the depth of this project (historically, culturally, politically), the efforts put forth by Councils to treat the transboundary watersheds as a unified political–cultural space may likely contribute to a wide acceptance of the "blurred" borders in the geographic imaginations of its supporters.

For the IJC's International Watersheds Initiative, the drive to cooperate at a binational level, will likely be region-dependent. Even where the IJC establishes a watershed board, it is unlikely that the IJC's involvement will foster a "borderless" geographic imagination for those involved. The IJC's presence, although ultimately in place to provide support at a watershed level, is still under the rubric of a nation-to-nation governance structure, which, in turn, reifies colonial constructions of space.

Conclusions and reflections

In this chapter, I explored the role of subnational actors in transboundary water governance through an analysis of the IJC's new International Watersheds Initiative. IJC's International Watershed Boards provide an opportunity for a more regional approach to transnational environmental cooperation. Since the inception of the International Watersheds Initiative in 1997, the IJC has helped to form four international watershed boards across the Canada–U.S. border. The new boards represent, in many ways, the shift from "government" to "governance" and an increased involvement of subnational actors as environmental actors. It also represents a broadening of responsibilities, which addresses water quality and water quantity issues simultaneously. However, despite the expanded role of the IJC's watershed boards, several regions have yet to participate at the local level, including the Pacific.

The development of the IWI approach is consistent with wider trends of multijurisdictional cooperation and increased participation of local actors in environmental governance. The Initiative was particularly noteworthy as it marked a distinct departure from the IJC's largely federally oriented governance style. Although the Initiative has not been widely adopted, it does show an institutional willingness on the part of the IJC to adapt to changing socio-political conditions, specifically the increased demand for civic engagement in natural resources issues.

I began the analysis by detailing the proposed composition of the Watershed Boards. Specifically, I showed how the Boards build on the strengths of the established IJC governance mechanisms, such as the References, fact-finding roles, and Water Quality/Quantity Boards. I described how collaboration, committee work, and shared goals have helped establish trust between the actors – a key element of being "a good upstream neighbor". Furthermore, I have suggested that the IJC's role in creating neutral platforms would likely remain a main asset for the Watersheds Initiative.

I then turned to the numerous critiques of the watershed approach. In particular, I questioned the long-term sustainability of the transboundary watershed group if it remains a federally-controlled process, particularly in times of non-crisis. A key argument throughout this analysis is that when the primary mechanism for transboundary water governance is state or federally-controlled, the nation-state boundaries are inherently reified. Even if the stated purview of the state/federal agency is "transboundary", they are defined by systemic nation-state boundaries and associated policies that are colonial relics. The work towards collaborating with partners on the *other* side of the border continues to reinforce national identities and national interpretations of landscape. They do not (and cannot) genuinely include connected ecosystems, nor traditional territories for Indigenous communities. Although some gains have been made within the IJC for greater inclusion of Indigenous peoples in the decision-making process (such as the Rainy Lake of the Woods Watershed Board *explicitly* including a seat for Indigenous representatives on their Board – something that the previous boards have not done) room remains for greater inclusion and diversity.

In the next Part, I explore the impacts of divided spaces on connected ecosystems and communities (as seen with the Boundary Bay case, Chapter 5), Indigenous-led formal mechanisms (such as the Coast Salish Gathering, Chapter 6), as well as performative techniques (such as the Canoe Journey, Chapter 7, and the Water Walkers, Chapter 8). Lastly, I explore the ongoing challenges of worldviews and governance through the complex case of Luna/*Tsu-xiit*, which challenges governance mechanisms both jurisdictionally and through a blurring of animal–human lines (Chapter 9).

Notes

1 Mitchell, 1990; Montgomery *et al.*, 1995; McGinnis, 1999; Leach and Pelkey, 2001; Kliot *et al.*, 2001.

2 This is based on interviews and feedback from the 2008 transboundary water governance workshop held at the University of British Columbia, Vancouver. The case studies represent an analysis of qualitative and quantitative data drawn from interviews with water managers on both sides of the border, participant observation in transboundary water governance activities, and a comprehensive database of transboundary water governance instruments. Specifically, for this chapter, the interviews with IJC officials occurred in Ottawa in January 2006 and DC in April 2006. The phone interviews occurred in 2007 and 2008. Overall, this research represents 54 interviews from cross-sectors of jurisdictions of actors involved in the governance of transboundary waters. For more information on methodology, please see Norman (2009).

Part Two

Indigenous water governance

Re/ordering transnational space

5 Shellfish harvesting in Boundary Bay

Transboundary environmental justice and the politics of counting

On a summer day in 1997, several members of the Semiahmoo First Nation travelled to the tidal waters of Boundary Bay, a small body of water on the Pacific coast of North America, to harvest shellfish. Across the bay, members of the Lummi tribe were also harvesting shellfish. This situation was not out of the ordinary: for centuries, Coast Salish communities relied successfully on these waters as primary sources of food, with clams, crab, oysters, shrimp, and many other species readily obtainable for harvest year-round.

However, what made this situation unique and important is that, on one side of the bay, the Semiahmoo community members were "breaking the law", while, on the other side, the Lummi community members were harvesting "legally". At the day's end, several members of the Semiahmoo band were fined for "illegally" harvesting shellfish, while the Lummi tribe continued harvesting without interruption. The reason for this discrepancy is simple: the Semiahmoo members reside in Canada, while the Lummi reside in the United States.

These divergent experiences stem from distinctive colonial histories after the establishment of the international border on the 49th parallel, reflecting different legal regimes that were created around respective American and British interests (see Textbox 2.1). To this day, these different framings continue to impact how communities relate to natural resources. In Boundary Bay, the tidelands have been summarily closed to shellfish harvesting since 1962 in Canada, but have been opened conditionally since 2004 in the United States as a result of monitoring and restoration.

Asking the simple question "who's counting?", both in terms of shellfish numbers and pollution inputs, provides insight into the spatial politics of ecosystem management, particularly in relation to Indigenous rights to access culturally relevant food. In this chapter, I explore the ways that historically connected Indigenous communities are divergently impacted by shellfish regulations and water pollution. I describe how ecocolonialism employs a series of political technologies (including calculative techniques such as the enumeration of contamination levels) that have significant political effects on Indigenous communities. Unpacking what Gregory calls "the extraordinary power and performative force of colonial modernity" (2004, p. 4) helps to shed light on critical environmental justice issues tied to ecosystem protection and access to traditional food resources.

For the purpose of this chapter, I employ Watson's definition of ecocolonization: "the process by which Indigenous people collaterally suffer the effects of the seizure and destruction of their natural resources by an outside political force" (2009, p. 4). This definition builds on earlier concepts of green imperialism, which link imperial expansion to environmental degradation (Griffiths and Robbins, 1997; Grove, 1997).

I suggest that ecocolonization occurs in three central ways in Boundary Bay: first, through the bordering of space that ties Indigenous communities to small parcels of land (reserves in Canada and reservations in the U.S.) under different political regimes, and with limited access to marine resources; second, through "extraterritorial" pollution inputs that compromise culturally significant marine resources; and third, through the politics of calculation.

The first two points are relatively well examined in existing literature at the intersection of political ecology, environmental justice, and political and

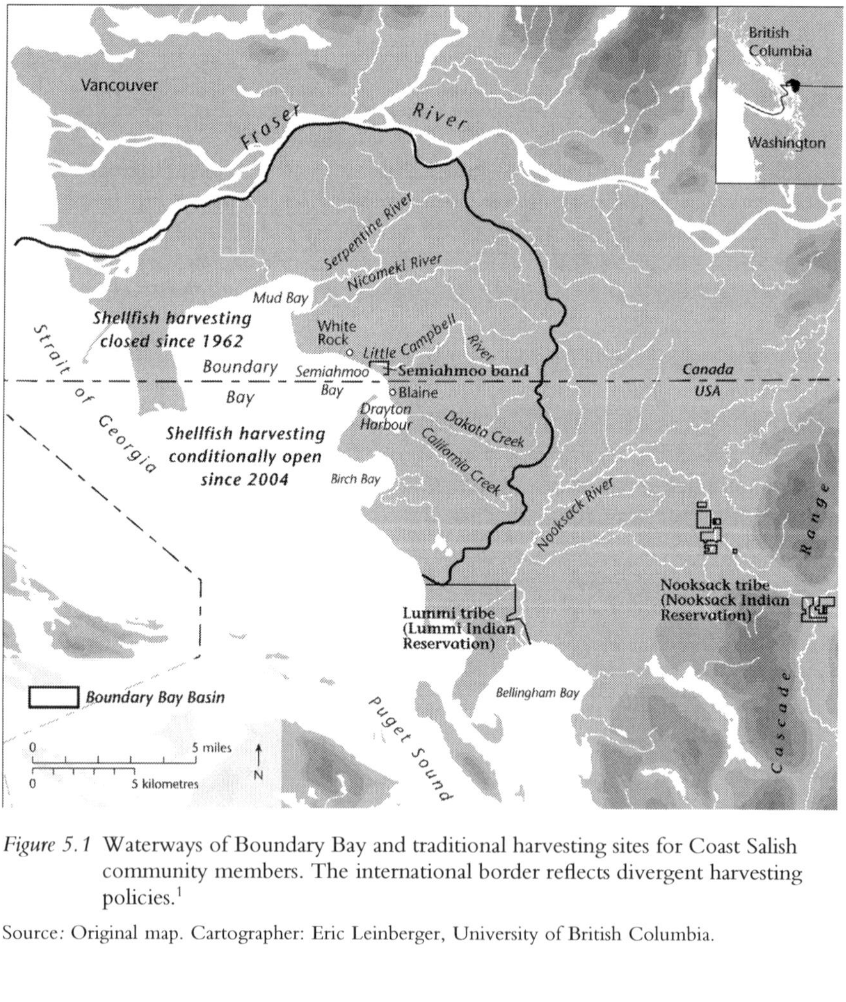

Figure 5.1 Waterways of Boundary Bay and traditional harvesting sites for Coast Salish community members. The international border reflects divergent harvesting policies.[1]

Source: Original map. Cartographer: Eric Leinberger, University of British Columbia.

environmental geography.[2] However, the third point, which links the politics of calculation to ecocolonization, is less developed and is the central focus of this chapter.[3]

Politics of b/ordering and counting

This chapter suggests that much is to be gained by exploring how political and legal regimes of resource management are operationalized on the ground and how these regimes impact historically connected communities in different ways. Unpacking the tensions between the fixity of modern political borders, the fluidity of natural resources (and pollution inputs), and the socio-political implications of "counting" and "dividing" ecosystems provide more nuance to the practicalities of governing resources in a b/ordered landscape.

For many Indigenous communities throughout the world, fragmented post-colonial landscapes, a rapidly changing physical environment, and social equity issues complicate access to food (Kauanui, 2008; Robbins, 2012). The Boundary Bay case demonstrates that technologies of power associated with the politics of calculation have considerable impacts on Indigenous communities.

Politics of calculation

This chapter stems from and enriches the existing body of geographic literature that critically examines the interrelationships between space, politics and calculation.[4] Mitchell (1991), in particular, helped to lay the foundation for the critical inquiry of spatial politics in *Colonising Egypt*, which relocated Heidegger's notion of enframing and Foucault's work on governmentality to a global context. Mitchell (2002) furthered his analysis in *Rule of experts* by linking the modern technologies of power with the politics of calculation (or "techno-politics") of Egypt. Additionally, Elden (2007) described the crucial role of calculation in ordering the spaces and social processes of modernity. The construction of "calculating subjects" as a mechanism to create national identities and translocate value systems is a well-documented form of colonization (Said, 1979; Gregory, 2004). Thus, as Crampton and Elden (2006) suggest, elucidating relations between the political and the calculative helps illuminate the political and social costs of enframing or "othering". The distinction between quantitative methods of geography and the geographies of calculation lie in the rationalities associated with the process of enumeration (Mitchell, 2002; Rose-Redwood, 2012). The former utilizes calculation as a geographic method, whereas the latter takes calculation itself (and its political effects) as the "object" of critical geographic analysis. From this rich body of work, I examine the politics of calculation to inform my analysis of ecocolonization in Boundary Bay.

The situation in Boundary Bay reflects all aspects of these imperial constructs, but particularly demonstrates the impacts of calculation on maintaining a traditional way of life in which access to marine resources is central to identity. Enumerating and tabulating shellfish, rendering pollution inputs "uncountable", and governing who can and cannot access these resources are exercises of State authority. This process of "calculative rationality" resonates with Miller's (1997) observation that calculative systems (including accounting conventions) always involve the prioritization of some criteria over others. It is the process of prioritization that is at the heart of ecocolonization – through which frameworks are often established and voices are privileged or overshadowed, as is the case for the Coast Salish communities in Boundary Bay.

Coast Salish peoples and connection to marine resources

Numerous scholars have contributed ethnographic details of the political and societal structure of the Coast Salish communities.[5] These discussions help lay a foundation for examining the inconsistencies in access to marine resources for people who share a common ancestry and a long-standing connection to land and water. One issue central to the focus of this chapter is that people Indigenous to the Pacific coastal area have a deep and sustained relationship with marine ecosystems, but due to contemporary political framings and extraterritorial pollution, access to these resources is limited. The traditional way of life for Coast Salish people centres on the ability to harvest resources from a marine environment. The connection to these resources is not merely economic or dietary, but rather part of a long-standing tradition that is integral to cultural identity (Suttles, 1974). The importance of this connection was continually reinforced in interviews and meetings, as indicated by the following quotes from Coast Salish community members: "Our people have always relied on the sea for our food . . . harvesting from the sea is our way of life"; "To us, it is not about money or jobs, it is directly related to what it means to be a Salish person". In addition, archaeological records clearly show the overall long-term importance of shellfish in the Boundary Bay regions, dating back thousands of years (Matson, 2010).

These statements and records demonstrate that severing access to traditional foods has immediate and significant impacts on the physical and cultural health of a community. Reduced access occurs through a number of stressors. Pollution inputs, global climate change, and changing land use patterns all affect the quality of the marine environment, including food sources. In Boundary Bay, marine resources such as shellfish have decreased significantly since European contact, and continue to be compromised both in terms of quality and quantity (AFN, 2007; Donatuto, 2008).

Shellfish harvesting: British Columbia, Canada

Closures of shellfish harvesting sites have increased steadily in British Columbia over the past three decades. As of 31 December 2004, Environment Canada had reported 123,832 hectares closed to harvesting of shellfish in British Columbia (BC). The majority of the closures appear in the heavily populated Georgia Basin region (71,818 hectares), with some of the largest closures occurring in Boundary Bay (Figure 5.1). The closures result from nonpoint source pollution inputs associated with excessive runoff from the upland catchment occurring particularly after major storm events. Although shellfish are not harmed by fecal coliform bacteria pollution, these bacteria pose a risk to human health when consumed (Picot *et al.*, 2011). Due to such concerns, the intertidal shores north of the international border of Boundary Bay, Mud Bay, and Semiahmoo Bay have remained closed since 1962. The Semiahmoo band, whose traditional territory (and modern reserve) centers on Semiahmoo Bay, has actively fought for stronger regulations to limit pollution and argued against the "blanket" closures. The Semiahmoo have engaged in subsistence and cultural shellfish harvesting for thousands of years, and argue that rendering the tidelands summarily "closed" without periodic review is a violation of their inherent right to harvest and has insidious impacts on the well-being of their people.

As one community member noted:

> Closing the tidal waters altogether means that the people have given up on the tidal waters. Protecting it and caring for it is no longer a priority. We have not given up on the water. We can't give up. This is our home and harvesting from the sea is our way of life.

Closing the areas plays into what Warry (2008) argues is an underlying politics of denial related to Indigenous issues. For Boundary Bay, the denial acts to limit the recognition of the scope, importance, and nature of shellfish harvesting for First Nations. Ideally, habitat restoration practices and enforcement of land use policies would eliminate the need for closures altogether. However, for immediate purposes, the removal of blanket closures would allow the Semiahmoo First Nation to fulfill their right to harvest legally. Canadian First Nations' customary rights to fish and harvest marine resources are protected by a number of mechanisms, including the Constitution of Canada, court rulings, a federal Aboriginal Fisheries Strategy, as well as land and sea settlement agreements (Harris and Millerd, 2010). The Supreme Court of Canada affirmed the right to fish for sustenance, social and ceremonial uses (R. v. Sparrow 1990). However, the Canadian government (supported by the courts) takes the position that the rights must be proven case-by-case. The burden of proof related to customary rights lies with the First Nations and until it is proven in court, the rights remain "potential rights" (McNeil, 2008). For the Coast Salish First Nations, the extraordinary expense of litigation has proven prohibitive to bringing the shellfish issues to trial. In addition, when closures are associated with health risks, the ability to exercise these rights is limited further. As a Department of Fisheries and Oceans (BC) official noted, "The sport fishery regulation closes Boundary Bay to shellfish harvesting. There is no exception for the Semiahmoo band – it is a shellfish contamination closure and the shellfish is deemed unsafe for anyone to consume". However, many Coast Salish People disagree with this interpretation: "Having someone tell us where we can harvest and when goes against our inherent right to harvest". The issue of who determines (who calculates) when an area is open or closed is wrought with power dynamics and is at the heart of ecocolonization. Since the federal regulatory agencies in Canada have limited funds to conduct routine water quality and shellfish toxin testing, no one is able to harvest shellfish legally in Boundary or Semiahmoo Bays. The administrative decision to uphold a blanket closure rather than conduct ongoing tests affects everyone interested in harvesting. However, this decision has disproportionate impacts on Indigenous communities such as the Semiahmoo First Nation.

Framing this issue in terms of environmental justice helps to crystallize the links between contamination events, the lack of institutional capacity and fiscal priority to conduct ongoing routine water quality testing, and the restricted access to a food source integral to diverse senses of well-being within Indigenous communities. Thus, the government's decision to render the Bay "incalculable" has considerable political effects on local Indigenous communities.

This chapter asserts that the inability of the Semiahmoo First Nation to harvest "legally" – both due to environmental degradation of the waters and the lack of ongoing water quality tests – is a form of ecocolonization. This injustice is further complicated at the site of the border, where the divergent right to harvest shellfish comes down to which side of the border family members ended up on during relocation of families to reserves. To the members of these communities, the provincial government's lack of financial priority to test the waters appears to be extremely unjust.

Shellfish harvesting: Washington, United States

The contaminated tidelands of Boundary Bay also threaten the tradition of shellfish harvesting in the U.S. However, because of significant clean-up efforts on the U.S. side of the bay (and a willingness by the State to routinely test), Drayton Harbor has been open for conditional use in Washington State since 2004. This means that certain groups, including Indigenous groups and licensed commercial harvesters, are able to harvest when environmental conditions are deemed safe.

In the U.S., the legal right that Washington State Coast Salish people have to harvest shellfish lies within a series of treaties signed with representatives of the federal government in the 1850s. These treaties recognized legal rights for western Washington tribes to access fish in all usual and accustomed grounds (NWIFC, 2010). These treaties represent a negotiation between the newcomer and the Indigenous communities, and a political structure imposed on communities with established governance systems. Since shellfish are considered fish within the meaning of treaties, they fall under the same rights as other fish such as salmon (Boxberger, 1989).

Therefore, federally recognized tribes in the U.S. such as the Lummi are legally able to harvest shellfish for sustenance and cultural purposes in their usual and accustomed areas (Boxberger, 1989, 1993). These rights were upheld by U.S. District Judge George Boldt, who interpreted "in common with" to mean "sharing equally the opportunity to take fish . . ." between treaty and non-treaty fisherpeople. A central aspect of the Boldt decision in the context of Boundary Bay is not only the fixed allocation, but also the right of the tribes to manage their share (Boxberger, 1989). Although harvesting has reopened conditionally for federally recognized tribes in Washington State, the Indigenous communities remain impacted by the politics of calculation. In order to participate legally in the harvest, the tribal members must navigate a foreign bureaucracy with a matrix of rules and regulations. The particulars of when, where, how, whom, and how much are all meticulously outlined and governed by state officials such as the Washington State Department of Fish and Wildlife and the Washington State Department of Health. The wording and procedures of the regulations reflect a Western scientific approach to wildlife management rather than a Traditional Ecological Knowledge approach, which shifts the process of harvesting from an inherent right to a conditional right – a fundamental distinction (Cajete, 2000; Little Bear, 2000; Nadasdy, 2004).

Participating in population surveys and estimates, reporting catch and providing written notification of intention to harvest are all management techniques that place the right to harvest in the context of a policed system (Nadasdy, 2004). To many Coast Salish community members, the old adage, "when the tide is out, the table is set" is seen as a fundamental part of the traditional family-based tenure practices for harvesting this resource. Similarly, as one fisherwoman recalls, "When we needed fish for our family, we set out our nets and had food on our table in the evening. We did not need to wait for someone to tell us that the season was 'open' and then have to report our 'catch' to an external agency" (personal communication with author, 2009). This continual monitoring is perceived as a form of colonization and an affront to core values associated with what it means to be a Coast Salish person (Bierwert, 1999). The rules for harvesting are both internally and externally policed. The tribes themselves are responsible for working within the defined foreign system and reporting "aberrant" behavior. For the foreign system to function within tribal territory, the tribal members have to accept or internalize the regulations, thereby reinforcing the norms of a colonial present. Participation in surveys, calculations, and reporting transforms the act of shellfish harvesting into a Western-based science. For the Coast Salish fisherperson, however, distinct rules for access to resources are embedded in cultural norms and passed down through generations. In this system, in which an intricate organizational scheme exists within a tribe and inter-tribally, everyone in the community has a role in harvesting, from net mending to cooking and all family members are provided for (Suttles, 1954, 1990; Boxberger, 1989).

However, working within the usual and accustomed system, shellfish are treated as countable objects, disconnected from traditional rights of access. This reporting system also reinforces distinct power relations in which State bureaucracies control key aspects of the harvest. The physical demarcation of political borders – the Canada–U.S. border, reserve boundaries, and usual and accustomed harvest areas – separates cultural landscapes and further contributes to the weakening of the historical–cultural act of harvesting. Each of these bordering practices, although serving different means, are interrelated in that they create a paradigm of regulation over resources. This is problematic particularly in Washington State, where the tribes must access the tidelands through private lands.

The process of enumerating shellfish further places the harvest into a quantifiable framework, reducing the complexities of shellfish harvesting into a calculable (and manageable) quantity (Mitchell, 1991, 2002). This framework lends itself to regulation by the State and has significant political consequences (Demeritt, 2001). As Hannah (2000) observes, the politics of calculation tend to have greater impacts on under-represented and marginalized populations such as Indigenous people living on reservations. Such disproportionate impacts demonstrate how the internalization of borders can manifest itself into ecocolonization.

Identifying the techniques of ecocolonization (such as enumeration of catch and contamination levels) is an important step towards decolonizing space (Harris, 2002), both for the tribes and bands themselves and for the external agencies involved in resource management.

Regulations and resistance

As described above, the politics of calculation impact Indigenous communities differently, depending on which side of the international border they reside. The divergent policies put in place after the demarcation of the Canada–U.S. border also complicates intertribal negotiations. In Boundary Bay, the communities face many hurdles to working cooperatively, despite their historical connectedness. Divergent policies in the U.S. and Canada have perpetuated an internalization of "foreign" borders in Coast Salish communities, where differential access to limited resources based on political borders accentuates divisiveness (Thom, 2010). This division is exacerbated by the limitations to physically crossing the Canada–U.S. border and divergent resource management practices, both of which are complicated in a post-9/11 context (Miller, 1996–1997, 2006). The difficulty of crossing the border is continually referenced as an impediment for living and working within the traditional Coast Salish territory. For example, it is common for community members to travel many kilometers out of their way to go through what is considered "a more friendly border post" than the main point of entry. Over the years, I have heard many reports that the harassment and feeling of unease that people feel while crossing the international border has greatly limited their travel. This is particularly important for Coast Salish community members, with regard to their sense of connectedness between tribes and bands that span the border.

Furthermore, the nesting of tribal governance systems within a nation-state framework intensifies this divisiveness. One tribal employee reflected on her experience participating in a transboundary environmental committee:

> Right now, [our tribe] is recognized by the [U.S.] federal government as having treaty rights to harvest shellfish in what we call the usual and accustomed location. . . . And that's very important to the tribe that these rights are protected and that we want to ensure that they continue. So when I've reported back that the [Canadian band] is trying to make overtures to work in the waters on this side of the border, too, there's a strong reaction with respect to the fact that they do not have those same federally recognized rights on this side of the border. And if they wish to secure those rights, which is not a small task, they need to be making overtures and meeting with the tribes themselves. A discussion with me, at that table, is not adequate to do that. They have to be talking to our leaders.

Here, divergent policies in the U.S. and Canada have perpetuated an internalization of "foreign" borders within the Coast Salish communities. Differential access to limited resources based on political demarcations accentuates the reality. Though Canadian Coast Salish peoples may want to exercise traditional rights in U.S. waters because they are not "closed" for contaminants, the rights are not recognized across national borders, which serves as a double-exclusion for Canadian Coast Salish peoples.

However, Coast Salish leaders have made strides in re-imagining a "unified space" that provides a counter-narrative to postcolonial constructs of space. This has occurred through the creation of new transboundary governance mechanisms, such as the Coast Salish Gathering (Chapter 6), and the use of counter-mapping and critical cartography to re-imagine a unified space through the "Salish Sea". The Gathering provides an important mechanism to start addressing issues of shared concern in a unified Coast Salish voice, rather than tribe-by-tribe, band-by-band. For governmental employees and policy makers, this means "seeing" the waters and tidelands of Boundary Bay as a connected ecosystem and part of the wider Salish Sea. The participants of the Coast Salish Gathering call for increased capacity to govern and protect natural resources such as shellfish for the benefit of historically connected cultural groups (Thom, 2010). The 2010 naming of the Salish Sea as a supplement to the Georgia Basin–Puget Sound raised the political profile of such divided landscapes. This cartographic construct had a dual purpose: to honor the traditional territory of the Coast Salish communities and to acknowledge a connected aquatic ecosystem (Rose-Redwood, 2011). The Salish Sea naming, the development of the Gathering, and the Canoe Journeys may be preliminary steps in a political re-imagining of the territory as a connected region, indicating a movement towards "decolonizing the landscape". For Coast Salish community members, this means realigning governance mechanisms to reflect unified conceptions of place. Both the naming and the new governance structure de-emphasize the line that has made shellfish harvesting legal only to those on one side of the border, and that has reified a colonial construct counter to the Salish sense of space/place and counter to intact ecosystems. Whether these changes will translate into a re-evaluation of relevant policies and procedures in Boundary Bay is yet to be determined.

Conclusions and reflections

In this chapter, I suggest that jointly examining the politics of calculation and concepts of ecocolonization is helpful in the ongoing effort to unpack the complexities of the colonial present. By investigating shellfish closures for Boundary Bay, I show that Indigenous rights to harvest traditional foods are being compromised by a polluted ecosystem, a lack of government funding to monitor tidelands and protect habitats, and calculative techniques.

I have shown that the nation-state project of occupation continues to reify and entrench borders, rules, and regulations that are often incongruent with historical and cultural practices of Indigenous communities. Exacerbating these challenges is that the politics of calculation occur differently on either side of the international border. In Canada, the tidelands are deemed "incalculable". In the U.S., the tidelands are "open" but under strict control. In both situations, ecocolonization occurs as the process of harvesting shifts from an inherent right to a conditional right, and extraterritorial pollution inputs and degraded habitats limit access to a culturally relevant food source.

I suggest the need to decolonize our understanding of calculative techniques as it relates to ecosystem management, and offer a more nuanced interpretation of space that accounts for both traditional boundaries and ecosystems. The following questions can serve as next steps in this project:

- How could the Indigenous practice of shellfish harvesting be characterized as a "right" in the Canadian context?
- What will it take to minimize the impacts of public safety problems on the exercise of these rights (i.e. increased monitoring and sampling, compensation for degraded habitat, improved access, stronger anti-contamination laws, coordinated harvesting arrangements with other First Nations)?
- Will the development of the governing bodies such as the Coast Salish Gathering and cartographic constructs such as the Salish Sea contribute to the decolonization through discursive means?

Examining such issues would contribute to wider discussions of decolonizing space, and help communities such as the Coast Salish advocate for legal access to the resources that are necessary for their traditional way of life. Great need remains for revised policies, management plans, and longer-term conservation planning. However, asking the question "who's counting?" is a step towards addressing issues related to environmental justice, ecosystem management, and Indigenous rights.

In the next chapter, I investigate the counter-hegemonic practices of, and counter-narratives produced from, the Indigenous-led Coast Salish Gathering. This investigation helps to answer the third question related to the possibility of decolonization through discursive means, in addition to the wider questions related to increased self-determination and governance.

Notes

1 Thanks to the Royal Geographic Society for permission to reprint portions of the article by Norman (2013) Who's counting? Spatial politics, ecocolonization, and the politics of calculation in Boundary Bay, and for permission to reprint Figure 5.1.

2 See Sparke, 1998; Barman 1999; Clayton, 2000; Harris, 2002; Heynen, 2003; Miller, 2006; Simpson, 2007; Kauanui, 2008; Holifield *et al.*, 2009; Huhndorf, 2009.

3 For exceptions see Demeritt, 2001; Nadasdy, 2004, 2005.

4 Mitchell, 1991, 1999, 2002; Braun, 2000; Hannah, 2000, 2009; Duncan, 2002; Crampton and Elden, 2006; Elden, 2006, 2007; Ettlinger, 2011; Rose-Redwood, 2012.

5 Suttles, 1954, 1974, 1990; Verma, 1956; Allen, 1976; Boxberger and Miller, 1997; Harmon, 2000; Kennedy, 2007; Angelbeck, 2009.

6 "We are the ones that we are waiting for"

Indigenous leadership in transborder environmental governance

In November 2005, the first annual Coast Salish Gathering was held at the Jamestown S'Klallam Tribal Center in Sequim, Washington. This Gathering brought together First Nation Chiefs, Tribal Chairs, and Council members from around the Salish Sea of the coastal Pacific region of North America. Invited delegates from Canadian and U.S. governments and environmental organizations also participated in the dialogue with the tribal leaders in an attempt to address environmental issues of shared concern, particularly issues related to the protection of salmon habitat.

"It has been a long time since we have all come together as tribes", reflected Tom Sampson, prominent Coast Salish elder and tribal leader on the first day of the Gathering in Jamestown S'Klallam (2005). "The last five hundred years", he stated solemnly, "have not been great ones for our people". The elder reminded the audience that the words spoken today "are the words from our ancestors" and that the purpose of the Gathering was "to talk about the future of our children and the children yet to be born".

The opening statement addressed several interrelated topics: tribal governance, ancestral rights, environmental degradation, and the connectedness of the Coast Salish people. Although the words were spoken softly, they filled the longhouse in its entirety. Each one of the 200 participants listened intently as one of the most revered tribal leaders of the Coast Salish communities opened the discussions.

At the end of the 3-day Gathering, the Coast Salish leaders committed their communities to finding solutions to the pressing environmental issues they face, particularly those related to protecting the waterways of critical salmon habitat. The leaders agreed that the most effective way to accomplish this goal was to establish their own governing body and speak with a unified voice. As a result, the Coast Salish leaders agreed to the formation of an Indigenous-led governing body that would meet annually at the Coast Salish Gatherings.

Through the development of the Gatherings, the tribes and bands throughout Coast Salish territory have committed to working together to address shared environmental issues, drawing on a strong connection to their land, shared ancestors, and a commitment to the revitalization of their culture. As a group, they share the goal "[t]o protect the environment and natural resources of the Salish Sea for the sustainability of the Coast Salish peoples". The Coast Salish Gatherings represent more than seventy tribes and bands that span and pre-date the Canada–U.S. border, encompassing approximately 72,000 square kilometers of the Coast Salish region. The creation of the Salish governing body does not replace participation in other environmental fora; rather, it provides an organization designed for and by Salish people that places the Coast Salish belief system at the forefront of the governance structure.

A key issue that the Gatherings address – and a central theme in this book – is creating governance mechanisms commensurate to a scale that makes sense, ecologically and culturally. The protection of the watercourses of the Salish Sea is also a practical matter of preserving traditional lifeways. The bioaccumulative effects of pollution coupled with years of overharvesting have placed tremendous strain on the natural resources of the Salish Sea Basin, thereby disrupting the political, economic, and cultural fabric of many Coast Salish communities (Donatuto, 2008). Understanding the importance of these Gatherings provides valuable insights into the scalar politics of transboundary water governance. That the new governance mechanisms are, at their foundation, based on Coast Salish territorial boundaries, rather than institutions representing Canada or the United States, challenges implicit assumptions regarding constructions of scale, particularly in a postcolonial context.

This chapter explores the mechanisms that the Indigenous leaders are using to challenge colonial scalar constructions. Coast Salish Tribes and First Nations are (re)creating a shared sense of identity congruent with traditional territory and that reinforces cultural values through techniques that scholars and activists call "critical cartography" and "strategic essentialism". As found throughout this book, exploring scalar politics provides critical insights into the power dynamics often implicit in water governance, particularly for watercourses that transgress political boundaries. This case, which encompasses multiple jurisdictions and interpretations of spatial constructs, provides an interesting avenue to analyze scalar politics from the lens of transnational politics for Indigenous communities because Indigenous leaders are using shared cultural identities to challenge colonial boundary-drawing (see Figure 6.1).

Drawing the line: borders, power, and Indigenous space

As seen in the previous chapters, the delineation of the Canada–U.S. border and its subsequent provinces, states, and regions is part of the construction of a cultural landscape and identity built by culturally specific meanings. The centuries-old negotiation of territory that is now deemed Canada and the United States were part of a series of negotiations, disputes, and treaties that defined and redefined territories as separate spaces. Although documenting the historical processes that defined the modern Canada–U.S. border is beyond the scope of this chapter, it is important to acknowledge that the construction of political borders is part of wider geohistorical processes (see Textbox 2.2).

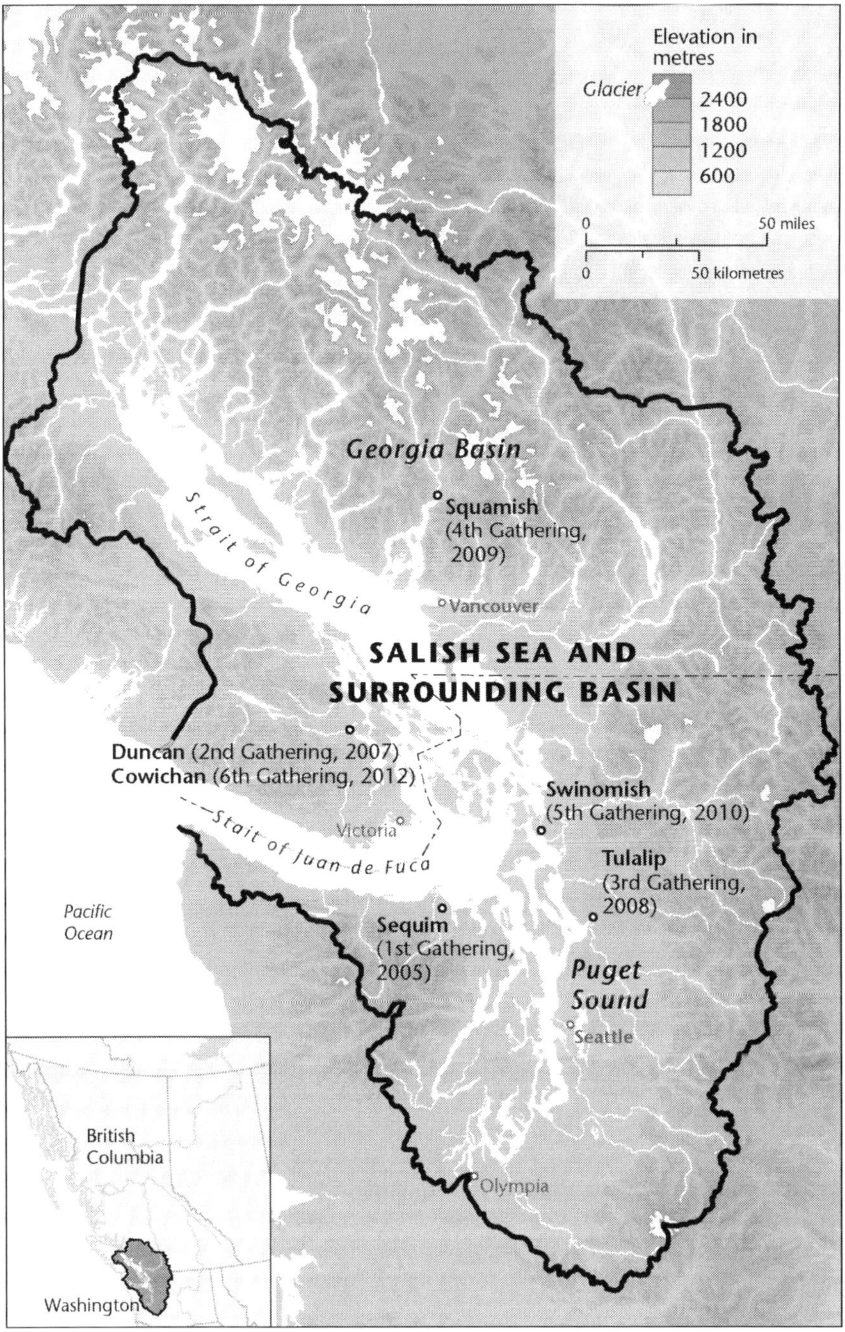

Figure 6.1 Map of Salish Sea Basin and locations of Coast Salish Gatherings.

Source: Original map. Cartography by Eric Leinberger, University of British Columbia.

As Canada and the United States built their cultural identities as bounded nations, the identities of the Indigenous communities spanning the border were impacted by the changing political geography. The production of sovereign political systems in Canada and the United States affected and continues to affect environmental governance, particularly access to and management of resources for Indigenous communities. The colonial political demarcation not only severed a cultural continuum that spanned and pre-dated the international border, but also created different national identities, rights to ownership of land, and land and resource policies that continue to impact Indigenous communities (Boxberger, 1989; Harris DC, 2000, 2001; Harris C, 2002). As the divergent political systems strengthened and developed national identities, Indigenous communities, whose traditional territory spanned the international divide, became increasingly fragmented.

Shortly after the 1849 demarcation, yet another politically-defined construction of space occurred in North America. The establishment of the reservation system was a physical and political restructuring of Indigenous communities, which greatly impacted access to culturally relevant resources such as salmon and shellfish and impacted hunting and gathering practices throughout Coast Salish territory (Boxberger, 1989; Harris, 2000). A new tribal system was imposed on a cultural group based on family units unified by cultural practice, language, and intermarriage (Suttles, 1974). As noted Coast Salish scholar Wayne Suttles (1960, p. 296) reflects, groups of villages in the Coast Salish region were linked by "common dialect and traditions as 'tribes' but in recent generations these village groupings were certainly not separate 'societies'". The creation of the reserve system significantly altered settlements, migration patterns, and access to resources for the Salish communities (Boxberger, 1993; Miller, 1997, 2006; Barman, 1999).

The political demarcations drastically changed participation in subsistence activities not only throughout Coast Salish territory, but wherever the Indigenous communities would seek to harvest resources. Access to natural resources, including hunting, gathering, and marine and freshwater resources, was regulated under divergent sets of codes, laws, and principles. The implications of the changed governance structures post-contact are especially acute in the management of mobile resources, e.g. salmon that migrate between the newly demarcated borders. In many cases, the salmon spawn on one side of the international border and migrate to the other side during their adult life. This migration complicates fishing rights and access during the harvest season. The access to, and distribution of, salmon are integral components to the societal make-up and identity of Coast Salish communities (Suttles, 1974; Boxberger, 1989). The shift from internally-governed systems (pre-contact) to externally-monitored systems (post-contact) has ongoing consequences and implications for cultural preservation. This restructuring also has far-reaching impacts related to preservation of family structures. Limiting the ability to subsist on natural resources, and therefore limiting the ability to support Indigenous communities, causes extraordinary stress on families and ultimately comprises the wellness of intact family structures.

Beyond rights of access to marine resources for individual families, the political reorganization of the Salish Sea basin has had dramatic impacts on relationships between tribal members and non-tribal members, and between tribes themselves. For example, the contentious relationships, known as the "salmon wars" in the Pacific Northwest (Findlay and Coates, 2002), fueled the shifting economic structures that supported competing for resources (as sources of cash) rather than cooperation for subsistence (Singleton, 2002). Adding to the tensions are the extraterritorial impacts of environmental degradation on critical fish habitat (spawning grounds) and the negative impacts of global climate change on fish populations.

In the Coast Salish case (similar to other Indigenous communities throughout the world), social restructuring adversely impacts the cultural fabric of the population. As such, the Gatherings are not just about addressing environmental issues; rather, the governance structures have far-reaching goals that include language revitalization and self-determination. Thus, the work of the Coast Salish Gatherings is part of the process to reclaim and rebuild some of the internal control of decision-making and governance. It is also about strengthening the individual tribes and bands to think beyond the limits (geographic, economic, political, etc.) that were placed on them during colonial times.

The Gatherings are deliberate attempts to rebuild the cultural structures and characteristics of the Coast Salish communities. This work is achieved, in part, through the "scaling up" of individual bands and tribes to a singular nation. In this case, the process of reconstructing the scale based on wider Coast Salish territory is occurring through the employment of techniques such as strategic essentialism, performativity, and counter-mapping.

Challenging bounded space – rethinking citizenry

Analyzing the Gatherings as governance mechanisms provides three entry points into understanding how reconstructed borders (and re-imagined scales of governance) might usefully inform water governance. First, governance mechanisms such as the Gathering can socially reconstruct a new geographic region (the Salish Sea basin), thereby challenging and disrupting imposed nation-state borders and facilitating more coordinated water governance across jurisdictions. Second, the development of the Gathering is motivated by a concern for the social and cultural implications of a degraded physical environment, and is achieved by reconnecting (politically, socially, and culturally) with bands and tribes spanning the nation-state borders and increasing capacity for improved water governance throughout the Salish Sea Basin. Finally, the development of governance mechanisms based on traditional protocol can help to reinforce goals of self-governance and self-determination, as has been articulated by scholars such as Deloria (1984), Deloria and Wilkins (1999), Little Bear (2000), Wilkinson (1987), La Duke (1999), and Borrows (2002). Improved self-governance and empowerment will lead to greater capacity to carry out effective water governance throughout the Basin.

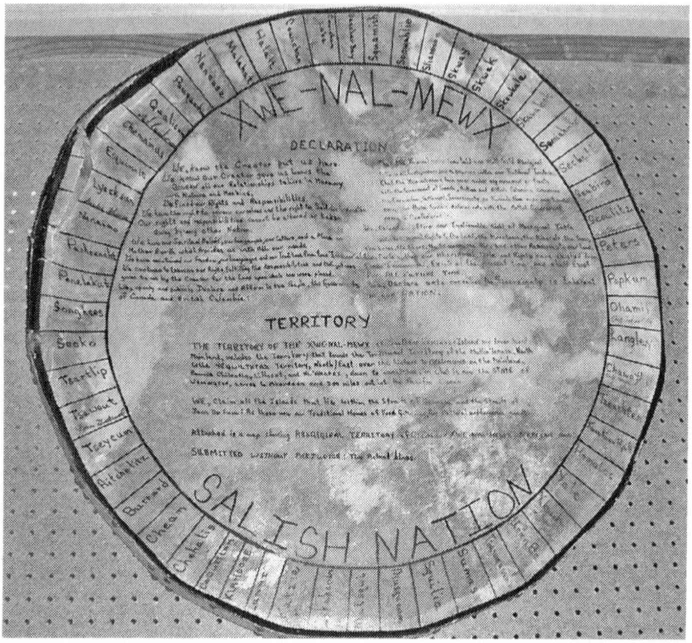

Figure 6.2 Photo of Coast Salish declaration drum.

Source: Photo taken by E. Norman, Coast Salish Aboriginal Gathering, Tulalip, Washington 2008.

Critical scalar construction: the development of the Coast Salish Gatherings

Understanding the context in which the Gathering was developed provides insights into the construction (or reconstruction) of a shared identity and the importance of including cultural politics in analyses of borders, water governance, and scale. This story shows the deliberate intent to rescale governance by "scaling up" identities from individual bands and tribes to a collective Coast Salish Nation. This is an important consideration, as rescaling is often thought of as scaling *down*. The conscious effort to unify groups on either side of the border draws simultaneously on historical connectedness and the shared desire to address issues of environmental degradation. In so doing, the participants of the Gathering are rejecting scales of governance that bifurcate the Coast Salish community (based on the nation-state system) and adopting a scale of governance commensurate with traditional Coast Salish territory (the Salish Sea Basin).

As First Nations leader, Tom Sampson, noted at the 2008 Tulalip Gathering: "When [Former Premier of British Columbia] Harcourt asked how we communicated with each other, we said, 'Ceremonies bring us together. We have our agreement, we have our drum'". The drum declaration, signed during one of the original meetings, outlines the inherent right to the lands, waters, and resources

XWE–NAL–MEWX: Salish Nation

DECLARATION

We know the Creator put us here. We know our Creator gave us laws that govern all our relationships to live in harmony with nature and mankind, defined our rights and responsibilities. We have the right to govern ourselves and the right to self-determination. Our rights and responsibilities cannot be altered or taken away by another Nation. We have spiritual beliefs, our languages, our culture, and a place on Mother Earth which provides us with all our needs.

We have maintained our freedom, our languages, and our traditions from time immemorial.

We continue to exercise our rights fulfilling the responsibilities and obligations given to us by the Creator for the land upon which we were placed. We, openly and publicly declare and affirm to the people, the governments of Canada and British Columbia:

That the Xwe-nal-mewx have held and still hold Aboriginal title to all the lands, waters and resources within our traditional territories. That the Xwe-nal-mewx have never rendered any agreement or Treaty with the Government of Canada, Britain, and British Columbia concerning the occupation, settlement, sovereignty or jurisdiction over our Lands except those treaties entered into with the British Government prior to Confederation.

We declare and affirm our Inalienable Right of Aboriginal Title of Aboriginal Rights to the lands the mountains, the minerals, the trees, the lakes, the rivers, the streams, the air, and other resources on our Land. We, declare that our Aboriginal title and rights have existed from time immemorial, exists at the present time and shall exist for all future time. We, declare unto ourselves that sovereignty is inherent in our Nation.

TERRITORY

The territory of the XWE-NAL-MEWX of Southern Vancouver Island and Lower West Mainland, includes the territory that bounds the traditional territory of the MUTHA'LEMEXIT, North the YEQW'LWTHTAX Territory, and NL'AKAPAX, down to Jenatchee, in what now the state of Washington, across to Aberdeen and 250 miles out into the Pacific Ocean.

We, claim all the Islands that lie with the Straits of Georgia and the Straits of Juan De Fuca: As these are our traditional homes of food gathering, for cultural and economic needs.

Attached is a map showing ABORIGINAL TERRITORY of Claim for XWE-NAL-MEWX NATIONS and SUBMITTED WITHOUT PREJUDICE: The Actual Lines.

Figure 6.3 Text of the Coast Salish declaration drum.

within the Coast Salish traditional territories (see Figures 6.2 and 6.3). This declaration is important for a number of reasons. First, it declares that these rights have existed since time immemorial. Second, it specifically outlines the territory of the Coast Salish region. Third, it commits the Salish Nations to govern these resources for future generations with the spirit of sovereignty as a connected nation:

> We declare and affirm our Inalienable Right of Aboriginal Title of Aboriginal Rights to the Lands, the Mountains, the Minerals, the Trees, the Lakes, the Rivers, the Streams, the Air, and other Resources on our Land. We, Declare that our Aboriginal title and rights have existed from time Immemorial, Exists at the present time and shall exist for ALL Future TIME. We, Declare unto ourselves that Sovereignty is Inherent in our NATION.

As a connected Nation, inherent rights and title to the land, water, and resources are articulated. The signing members articulate their vision, territory, and membership. This process is central to the rescaling process that includes aligning themselves under a reconnected nation and agreeing to common terms.

Signing the drum declaration serves as a symbol of the leaders' commitment to ongoing cooperation throughout the Salish Nation. As Tom Sampson reflected, "Signing the drum was one of the best things that we have done. I believe there is cause again to reaffirm that relationship". "After all", he continued, "that continuity lies in the heart and minds of our people". The drum continues to serve an important role in the Salish Gatherings.

Uniting individual tribes and bands under a single Nation (represented as a singular drum that declares and asserts the rights of a Nation) serves as a discursive tool towards the "performativity" (and actualization) of unification. These connections are reaffirmed every year, as the Coast Salish Gatherings rotate between communities. The drum is displayed prominently at the meetings and referenced frequently.

Self-determination and governance

Furthermore, the Gathering places the Salish people at the locus of power for the management and protection of their natural environment. This organizational structure reinforces a governance model in which Coast Salish people govern the resources for their community. The Gatherings serve as a place for Coast Salish community leaders to identify key priorities for the Coast Salish Nation. These priorities are then brought back to the communities and integrated into localized efforts. In addition, the Gatherings serve as an important place for information exchange, and reaffirmation and revitalization of shared identity. The Gatherings keep the momentum for the work ahead, and keep the goals aligned.

A growing number of scholars have written extensively on the need for Indigenous communities to reclaim their governance mechanisms, breaking away from systems that perpetuate a dependence on federal governments (Deloria, 1984;

Wilkinson, 1987; Little Bear, 2000; Wildcat 2011). For example, Deloria (1984, p. viii) writes:

> Citizens and tribal members often chafe at regulations and restrictions, not realizing that the burgeoning population has created a need for government to serve large numbers of people in a rather impersonal way. Some means must be found to humanize social and political institutions once again. Here traditional Indian customs, if properly incorporated in the functions and mission of government, can prove effective and important.

The spirit of Deloria's words come through at the Coast Salish Gatherings. The Gatherings are organized carefully – both in structure and language – to preserve and revitalize Coast Salish cultural practices. Unlike other transboundary environmental meetings, the Gathering does not immediately delve into policy talks and action items. Rather, the organizers design the entire first day of the Gathering to "rekindle the relationship of Coast Salish First Nations and Tribes through traditional practices" (Coast Salish Gathering, 2012).[1] The program for the Tulalip Gathering outlined the significance of this first day:

> The ceremonies are an important traditional process that is valuable in unifying the Gathering and will include the introduction and honor of the Coast Salish leadership's gallant triumphs that support the efforts to protect our aboriginal rights.

Through an intricate web of ceremony, blessings, and introductions, the participants at the Gathering become "mentally and spiritually prepared" to participate in the coming days' policy talks. The Gathering achieves this by following protocol such as blessing the four corners, calling of witnesses, and praying for the participants and their families. "This is important work", noted Chairman of the Northwest Indian Fisheries Commission, Coast Salish leader, Billy Frank Jr., and "we all need to be fully present – in mind and body – to do the work for our ancestors and children". After the ceremonies and blessings, the rest of the days are open for introductions and testimony.

For example in the Tulalip Gathering, the Council members,[2] elected officials, invited guests, veterans, and elders each had the opportunity to introduce themselves and reflect on the purpose of the meeting. The introductions often included their English and Salish name, the tribe or band they represented, and a declaration that they recognized the land that they stood on as the traditional territory of the host tribe. The Gatherings also follow traditional longhouse etiquette. The use of traditional Coast Salish language throughout the conference underscores (and embodies) the desire for cultural preservation, and is used as a way to challenge former practices of cultural dominance and forced assimilation. The deliberate planning for the Gathering helps achieve many of its goals, employing innovative strategies to transcend the political geographies of imposed borderlands to reach cultural and environmental goals.

The material impacts of a fixed border: governing across a colonial construction of space

Although the Coast Salish communities identify themselves as a connected group, the realities of border-crossing serve as harsh reminders of the politics of occupation and colonially-constructed space. In fact, many Coast Salish people do not recognize the border as a matter of principle. Some even go as far as not declaring U.S. or Canadian citizenship when crossing the border, choosing rather to self-identify by family or tribe.

Testimonies of participants attending the Jamestown and Tulalip Gatherings reflect the hardships of the border and the ongoing impacts of political fragmentation on resource management. At the Gatherings, participants provided testimony on the continued impacts of, consternation for, and resistance to their bordered homeland. In discussions, many participants described the border (or "the line" as it is commonly called by Coast Salish community members) as something that needed to be "overcome". The demarcation of this line was often viewed as something that was separating their communities: "Like the Great Wall of China, [the line] is separating us". In addition, the construction of reservation borders was also voiced as a major concern. As one elder from the northern Coast Salish territory indicated: "Our people once controlled over 600,000 [square] miles of ancestral land and now we live on reservations and they expect us to plan for the future of our children on small plots of land". In addition, the physical passage through the border brought up strong emotions related to identity and power: "Having to state, 'I'm American' or 'I'm Canadian' isn't right. 'No!' I say to the guard, 'I am Coast Salish!'".

The testimony also reflects that the Gathering provides a sense of (re)connectedness, allowing families that span the border to come together. Several of the participants voiced this as an opportunity to reconnect with family and community throughout Coast Salish territory: "We are able to bring together our relatives. That border separates us, but we are connected in many, many ways". The recognition that this was an opportunity to reunify and strengthen their voice was also noted: "We need to speak with one voice. We need to continue to build upon that foundation of shared history. That is what we are doing. We are learning to speak with one voice again." This quote is an example of how strategic essentialism is employed to push forward goals associated with a unified Coast Salish Nation, both in terms of self-determination and the capacity to serve as stewards of the shared natural environment.

In the discussions, the border was often linked to wider issues of natural resource management. As one participant reflected, "Natural resources bring us together. It bothers me that we have to *compete* for natural resources because we have always worked together. The way the system is now, we are set up against each other." The above statements capture a central driver of the establishment of the Gathering. They also reinforce observations by Thom (2010) on the changing fabric of the Coast Salish community and the efforts to reconfigure strategically for a common purpose. Historically, Coast Salish communities worked collectively to ensure adequate provisions for all family members. Intricate socio-economic networks based on trade and ceremony helped in the distribution of wealth and basic resources throughout the extended communities (Suttles, 1963; Boxberger, 1993; Kennedy, 2007).

Performing unity and counter-mapping

In an effort to mitigate the historical (and contemporary) divisiveness of the constructed international border, the organizers of the Gathering employ strategic exercises to help reinforce cultural connections. In addition, they use discursive tools (i.e. maps, media coverage, literature) to empower communities and reframe governance structures. For example, the facilitator of the Tulalip Gathering suggested that, during the introductions, every participant add the phrase "And I am Coast Salish" after their name. As the leaders affirmed their status, the powerful words became increasingly impassioned: "I *am* Coast Salish . . . We are the same". Some respondents uttered their statements with such passion that applause, cheers, and "whoops" would spontaneously erupt. This "performance" of unity helped align the material and the symbolic concept of a (re)connected community. Interestingly, this exercise plays on the very successful ad campaign by Molson, a Canadian beer company that used the patriotic phrase "I am Canadian" to sell their product, as described by Seiler (2002).

This exercise was also a way of establishing consensus. By repeatedly emphasizing the connectedness of the community, the aim was to rewrite the discourse of a fragmented community. As one participant of the Gathering reflected, the affirmations remind the participants "regardless of which side of the border our relatives happened to land, we are all interconnected". A Coast Salish leader further explained:

> You might ask what we did today . . . We are learning to trust each other again. There are no hidden agendas. If we agree as to who we are, we are able to protect who we are. It is up to you to reach back and remember the works of our ancestors and bring it forward. We have to bring hope and life to our children.

Although the tribes and bands had and continue to have their own priorities, the intricate relationships and shared connection to the land and water are important components of the creation of the Gatherings and of the dedication to address the environmental issues facing their respective communities and the Salish Nation as a whole, particularly the decline in salmon.

In addition to re-establishing cultural continuity, the Gatherings provide the space for the Coast Salish leaders to collaborate and speak with one voice. Establishing consensus within the Salish communities serves an important purpose. It helps prioritize issues and strategically organize efforts to tackle increasingly complex and multijurisdictional environmental issues. The ongoing dialogue between the Indigenous leaders at the Gathering helps to identify these critical areas. The objective is clearly stated in the literature put forth by the organizers of the Gathering:

> The objective of the Gathering was to provide a forum for Tribal and First Nation leaders to collaborate on environmental issues and share that information with governmental policy makers to assist them in making more protective and culturally sensitive decisions concerning the future of this richly endowed, yet fragile, region that we share, the Salish Sea.
>
> (Coast Salish Gathering Program, 2008)

With a unified voice, the Tribal and First Nations leaders who participate in the Gatherings have committed to meeting a series of goals. For example, through the development of an environmental action plan, the Gathering aims to "Conserve and restore the Salish Sea ecosystem to a level that ensures the sustainability of the Coast Salish People and our cultural lifeways" (Coast Salish Gathering, 2008). A number of priorities are identified in the plan, including the provision of adequate clean air, water, and land to sustain and protect the health of the Coast Salish people. These priorities represent the general pairing of environmental and cultural protections in the contemporary Coast Salish governance model. It also highlights how protecting water resources (both marine and freshwater) directly supports subsistence, cultural, and economic activities.

Establishing consensus among the Coast Salish tribes and bands also helps in coordinating with external agencies. The regional director of the United States Environmental Protection Agency expressed this point of view at the Tulalip Gathering: "The more unified your voice, the more support we can give you". The director further explained that although the department is "sensitive to the needs of individual bands and tribes, establishing a common position aids in the navigation through large bureaucratic systems". Thus, the creation of a unified voice among Coast Salish communities and a (re)constructed space serve important roles both internally and externally.

Representative of this shift is a recent collaboration between Coast Salish communities and the United States Geological Survey (USGS) to conduct water quality sampling on the annual intertribal Canoe Journey (see Chapter 7). The Canoe Journey is listed on the USGS website as a unique new multijurisdictional partnership, which "blends science and tradition".

Indicative of this coordinated project, the Coast Salish Gathering website provides an electronic link to the water quality sites and real-time information on the data collection (as well as video clips of the daily progress of the Canoe Journey). This is, perhaps, one of the first of many tangible outcomes of the creation of the Gathering in terms of multijurisdictional collaboration. The partnership has occurred on an annual basis since 2008, with increased participation and collaboration reported by the participants.

Beyond stakeholders

The development of a distinctly Indigenous governing body is also based on the need to be more than just "stakeholders" in the governance process. By taking ownership of the governance process, the power shifts back to the tribes and bands of the Coast Salish communities. Including governmental and non-governmental representatives in the Coast Salish Gathering helps the Community meet their goals while remaining in control of the governance process. It also supports a collaborative governance process without weakening the cultural emphasis. One example of this balance was the delineation of an "executive session" for which the room was open only to Coast Salish members. Maintaining these clear boundaries situates the Coast Salish people at the centre of their own governing process. It also provides space for Coast Salish participants to speak freely within their own Community and to continue to build trust between Communities.

Maintaining ownership over the governance process also allows the Gathering participants to follow traditional protocol. Although multicultural training is increasingly prevalent in governmental offices throughout the Pacific west (and beyond), cultural inclusion can often lead to cultural misunderstandings. Despite good intentions, sometimes this process of cultural inclusion comes off as cursory, tokenized, or even insensitive.

One striking example of this occurred during a transboundary environmental conference held in Seattle, Washington in 2005. In this case, the conference organizers had invited members of the Tulalip tribe to provide a traditional welcome at the conference, where they were to bless the four corners of the room. As part of the ceremony, the Tulalip members shared the meaning and origin of the song with the conference participants. The welcome took longer than was allocated on the agenda, and the facilitator grew visibly agitated, looking at her watch and pacing the room. After the Tulalip group had blessed only one corner, the facilitator interrupted the ceremony and suggested that the group finish in the hallway "because they were running behind schedule". The Tulalip drum-leader brushed off the suggestion with a laugh.

After an awkward public negotiation between the facilitator and Tulalip tribal member, they finally agreed that the group would complete one more song. This insensitive act was particularly poignant considering the conference literature had replaced the Georgia Basin–Puget Sound logo with "The Salish Sea". The public overtures of the organizers to frame the conference in a Coast Salish perspective suggested a greater sensitivity to Indigenous issues. However, this incident, coupled with the general lack of involvement of and engagement with issues facing Indigenous communities, suggested otherwise. Since this incident, much work has been done to revise these conferences for greater inclusion of Coast Salish members in the planning. The 2014 conference, for example, was much more inclusive and was very deliberate about consulting with, and integrating Indigenous leadership into the planning process. However, the deficits of these earlier conferences helped provide an incentive to prioritize the establishment of Indigenous-led governance mechanisms.

As Charlie O'Hara, Planning Director for the Swinomish Indian Tribal Community, reflected after the incident, "It never works to bring Tribal members into conferences like this. . . .We need to bring them (non-tribal members) into our own meetings in order for them to understand our perspective". The problem, he surmised, was one of worldviews:

> Westerners think that environmental issues will be solved only by removing humans from the equation. Natives, on the other hand, treat human and environmental issues as one and the same.

Setting up a Native–non-Native binary is clearly problematic. However, this example serves to underscore the importance of power and position in the governance process. An invitation to participate in a governance process already defined for the actors is very different from creating one's own governance system. For the Coast Salish Community, which is actively trying to restore and revitalize a cultural tradition while addressing pressing environmental issues, this distinction is fundamental.

Building bridges

Governmental offices and First Nations/Tribal communities are increasingly collaborating in multijurisdictional governance projects. However, as the above example illustrates, this multicultural partnership requires clear communication between partners and enhanced cultural awareness. Another example of this effort includes the Coast Salish Sea Initiative – a partnership between Environment Canada and Coast Salish communities in British Columbia. The design of this program aims to "facilitate meaningful engagement of Coast Salish with the Georgia Basin Action Plan". The project also indicates a priority of cross-cultural exchange and respect for divergent worldviews. For example, the projects emphasize training programs where Environment Canada employees are trained in Traditional Ecological Knowledge methods and First Nations community members are trained in water quality testing:

> Together we have undertaken water quality assessments, reopened Baynes Sound to shellfish harvesting and are working towards having a comprehensive management plan for the Nanaimo River Estuary. We have trained First Nations members as samplers, data collectors, and maintenance for Squirrel Cove pump out station. We have improved the way the scientific and First Nation community work together through important Traditional Ecological Knowledge (TEK) conferences.

In addition, cross-cultural training has been provided to Emergency Awareness and Enforcement officers resulting in a better understanding of how to work together with First Nations and Traditional Ecological Knowledge. In this case, the governmental agencies clearly acknowledge the importance of cross-cultural training and the engagement of TEK in their programming. At a federal level, the U.S. Environmental Protection Agency (EPA) publishes a Tribal Environmental newsletter to enhance communications with tribal communities. The EPA designed the newsletter as a forum for the EPA and tribal communities to share information in a timely manner. As editor Mary Lauterbach explained, the newsletter also helps Indigenous communities deal with pervasive environmental issues by curbing limited institutional capacity. Lauterbach notes:

> Many at EPA have heard from Tribes that improving our ways of communication would be greatly beneficial to EPA and Tribal partnerships. It is fairly well known that Tribal environmental programs and office staff are often overwhelmed with information from numerous and varied sources. Tribes have expressed the great difficulties for their limited Tribal staff to sort through and select pertinent information in a timely fashion. Many Tribes do not have the size or infrastructure to deal with the many diverse office and media programs sources of information. Tribal representatives have continued to advise EPA that Tribes tend to relate to the environment differently as they view the world in a holistic fashion, and would prefer the Agency decrease its use of administrating Tribal environmental protection programs through its traditional "stove piping" approaches, such as air and water. Since many Tribes view all things as being inter-related, it may be better to learn about the environment holistically.

Later in the newsletter, Lauterbach names a litany of environmental concerns, and subsequent health effects, facing tribal communities. For example, environmental health experts link mining, industry, and development activities to a decline in air and water quality and growing health issues such as increased rates of asthma, cancer, and diabetes. Despite the daunting statistics, Lauterbach expresses optimism that the partnership between federal agencies and tribal communities will lead to a better future. Drawing attention to the importance of TEK, she notes:

> Amazingly, they use their knowledge of the past to make a better future. Thousands of years of experience, information, and science are resulting in outcomes that we all need to pay attention to for our world. Through Indigenous knowledge, along with some of the best science in EPA, we will sustain the Tribes and all people in the future. The development of the tribal environmental newsletter is one example of a governance mechanism designed to foster better communication and build on each other's strengths. The (scientific) capacity of the federal government and the traditional knowledge of the Native communities work together to help address issues of shared concern. When used in conjunction with a commitment to greater cultural understanding, this is a positive step in cross-cultural, multijurisdictional governance.

Discussion and conclusion

This chapter has explored the politics of scale of water governance in a post-colonial context through the analysis of the Coast Salish Gatherings. In this chapter, I explore how collective rights (treaty and Indigenous) are being "scaled up" from individual "tribe" or "band" to "Nation". This rescaling, I suggest, contributes to the nascent discussions of politics of scale within water governance and complements other critical scholarship (see, for example, Cohen and McCarthy, 2014; Norman *et al.*, 2015). In addition, the chapter responds to a call from political geographers and borders scholars to look more closely at how power is mobilized at the site of the border (Paasi, 2002, 2009; Agnew, 2007, 2010; Popescu, 2012). I argue that including cultural politics in the investigations of borders, environmental governance, and scale provides greater nuance to understanding water as a socio-natural hybrid. This call for greater inclusion of cultural politics in transboundary governance, contributing to earlier insights put forth by critical scholars Don Mitchell (2000) and Kay Anderson (2007). Applying these insights to the context of Indigenous water governance provides an important contribution to these earlier discussions.

This chapter is noteworthy given that the governance structure of the Coast Salish Gathering presents an apparent contradiction: it is both transnational (as it spans the Canada–U.S. border) and national (as it represents a singular Coast Salish Nation). The establishment of the Gatherings thereby serves as a counter-narrative to a bordered geography by emphasizing the connectedness of their communities, rather than the differences in national identities. The efforts to employ strategic essentialism and counter-mapping at the Coast Salish Gatherings are in line with other documented efforts within political geography to construct or reconstruct scale that is meaningful to the user (Harris and Hazen, 2006; Cohen and Harris, 2014).

There is a growing movement within Indigenous communities to reclaim traditional governance processes. As John Waterhouse, director of the Yukon River Inter-Tribal Watershed Council, who was also participating at the Jamestown Gathering, aptly noted, "We are the ones that we are waiting for". This chapter provides a starting point to evaluate larger issues of efficacy and power in tribal reorganization across State boundaries. Further research, however, is needed to continue evaluation of these efforts. Overall, these examples show how the aggregation of historically connected tribes and bands for the shared benefit of environmental protection and cultural reunification is a first step in reclaiming space and reconstructing traditional governance mechanisms.

This chapter marks a deliberate effort to include the cultural politics of the border in the investigations of transboundary environmental governance. I suggest that investigating how the administrative structures and physical boundaries of water governance are both socially constructed and politically mobilized provides for a more nuanced approach to discussions of transboundary environmental governance. This approach may also be useful for other studies engaging in issues related to borders, scale, and natural resource governance, particularly flow resources such

Box 6.1 The Sacred Water

© Tom Sampson (ttesaLaq)

Introductory Address and Welcome from Coast Salish leader, Tom Sampson at the Transboundary Water Workshop, Vancouver, British Columbia (2008).

(Tom Sampson served as Chief of Tsartlip First Nation for 24 years, Chairman of the South Island Tribal Council for 22 years, vice Chief of the British Columbia Assembly of First Nations, Chairman of the Assembly's Constitutional Working Group for Status Indians and chair of the Douglas Treaty Council and continues to be an important leader throughout Coast Salish communities)

(Reprinted with permission from Tom Sampson)

It said by our ancestors that when the Creator gave life to the First Nations of the Coast Salish Nations and their land; it is said that the Creator also gave them the language in which they could communicate with all of the other creations with which the First Nations would share the land, water, and air.

It is then that the Creator gave us our names known as NE,HI,MET; from this name would come our right to land ownership, and spiritual rights called XAXES,KAL sacred belief. This would include our sacred teachings called, SNI,NU. The SNI,NU includes our sacred ceremony called TEXTAN and the sacred song for each ceremony. Each ceremony had and still has its own discipline. It is the elder women who transfer these ceremonial songs to the daughters and granddaughters. The sons and grandsons dance the sacred masks of the family. Each of the families train their own children within their own lodge/big house. It is always the responsibility of the Heads of the Family to train and teach their own children and their families.

The ceremonies as it pertains to the water are a sacred belief. We know through the Grandmothers, that the water contains and holds the baby in place within our mothers. The Grandmothers taught us how to drink the water by way of blessing the water before we were allowed to drink it. The water had to be protected at all times because of this sacred belief. The water that came from the mountain is considered sacred and these mountains had to be protected, they are now called watersheds. The water was also used to bless our children, the boys and the girls as they changed from children to young adults.

The water is also used for the winter dancers and spiritual healers called FIFE. Water is used to give special blessing to the people at special ceremonies. The water provides us with our songs from the mountains, the oceans, the lakes, and the rivers. The tears that come from our eyes remind us of our families and our ancestors.

Sometimes it is the sadness or the happiness that comes to us in forms of songs and spiritual visions. We say that the mountain is sacred because it contains the sacred spirits of our ancestors. They return to us in forms of water and to our sacred bathing places where we cleanse our bodies. The water provides our bodies and our spirits with blessing each day of our life as it provides life to all of creations. We know that the water that flows from the sacred mountain will nourish all things that the Creator placed on our sacred mountain. The water that travels to the ocean will nourish and feed all of those things that live in the ocean – the fish, the shellfish, etc. It is the fragrance of the mountain, which guides the salmon back to its place of birth.

We as First Nations have seen water when it was clean and it is sacred to all of creation. We now see other governments and corporations seeking ownership to polluted waters and dying oceans/lakes/rivers/streams. If we are going to save the water and the land, we must change the way we see things and share the protected water so that all of creation will benefit from our true discipline, which was given to us by the Creator.

as water. Including a critical discussion of the cultural politics of borders (and border-making) helps to identify, and thereby address more effectively, the power dynamics constituted through postcolonial constructions of space and hydrosocial networks. In the next chapter, I explore the performativities of transboundary water governance through the enactment of the intertribal Canoe Journey.

Notes

1 The proceeding Gatherings in Duncan, BC (2007), Tulalip, WA (2008), Squamish, BC (2009), and Swinomish, WA (2010) also followed this protocol.

2 Largely comprising tribal chiefs and band leaders and elected officials, such as tribal chairs.

7 The Canoe Journey

Paddling for change

It is a powerful sight – hundreds of paddlers in brightly painted dugout canoes. The waterscape is transformed to a sea of black and red, the colours of the Coast Salish people.

The participants of the Canoe Journey have pulled (paddled) hard for the last several hours and they are ready to come to shore. They are tired and hungry, yet overjoyed at the sight of so many people waiting on the rocky shores to celebrate their arrival. Following traditional protocol, the pullers wait for the last canoe to catch up before seeking permission to land as a group. Facing the shore as a unified flotilla, the canoes gently rise and fall as the sea swells.

Once unified, the lead canoeist initiates protocol. She speaks clearly and loudly to the host tribe. First, the Creator is thanked for a safe journey. Then, the details of where they came from and what tribal communities they represent are reported. Lastly, the Speaker acknowledges that the paddlers are entering the traditional territory of the host tribe and seek permission to come ashore. The Speaker clearly indicates that they are guests of the host tribe, and will just be passing through. Much of this information transpires in song.

They are part of a canoe journey integral to the traditional lifeways of the Coast Salish people of Pacific North America. In times past, canoe travel was a primary way of connecting with relatives and tribes. It was also a time to share goods, pass on news, and build allies. In today's world, people can visit through more "efficient" means – cars, ferries make the journey across these waterways faster, and phones and computers make the news spread quicker. However, the Canoe Journeys are more than just a matter of transportation and information exchange. This is a way to maintain tradition and connections with a way of life, and a reconnection with the sacred water. What it means for water governance is an ongoing, explicit movement towards strengthening culture, reconnecting with the waters, healing communities, and training youth. The Journeys also help build allies, by raising the profile of their communities and building positive associations. All of these work towards strengthening transnational water governance (see Figures 7.1 and 7.2).

On the shores, there is a buzz of activity in anticipation of the disembarking. The host tribes have been planning the arrival for weeks, preparing the site, and the food. The drummers are ready to welcome the travellers and there is a tent

Figure 7.1 Intertribal Canoe Journey paddling at sunset.

Source: Used with permission from Jeff Bear, Urbanrez Productions, Producer of Water Stories, and www.samaqan.ca/www.samaqan3.ca/?p=657.

Figure 7.2 Photo of intertribal Canoe Journey participants waiting to land, paddle to Swinomish.

Source: 2011 Photo by Caroline J. Edwards (used with permission).

set up to play traditional stick games late into the night. It takes on the feel of a celebration, yet is rooted in ancient traditions.

As the paddlers bring their canoes on shore and unpack their goods to make camp for the night, there are a number of items that remind you of modern times. The youth have their iPhones and iPods carefully tucked away in waterproof bags, and the T-shirts may pay homage to favorite sports teams or music groups.

But one modern addition to many of the canoes is of particular significance to this book – a water quality probe and Global Positioning System.

Since 2011, the organizers of the Canoe Journey, the Swinomish Indian Tribal Community, and the United States Geological Survey have formed a unique partnership. What do the USGS and the organizers of the Canoe Journey have in common? Both are concerned with the protection of the Salish Sea Basin; however, their practices of documenting and recording information are different. This new relationship becomes a hybrid space, where ancient traditions, Western science, and Traditional Ecological Knowledge mingle.

The Canoe Journey holds many avenues to explore/investigate the central questions asked in this book. The ongoing relationship with partners such as USGS

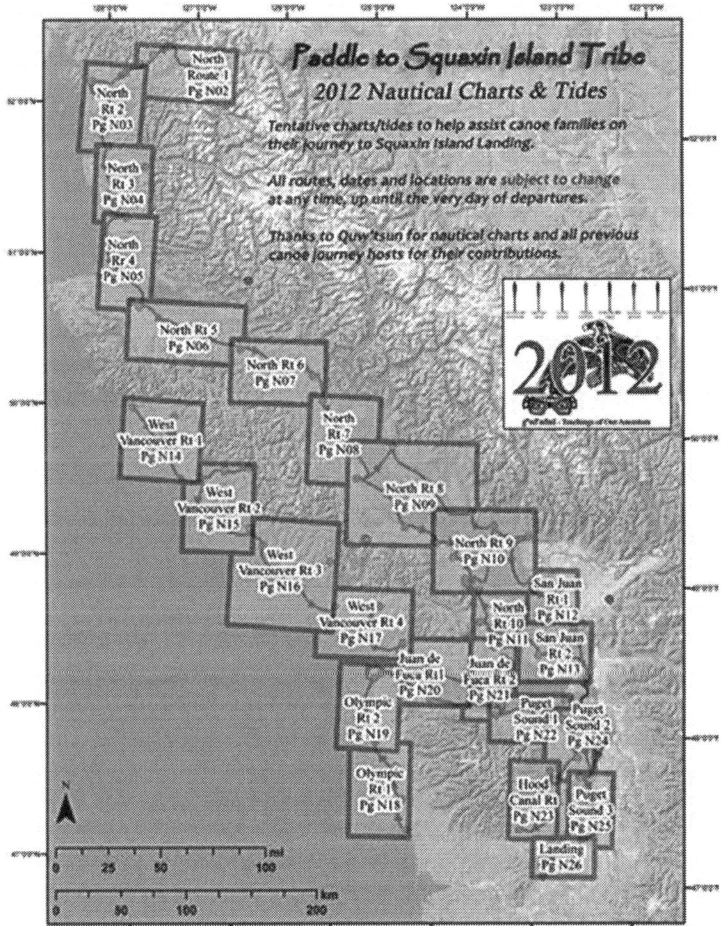

Figure 7.3 Map of 2012 Intertribal Canoe Journey route.

Source: Intertribal Canoe Journey paddle to Squaxin organizing committee.

helps to answer "what makes a good upstream neighbor?" while the act of participating in (and training for) the Journey exhibits how conceptualizing a postcolonial/borderless waterscape may foster better water governance.

This chapter provides an opportunity to highlight the new partnerships that are developing to work towards goals of protecting sacred waters. It also provides counter-narratives of hydrohegemony and fosters Indigenous-led methods for governance. Foundationally, it is about connecting to the waters, but also about personal growth and cultural revitalization. As Kelly John, an elder of the Kyuquot First Nation in British Columbia and a canoe leader, notes "We look at this journey as a very personal quest" (Briggs and Alexander, 2006). This Journey is personal (many kick habits, find cultural roots, find love) but it is also foundationally about exercising inherent cultural rights and revitalizing cultures. As Chief Jerry Jack, of Mowachaht/Muchalaht First Nation believed, a healthy tribal nation is one inexorably tied to its ceremonies and, in this case, the ocean-going Canoe Journey (Briggs and Alexander, 2006). This is particularly profound considering the outlawing of the potlatch tradition of the Northwest coast tribes, which had detrimental impacts on the social networks of the coastal traditions. The work of cultural revitalization and self-determination that Chief Jerry Jack committed his life to, through leadership, continues through these journeys. Jack sadly passed away on the 2006 Canoe Journey after his boat capsized in the open waters (the first death associated with the Journey).

History of the Canoe Journey

Canoe travel has been integral to the Coast Salish culture since time immemorial. The Coast Salish people have traditionally lived close to water, providing year-round access to plentiful marine resources and transportation routes. During the summer months, the communities would take to the waters to trade, reconnect with familial relations, and to set up fish camps.

However, many of these traditions and practices have been lost over the years. As discussed in Chapter 2, colonial practices of forced assimilation, loss of traditional territory, and movement onto reserves has had significant impacts on the spiritual, economic, and overall health of Indigenous communities. In particular, the outlawing of potlatch exchange (which only became "legal" again in the mid-1950s), the epidemic of child abuse and language loss that occurred in the boarding schools, and the associated multigenerational trauma associated with these events has made life difficult for Indigenous communities throughout the last century (Warry, 2008). These travesties have had, and continue to have, dire impacts on the social, economic, and political fabric of the communities.

In addition to the socio-political change, Indigenous communities are faced with degraded environmental conditions and extraterritorial pollution that impact traditional harvesting practices and disrupt traditional ways of living. Degraded water quality, overfishing, and temperature increases due to global climate change and loss of riparian habitat also continue to have tremendous impacts on marine resources. (Although overfishing is being curbed through regulatory mechanisms.)

However, mechanisms to revitalize and strengthen Indigenous communities have been increasing significantly over the past two decades. As discussed in Chapter 6, the Coast Salish Gathering is working towards goals of improving water quality throughout the Salish Sea, and leaders such as the late Billy Frank Jr. and Tom Sampson continue to provide inspiration and guidance to the Coast Salish peoples.

The Canoe Journey is also a notable example – both symbolic and performative – of strengthening ties and moving towards goals of shared water governance. Stroke by stroke, year by year, the Canoe Journey provides an important mark for reconnecting with shared waters and highlighting the ongoing efforts to reform intertribal relationships and re-imagine shared spaces.

One member of the Quinault tribe, which hosted the 2013 Canoe Journey, reflected:

> The Canoe Journey creates opportunities for tribal members to relearn, strengthen and reinforce their canoe traditions. There are many cultural values that are learned from the canoeing, some include: pride, cultural knowledge, learning how to paddle, respect, and sense of achievement.

The revitalization of the Canoe Journey started with a smaller-scale event. In 1989, a Quinault Tribal Elder, Emmet Oliver, organized the "Paddle to Seattle" as part of the Washington State Centennial Ceremony. The momentum gained from this experience was profound, with thousands of participants over the decades of Journeys.

Since the 1989 Paddle-to-Seattle, the Canoe Journey has become an important part of the cultural revitalization process, and similar to the companion journey in the Yukon River, it is often referred to as "the Healing Journey". The 2013 Coast Salish Intertribal Canoe Journey included 90 U.S. Tribes and Canadian First Nations, and included allies from as far away as New Zealand. The participation of the other Indigenous groups reflects the strengthening of inter-Indigenous movements throughout the world and reflects wider efforts of Indigenous cultural revitalization and self-determination.

Technological platforms have helped make the Canoe Journey more publicly accessible. The use of websites, Facebook pages, and Twitter also allows participants to exchange information related to the Journey such as training dates and locations, travel information, water conditions, as well as perpetuate a more unified (and publicly visible) experience. This type of networking is present throughout Indigenous movements (as seen in the Great Lakes and the Yukon River examples in Chapters 8 and 4) and assists in fostering allies and creating support. The public platform has been important to build allies and raise awareness of the contemporary Indigenous movement.

Canoe Journeys and enhanced water governance

At first brush, one might have a difficult time finding the connection between Canoe Journeys and enhanced water governance. However, recent experiences suggest that the Canoe Journey helps to promote effective water governance both internally (through increased self-determination, cultural revitalization, and empowerment) and externally (through partnerships and creation of allies).

Participating in (and training for) the Journey helps to strengthen community ties, rebuild networks, reconnect with the water, and expose the youth to positive life experiences that celebrate traditional cohesion and respect for each other and themselves. The material connections between the participants and the environment viscerally connect the participants with the ecosystem.

Second, the roles of partners and allies provide stronger community importance. This occurs informally through interpersonal relations and formally through curriculum development and partnerships with agencies such as the USGS.

Cultural revitalization and rebuilding connections

Culturally, the Canoe Journey helps to revitalize traditions. The Journey itself becomes a floating classroom, where lessons are passed down, on and off the water. The training for this Journey provides an important arena for the (re)establishment of governance frameworks, protocols, and lifeways that prepare the participants for life on and off the water. The connections between teacher and student, elder and youth, and between people and the environment are strengthened with each Journey.

The idea of unity is a common theme that runs through the Journey. In training, the paddlers learn that: the strongest canoes are the ones that pull in unison; the canoe is only as strong as its weakest member; and everyone needs to support and encourage each member in order to reach their potential. They also learn valuable lessons about communication and leadership. Under this framework, accountability, transparency, and support are fundamental pillars to ensure success, collectively. Following these steps is very important for the success of the canoe team, but it is also indicative of wider governance frameworks.

The benefits can loosely be categorized as "re/building connections" – connections between the individual and the environment, tribes and bands, agencies and allies, teacher and student, elder and youth, and between nations.

Suquamish youth puller, Shaylene Jefferson, who has been participating in the Journey for 5 years, noted that her favorite parts of the Journey are meeting new people and being on the water. Shaylene noted, "The best part of the Journey is sitting in the protocol tent, listening to elders" (Stephenson, 2013). Another member of the youth canoe team, Jazmine Lawrence, reflected on the power of the water. "The waves control you," Jazmine said. The 2013 Canoe Journey took the paddlers to the outer Pacific coast, which required significantly different training than in years past. The waters of the outer coast are much less predictable than the protected inland waters. This new route also influences the protocol of landing. Unlike in the inner coast, where the travellers seek permission to land while still in the boat, along the outer coast the canoes land bow first, unload, then, standing on the beach, the visitors continue the protocol of seeking permission to join the community. "It's probably how [our ancestors] did it a long time ago," Price noted, "you don't want your guests getting hurt".

Jazmine, who has participated in every Canoe Journey since she was a young child, and Shaylene, who has been participating since she was 11, are part of a new generation of Indigenous youth, in which the norm (rather than the exception) is to promote cultural revitalization. They are part of a generation with a unique vantage point where they are connected to a wider world in a way that many of their parents were not. Common throughout the stories told in this book is the promise of youth; the connections and groundings of the youth help address the complex issues facing the Indigenous nations (and the world more broadly). Their perspective – rooted both in tradition and a global perspective – holds the promise of breaching worlds to tackle complex problems. Many are concerned that traditions continue to die off with elders. But a resurgence of interest in Indigenous languages with the tribal youth holds promise for moving forward. The Indigenous communities from the Great Lakes region (Ojibwa) and the coastal Pacific (the Coast Salish) are two North American examples of language revitalization initiatives that focus on rebuilding communities through language immersion.

Connection to place

The Journey also becomes a place where lessons about the environment (tides, marine life, water quality) are passed on. These teachings occur organically, through questions around the campfire, while they are floating, pulled out on the beaches for lunch. They also occur through storytelling, passing on ancient tales that hold powerful and profound lessons. It provides an incredibly important classroom for reconnecting with water and the land through experience. Taking the "frog's eye view" as renowned Native American scholar David Wilkins calls it,[1] helps to provide an embodied experience where the participants gain a profound connection with the water and land of the Salish Sea Basin.

Creating allies

The public nature of this Journey is noteworthy. The Journey, arguably, is as important internally (for Indigenous communities) as it is externally (for non-Indigenous groups). How outsiders view and experience the Canoe Journey is an important way to reconstruct new space. How media report on the Journey amplifies the experience to the outside world. Thus, the performativity of the Canoe Journey helps to reconstruct the coastal landscape to include Indigenous acts as contemporary rather than relics of the past. The inclusion of Indigenous actors into the landscape and seascape helps to break down barriers. For the Coast Salish, these borders are both nation-state (between Canada and the United States), intertribal (between tribes), and Indigenous and non-Indigenous.

For example, in the 2013 Canoe Journey, lead canoe puller, Justin Finkbonner (Lummi), posted on his Facebook page: "Invited in for coffee and to use the bathroom from strangers on the beach today. We are used to being chased off the beaches – thank you kind strangers". In Washington State, one of the few states where beaches can be privately owned, the landing of canoes for non-scheduled breaks can be problematic. The positive exposure of the Canoe Journey, over the years, most likely contributes to better relationships between Indigenous and non-Indigenous residents. In years past, bitter racism fuelled by fishing rights issues made the waterways and beaches of the Salish Sea Basin a hostile environment for many Coast Salish members. Now, with the fish wars less heated, the fish allocation policies relatively normalized, and the reduction of commercial fishers (and fish), a new generation exists where respect mostly trumps racism. Part of the turning of the tide is the positive framing of the Canoe Journey. Other components include work in the classroom, and efforts for collaboration with governmental agencies such as USGS and Environment Canada.

Both the State of Washington and the Province of British Columbia have charges to include more curriculum with Indigenous content. This inclusion is occurring, school district by school district. For example, in Anacortes, Washington (the launching point to the San Juan Islands), there has been a recent push by educators and administration to include Coast Salish content in the classroom. In British Columbia, the Truth and Reconciliation Commission hearings have enhanced this effort. The introduction of curriculum to students that celebrates (rather than ignores or tokenizes) the long history of Indigenous peoples is an important step in creating communities that respect and honor the long presence of the Indigenous peoples of North America.

In addition to classroom education, public education comes through public art and exhibits. For example, a healing pole in Anacortes, Washington, was placed on the beach in 2011 after an oil refinery accident killed seven community members. This tragedy brought Indigenous and non-Indigenous community members together to focus on the need to heal, and also inspired renowned local carver and spiritual leader of the Samish Nation, Bill James, to donate a totem pole that he describes as a gift from the Creator. The pole serves as a way to honor the victims of the accident and also a way to raise multicultural awareness.

Hybrid spaces: U.S. Geological Survey and the tribal Canoe Journey

The partnership between the Salish tribes and the USGS is a noteworthy example of mechanisms that promote shared goals of improved water quality and governance. The partnership began in 2008 and continues to be described as a "blending of science and tradition". In the inaugural partnership, the project organizers lauded the unique relationship:

> In an exciting new partnership between the Coast Salish (Indigenous peoples of the Salish Sea ecoregion) and the USGS, members of western Washington Tribes and British Columbia First Nations will measure water quality in Puget Sound and the Strait of Georgia during the Tribal Journey, the annual summer canoe voyage. The project will provide a snapshot of current water quality conditions and data that can be compared with future measurements along successive journeys. This information is important to improve management of ancestral waters that are experiencing environmental decline.
>
> (USGS, 2008)

Five years later, the relationship continues to yield positive results:

> Since 2008, the Coast Salish Nation and Swinomish Indian Tribal Community in partnership with the U.S. Geological Survey has examined the coastal waters of the Salish Sea providing a new strategy that blends western science and Coast Salish culture to study water-quality and its effects on ecosystem dynamics.
>
> (USGS, 2013)

The partnership is designed to help identify some of the key areas where coastal water quality and habitat problems are affecting the marine resources of the Coast Salish ecoregion. The USGS scientists help to determine what approaches will work for assessing water quality, and deploy the instrumentation to measure and interpret the data. Educational outreach is also part of the process, training the canoe participants on how to use the equipment and participate in the science of water quality assessment.

When asked why this is important for USGS, the head USGS scientist and project coordinator Eric Grossman noted:

> [T]heir identity is tied to the Coast Salish ecoregion. And so, being able to maintain the function of that ecosystem is paramount to their culture and their existence. And so, for science and resource management, this journey offers a very unique way of conducting the science in an effective way behind a traditional canoe which doesn't disrupt the water, as instruments are deployed behind them measuring various water quality parameters and habitat traits.
>
> And so, this becomes a really interesting opportunity to blend tradition and science as well as traditional knowledge to better understand what are the environmental changes that are occurring today. Are they impacting some of the coastal resources that we depend on; resources like salmons that are – many species that are plummeting in their population today, a number of shellfish species and even endangered orca that are symbols of the entire Pacific Northwest.

In a short video on the partnership,[2] Eric Grossman and Brian Cladoosby, chairman of the Swinomish Tribe of western Washington, speak about the benefits of the partnership. Both Grossman and Cladoosby focus on the youth. Grossman reflects:

> The children are getting to know their environment. They have appreciation for it. They look for the animals. In fact along the way they're singing and playing games like "I spy a certain animal" and all the kids on the canoe end up looking for the same animal that the one called out. It will be interesting to see how this information can be used by those folks and the children especially to engage them in better understanding some of the water quality issues and their environmental problems for the future and hopefully they will be able to use it to develop better management practices.

Cladoosby reflects:

> I think the kids, just being here to be able to witness, seeing the probes and hopefully when we get back, to be able to show them exactly what they were able to do. And to explain to them in layman's terms what this means, what that means, is going to be cool. And to let them know that they were the genesis of this.

Both testimonies highlight the benefits of including youth in this process. The experience of the Canoe Journey is beneficial for connecting to place and learning on the water, as well as being part of something bigger – to participate in a project that will lead to a greater understanding of the quality of the water – but, perhaps, more importantly, letting the youth know that they are instrumental to this project is key. Simply, the project is equally about water quality data as it is about empowerment, building allies, and a cultural revitalization. For the youth to have a validation of blended worldviews and practices, in which Western science and traditional practice can contribute to better protection of the waters that are important to all, is of utmost importance. This, in turn, helps foster "good neighbors" through information-exchange and cultural awareness.

Ongoing legacies of colonial b/ordering

Despite the ongoing efforts to promote unity and cultural connectedness between tribes and nations, the political imprint of the international border is still very much present and influences both the Canoe Journey and the water quality program. For example, the involvement of Canadian partners, such as Environment Canada, has waned over the years. The decrease in involvement is largely due to budget constraints and limited staff ability. As the series of images below show, although the Canoe Journey continues to be a "transnational" experience, the purviews of the agencies are reliant on fiscal priorities and budgets and will not always carry over into the "international" spectrum. Note the first two images reflecting the years 2008 and 2009 include data from both Canada and the U.S. side of the Canoe Journey, whereas the latter images, for 2010 and 2011, only show data from the U.S. side. This is an important point to consider when looking at transnational governance and federally-funded projects. Ultimately, federal projects are limited to the scope and purview of their internal boundaries. The agencies can coordinate, but ultimately the implementation of transboundary projects is limited by the fiscal priorities set by the national government. This underscores the unique position of Indigenous communities to take leadership on transnational issues, whose scope and purview can transcend borders.

Although a key goal of the Canoe Journey is to highlight the shared traditions of the Coast Salish people and to participate in unifying traditional territories through the Journey itself, the presence of the international border is not erased all together. For the USGS, the presence of the border impacts the data collection. The border also impacts the participants in other more routine ways. For example,

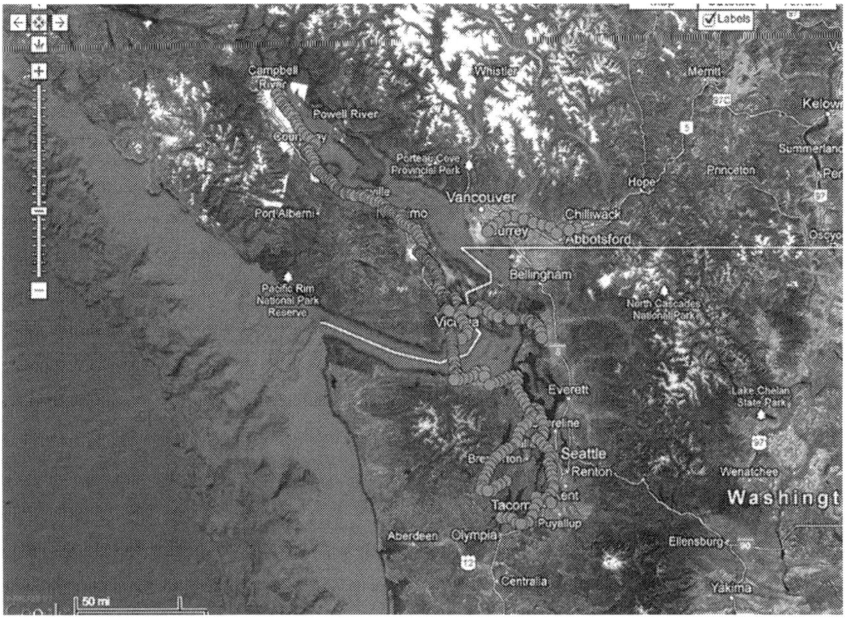

Figure 7.4 USGS Intertribal Canoe Journey data points, 2008.

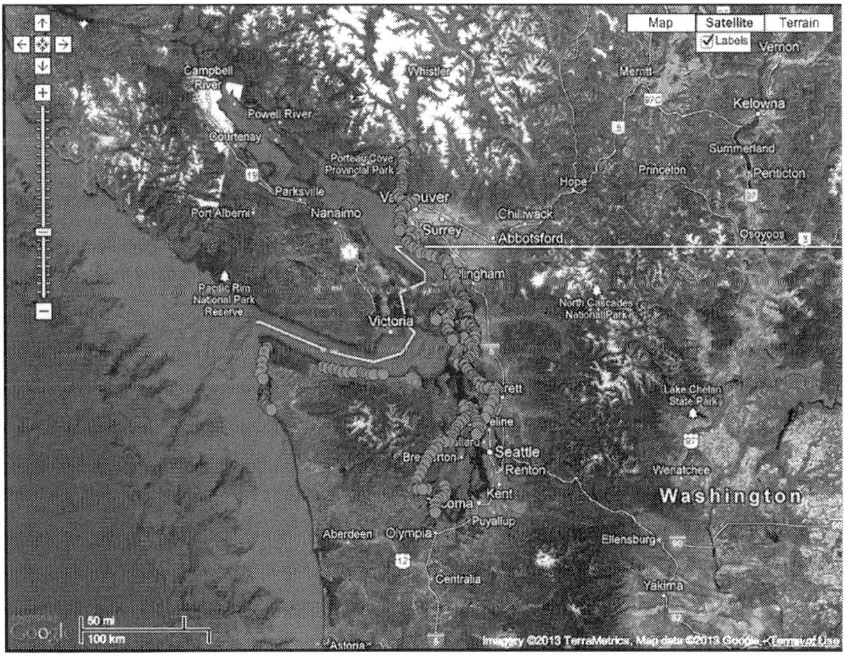

Figure 7.5 USGS Intertribal Canoe Journey data points, 2009.

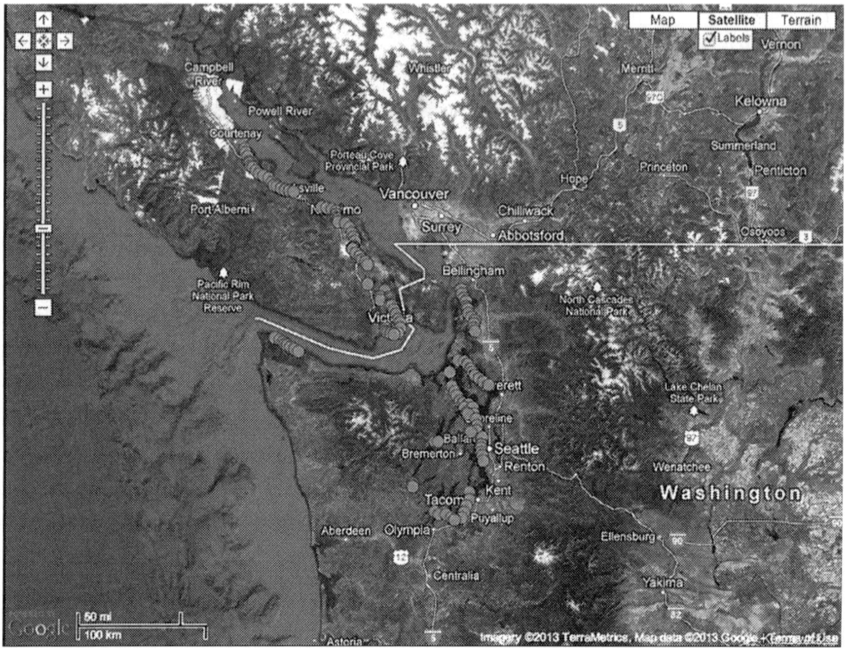

Figure 7.6 USGS Intertribal Canoe Journey data points, 2010.

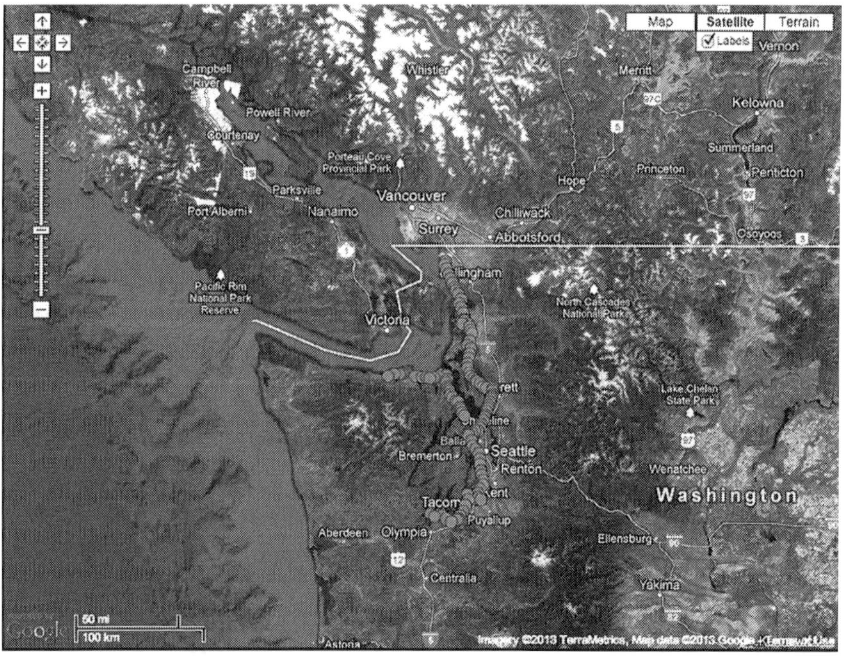

Figure 7.7 USGS Intertribal Canoe Journey data points, 2011.

Source: USGS, 2013.

in a website preparing the participants for the journey, rules and protocols associated with customs provide a backdrop of b/ordering.

The participants are reminded to bring the proper documentation:

> **CUSTOMS AND BORDER CROSSING – Between U.S. and CANADA**
>
> **U.S. CUSTOMS Port Angeles Office.**
>
> Documents needed for crossing border for Canoe Journey – Any of these will work, according to the U.S. Customs people in Port Angeles Office:
>
> - Native card (Tribal Issue) for adult or children.
> - Passport or valid driver's license or picture ID are best.
> - Birth certificate for minors.

They are also reminded what they are "allowed" to bring across the border:

> ITEMS ALLOWED TO BRING ACROSS:
>
> - Dried fish. . . Yes
> - Jarred fish and jams. . . Yes
> - Cedar bark. . . Yes if it's in the form of regalia or has been worked with for baskets or other items. (Not if it's "raw" cedar bark . . . unwashed or undried.)
> - Eagle feathers . . . Yes if in use by Native individuals, for Native purposes.

These rules and regulations, although relatively minor inconveniences, serve to remind the participants that they are, indeed, transgressing spaces, that they are between worlds, and the authority to cross over and through territory is held by someone else – a foreigner – and the rules under which the travel can occur is also not under their control.

Although the Journey has made tremendous strides in reconnecting communities, rebuilding transnational spaces, and building allies, subtle reminders continue to show the ongoing legacies of colonial forces. What these mean for water governance is the ongoing need to articulate and rearticulate boundaries that reflect intact ecological and social systems.

Conclusions and discussions

In this chapter, I explored how the intertribal Canoe Journey has helped reshape the geographic imagination of the Salish Sea Basin – both for the Canoe Journey participants, and their allies. The annual Canoe Journey has helped to create a counter-narrative of "divided nations" (in terms of both fragmented tribes/bands and the U.S.–Canada governments). The new narrative of a "Salish Sea Basin" helps to reconnect Indigenous participants (whose communities had been disconnected since the demarcation of the Canada–U.S. border). In this case, the performative act of paddling the waters of the Salish Sea Basin fosters multiple connections – connections between people and the water, between Indigenous communities, and between Indigenous and non-Indigenous people. Literally and metaphorically, the act of "pulling together" has helped foster unity. It has also helped to foster healing in relation to decades of multigenerational trauma associated with the legacy of colonization. Working together for a common cause, the connection with, and protection of, the Salish Sea water provides a common goal that places the water first, and minimizes the legacies of colonial constructions of space.

The power dynamics, in which Indigenous communities lead this project for Indigenous communities, help with goals of self-determination and governance on terms set by the actors. For example, the partnership with USGS and other governmental agencies helps with the healing, as it provides a shift in power, where the Indigenous communities are not only "at the table" – they set the agenda. The innovative partnering of USGS water quality probes and the intertribal Canoe Journey provides a partnership in which data collected will help scientists better understand the current state of the water. It also sensitizes the governmental agencies involved to the wider efforts, purviews, and traditions of the Coast Salish Tribes and First Nations. It joins the groups by engaging the participants in *knowing* the water through technologies and observation.

Thus, this chapter helps to address the second and third questions posed in this book – "How are the Indigenous-led governance mechanisms linked to the twinned goals of ecosystem protection and processes of self-determination, empowerment, and decolonization?" and the general question: "What makes a good upstream neighbor?"

In this case, a "good neighbor" is one that "pulls together" for a common cause. For the canoe to reach its goal, each of the paddlers needs to be equally prepared and strong. The paddlers need to pull in unison, and hold a shared vision. This lesson translates to governance, where a shared vision and equality of actors contribute to shared goals of ecosystem protection and cultural revitalization. In addition, "pulling together" contributes to wider, long-term goals of increased self-determination, empowerment, and decolonization through processes of reclaiming cultural heritage. In the next chapter, these twinned goals are further explored through the case of Water Walkers in the Great Lakes.

Notes

1 The concept of the "Frog's Eye View" was first introduced to me by Native American scholar and writer, David Wilkins. Wilkins attributes his use of the phrase to Gunnar Myrdal's influential book, *An American Dilemma: The Negro Problem and Modern Democracy* (1944).

2 For ebook Video Clip: see http://gallery.usgs.gov/videos/80 (2008).

8 Walking *Gichigami*

Mother Earth Water Walks and environmental advocacy

Mother Earth Water Walk

It's early morning. The sun is just rising over the calm waters of Lake Superior. Nokomis Josephine Mandamin, a 66-year-old grandmother and member of the Anishinaabe Nation, dips her copper bucket into the calm waters of Lake Superior, the largest of the North American Great Lakes (and the third largest lake, by volume, in the world).

She quietly, serenely starts the day as she has many times before with a prayer to the lake (or what Anishinaabe speakers call *Gichigami*, the big lake). *Gichigami* is seen as a spiritual entity, deserving both respect and reverence. Josephine prays for the health of the water, the well-being of her relatives and ancestors, and blesses the four directions. She then collects the water and starts her journey.

Josephine is a Water Keeper, and a member of the Ojibwa tribe of the Great Lakes of North America. In her people's tradition, it is the woman's responsibility to care for and protect the water – a responsibility that must, at times, seem daunting.

Over her lifetime, she has witnessed a significant decline in the water's health. She has seen ecosystems fail, coastlines degrade, and beaches close. She has seen industrial pollutants, agricultural runoff, and forest removal impact the health of fish and, subsequently, the health of her people. She has seen fish overharvested and exotic species threaten the survival of native species. She has seen bottling water companies such as Nestlé and Aquafina pose significant threats to the aquifers in the Great Lakes Basin. These issues are not isolated. The waters of her homeland are impacted by decisions made in far-off places. She knows, however, that she can do only so much from her home.

So, as a Water Keeper, as a mother, and as a grandmother, she does what she can. She walks. For the past 10 years Josephine has been walking along the shores of the waters she cares for so much. She walks to raise awareness of the sacred nature of water, to give voice to the pressing issues, and to inspire others to take suit. Without complaint, she walks mile after mile, kilometer after kilometer, building lore that celebrates water. Her schedule is dizzying:

Lake Superior. 2003.
Lake Michigan. 2004.

Lake Huron. 2005.
Lake Ontario. 2006.
Lake Erie. 2007.
Lake Michigan, again. 2008.
St. Lawrence River. 2009.
Four Directions Water Walk. 2011.
Lake Monona. 2012.
Mississippi Water Walk. 2013.

Each spring, Josephine and the other Water Keepers – mostly grandmothers from different clans around the Great Lakes – come together to start another journey. They come together in spring because it is seen as a time for renewal, regrowth, and rebirth for the natural habitat. It is a time to start afresh. They share a common goal – to raise awareness of the issues facing their sacred waters and to inspire action to remedy these travesties.

Their walks cross borders of all kinds – international, state, provincial, tribal – to reach their goals. Although they may not frame their work as "transboundary water governance", the Walkers' actions help to create, symbolically, a reunified territory. Similar to the work of the Canoe Journeys of the Yukon and the Coast Salish, the Great Lakes Ojibwa are consistently faced with fragmented landscapes and bifurcated policies related to colonial constructions of space, which directly impact the health of their water. The Grandmothers are also contributing to a growing discussion related to gender in water governance. For example, Harris (2009) calls for greater engagement from gender theorists on issues related to water resources and water governance. The Grandmother Water Walkers provide a substantial opportunity to make this link between the importance of gender in water and water governance, and the practicality of the role of women, historically in caring for and honoring water, which is particularly salient for Ojibwa communities (see Figure 8.1).

The Ojibwa (or Anishinaabe) are the largest groups of Indigenous peoples north of Mexico. Historically, the largest settling of Ojibwa communities are located mainly around the outlet of Sault St. Marie. However, the traditional territory ranges north into Ontario, Canada, into the U.S. states of Minnesota, Wisconsin, and Michigan, and as far west as North Dakota (Turtle Mountain). The language group, Anishinaabemowin, is still spoken today (although the number of speakers is sharply declining). During the European settlement period, the Ojibwa Nation set a precedent for their leaders to sign more detailed treaties. Notably, the Ojibwa tribes retained their hunting, fishing, and gathering rights in the 1837, 1842, and 1854 Treaties with the United States government. The coordination of these rights for eleven of the Ojibwa tribes in the U.S. is now managed through the Great Lakes Indian Fish and Wildlife Commission (GLIFWC), while the coordination of the 1836 Treaty fishing tribes is done through Chippewa Ottawa Resource Authority (CORA). In 1850, the signing of the Robson Treaty led the British to acquire all land north of Lake Huron from the Ottawa River to Lake Superior, which includes the land north of Lake Superior (in what is now Canada).

Figure 8.1 Photograph of Grandmother and Water Keeper, Nokomis Josephine Mandamin, along a small creek that flows into *Gichigami* (Lake Superior). Josephine is petitioning to Mother Earth for the water, and giving thanks for her beauty and kindness.

Source: Photograph taken by Brent Wesley, used with permission from Grandmother Josephine Mandamin who holds the copyright.

Walking *Gichigami*

It is apt, then, that Josephine started her journey on the shores of her home, the shores of *Gichigami*. For those that know the Great Lakes, Lake Superior is seen as the last "untouched lake" and is the most pristine. Its shores are still wild while the other Great Lakes' shores are not. However, this enviable status no longer holds water. Even the great Lake Superior is not immune from toxins. It is, in fact, what Mel Visser – chemical engineer turned environmental activist – calls a lake that is "Cold, Clear, and Deadly". In his book, Visser describes how synthetic pollutants such as dichlorodiphenyltrichloroethanes (DDTs), polychlorinated biphenyls (PCBs), and toxaphene are wreaking havoc on the biosystems of cold

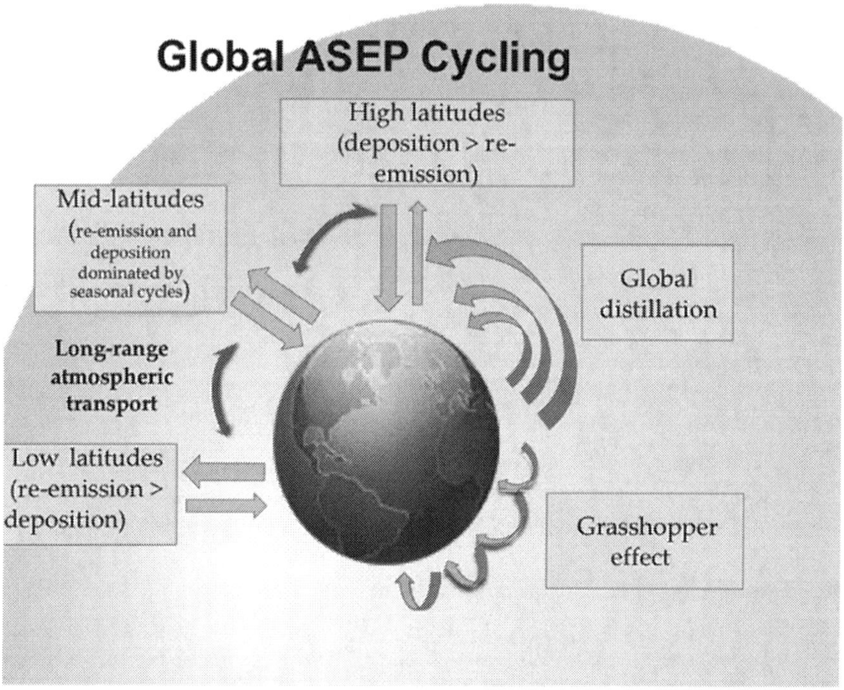

Figure 8.2 Schematic of global atmospheric transport of ASEPs.

Source: Schematic prepared by Tanvir Khan (Michigan Tech) reprinted and adapted from Wania and Mackay (1996). Copyright (1996) American Chemical Society.

water systems of Lake Superior and are impacting the health of those that rely on its bounty for sustenance (Visser, 2007). Acclaimed environmental historian, Dr. Nancy Langston, also describes the "body burden" of these toxins through her eye-opening – and chilling – book *Toxic bodies* (Langston, 2010a).

It is now known that the waters of what was once considered to be one of the most pristine bodies of water on earth are, in fact, not immune from the impacts of global pollution. In a complicated interchange between land, air, and water, pollutants known as "atmosphere-surface exchangeable pollutants", or ASEPs, are released in one site and end up great distances from the original release site (Perlinger *et al.*, 2014). Northern latitudes and higher elevations are particularly vulnerable to the accumulation of these pollutants, through processes known as the "grasshopper effect" (see Figure 8.2). Complicating matters, the pollutants tend to concentrate (and amplify) in cold water systems, making the consumption of cold-water fish particularly risky. Lastly, the pollutants stick around for a long time. Depending on the chemical, the pollutant can take hundreds, if not thousands, of years to break down. Known as legacy chemicals, or persistent organic pollutants (POPs), they are caught in a vicious cycle of atmospheric-hydrologic and sediment exchange (Perlinger, 2005; Lohmann *et al.*, 2007). So even if everyone across the globe stopped releasing these pollutants into the environment today, we would still be dealing with the pollutants for generations to come.

Dr. Judith Perlinger, a professor of environmental engineering who has spent her career studying these pollutants, defines the three distinct characteristics of ASEPs – semivolatility and re-emissions, resistance to rapid degradation, and a tendency to accumulate in cold water – that cause unintended, negative consequences for human and ecosystem health, and are separated both in time and space (Perlinger *et al.*, 2014). When you see the elevated levels of these pollutants in organisms feeding in remote waters not subject to direct emissions – such as the trout and sturgeon in the Great Lakes (Perlinger, 2005; Perlinger *et al.*, 2005) and the whales and seals in the northern waters (AMAP, 2011; El-Hayek, 2007)– the global nature of this issue truly becomes apparent (Wania *et al.*, 1998). For example, as Henrik Selin reports in his book, *Global governance of hazardous chemicals*, an average 9-year-old male beluga whale found in the St. Lawrence estuary has enough PCBs to be treated as hazardous waste under Canadian legislation (Selin, 2010). These PCBs are not released near the St. Lawrence estuary. Rather, they "grasshopped" there, accumulating in the cold waters, and intensifying as they progress through the food chain (Perlinger *et al.*, 2014).

Although thousands of chemicals hold similar characteristics – and many more are developed every year – there is a list of what the Stockholm Convention refers to as "the dirty dozen" (see Table 8.1). Some gains have been made in banning these chemicals, such as DDT and aldrin, but new chemicals are being developed yearly, many with similar damaging properties.

Equally troubling is the increasing amount of mercury (Hg) being released into the environment. Although naturally occurring, mercury is being released in processes and concentrations that are causing severe damage to both humans and ecosystems. The cycle of mercury deposition is very complex. It is released into the atmosphere either naturally through release of soils or sediments or through anthropogenic (human-induced) causes such as fossil-fuel burning – mostly coal – and incineration of municipal wastes (Nater and Gribal, 1992). It also transforms into multiple mediums (such as methyl-mercury), some forms of which are toxic and some are inert. Modeling studies indicate that present-day secondary emissions of mercury exceed those from pre-industrial times by a factor of two to four (Selin *et al.*, 2008; Obrist, 2012).

A spike in the release of mercury into the environment is largely linked to the recent gold rush in Central and South America. The increased price of gold in the global markets has contributed to a substantial increase in small-scale gold-mining operations in the Peruvian Amazon. In these operations, a common practice to separate the gold from the silt is to use mercury – a substance that is both cheap and readily available. The United Nations Environment Programme (UNEP) estimates that small-scale miners use approximately 1,350 tons of mercury each year – making it the single largest contributor of mercury pollution worldwide. The release of mercury has regional and global environmental and health concerns. Through a process of biomagnification, the fish found in regional markets near the site of gold extraction exceed the World Health Organization's standards seven-fold.

Table 8.1 The Dirty Dozen – persistent organic pollutants

Chemical or class	*Notes*
Aldrin	Pesticide widely used on corn and cotton until 1970. EPA allowed its use for termites until manufacturer cancelled registration in 1987. Closely related to dieldrin
Chlordane	Pesticide on agricultural crops, lawns, and gardens and a fumigant for termite control. All uses were banned in the United States in 1988 but still produced for export
DDT	Pesticide still used for malaria control in the tropics. Banned for all but emergency uses in the United States in 1972
Dieldrin	Pesticide widely used on corn and cotton until 1970. EPA allowed its use for termites until manufacturer cancelled registration in 1987. A breakdown product of aldrin
Endrin	Used as a pesticide to control insects, rodents, and birds. Not produced or sold for general use in the United States since 1986
Heptachlor	Insecticide in household and agricultural uses until 1988. Also a component and a breakdown product of chlordane
Hexachloro-benzene	Pesticide and fungicide used on seeds, also an industrial byproduct. Not widely used in the United States since 1965
Mirex	Insecticide and flame retardant not used or manufactured in the United States since 1978
Toxaphene	Insecticide used primarily on cotton. Most uses in the United States were banned in 1982, and all uses in 1990
PCBs	Polychlorinated biphenyls, widely used in electrical equipment and other uses. Manufacture of PCBs banned in the United States in 1977
Polychlorinated byproducts Dioxins and Polychlorinated Furans	Two notorious classes of "unintentional" pollutants, of incineration and industrial processes. Regulated in the United States under air, water, food quality, occupational safety, waste, and other statutes

Source*:* www.uspopswatch.org/global/dirty-dozen.htm.

Chemical pollutants and human and ecosystem health

Once released, these pollutants are deposited regionally, but they also find their way into the atmosphere and are eventually deposited into the cold waters of higher latitudes. Although not visible to the human eye, the toxins biointensify in cold water species such as trout and sturgeon in Lake Superior, and whales and seals in the Arctic. For the Indigenous communities that rely on the lake for food sources – such as the Ojibwa of Lake Superior, the Inuit of Baffin Island, and the Aleut of Northern Alaska – the outcomes are dire.

Increased cancer rates, infertility, miscarriages, and deformities have all increased substantially over the last several decades (Clarkson and Magos, 2006). Indigenous communities are disproportionally impacted, largely because their customary diets are reliant on food sources that are greatly impacted by the pollutants. Eating more contaminated fish, for example, leads to a significant increase in illness. Conversely, abandoning traditional dietary practices and moving towards processed and preserved foods (often high in sugars and fat) contributes to significant increases in heart disease and Type II diabetes.

The evidence linking these toxins with compromised human and ecosystem health has been mounting since the 1950s. In the groundbreaking book, *Our stolen future*, Theo Colbern, Dianne Dumansoki, and John Meyers (1996) show the extent to which synthetic chemicals have been disrupting humans and ecosystems, particularly in relation to hormone disruption. Using historical vignettes, they show how these pollutants have made appearances in documented environmental tragedies since the 1950s, for example, the bald eagles in Florida (1952), river otters in England (late 1950s), mink in Michigan (1960s), herring gulls in Michigan (1970), western gulls in California (early 1980s), alligators in Florida (1980s), seals in northern Europe (1988), dolphins in the Mediterranean (early 1990s), and sperm counts of men worldwide (1992). However, as Colbern *et al.* describe, understanding these links took years to fully comprehend, and drawing these scientific conclusions was, in many ways, a matter of detective work.

Increasingly, the links between exposure to mercury and the other ASEPs are being well documented in scientific journals and health literature. For example, mercury is found to cause damage to the central nervous system, cardiovascular system, kidneys, and other organs in humans (Clarkson and Magos, 2006). Polycyclic aromatic hydrocarbons (PAHs) cause numerous chronic human health effects including cataracts, kidney and liver damage, jaundice, inflammation, decreased immune function, respiratory illnesses, and cancer (Agarwal, 2009; Huang *et al.*, 2012). Human health effects of PCBs include a range of immunal, hormonal, nervous and enzyme system effects (Huang *et al.*, 2012) including skin lesions, cancers, and reduced IQ in the offspring of parents who consume food tainted with PCBs (Schantz *et al.*, 2003).

Although the health impacts are well known, identifying governance mechanisms to address the negative impacts of these extraterritorial pollutants is far from straightforward. The global nature of this issue requires coordinated, multinational mechanisms. Yet, because the impacts of these pollutants are felt unevenly (intensified in the polar regions) and the economic benefits remain great (particularly for industrialized/ing nations) coming up with a comprehensive strategy has proven difficult. A range of governance mechanisms, agencies, and organizations (from supranational to local) are involved in the management of these pollutants. The most well known of these is the United Nations Stockholm Convention on Persistent Organic Pollutants (known simply as the Stockholm Convention) which was adopted in 2001, and came into force in 2004. The Stockholm Convention was designed as a global attempt to ban the most injurious of these persistent organic pollutants. But a successful international treaty requires the buy-in from all.

Although 179 nations have ratified the Treaty as of 2014 (and hold themselves legally accountable), the United States is noticeably absent. The U.S. signed the convention, but did not ratify – arguably the ratification was halted when dioxin was included for elimination (Visser, 2014). Other complementary treaties include the Basel Convention on the Control of Transboundary Movements of Hazardous Wastes and their Disposal (Basel Convention) which is designed to reduce the movements of hazardous waste between nations, particularly as a way to protect lesser developed countries from the impacts of uneven development. The Basel Convention came into force in May 1992. As of October 2013, 179 states and the EU had ratified the Basel Convention (the U.S. and Haiti have signed, but not ratified). Third, the Rotterdam Convention (known formally as the Rotterdam Convention on the Prior Informed Consent Procedure for Certain Hazardous Chemicals and Pesticides in International Trade) is a multilateral treaty that aims to promote open exchange of information related to the importation of hazardous chemicals – including proper labeling, safe handling instructions, and known bans. (For a list of substances covered under the Convention, see Appendix B.)

Organizations such as the Arctic Monitoring Assessment Program (AMAP), Alaska Communication Action on Toxins, and Indigenous Environmental Network are research and advocacy networks that seek to understand and document the ecosystem and human health impacts of these ASEPs. Federal Agencies such as the U.S. Drug and Food Administration, the U.S. Environmental Protection Agency, Environment Canada, and Health Canada each have roles within their institutions though budget cuts and decentralization continue to compromise their ability to handle these complex, global issues. At the state and provincial levels, governmental agencies such as the Michigan Department of Community Health and Ontario Natural Resources try to make the risks known to the public. Thus, at the local level, the issue largely becomes one of "informing people what they can and cannot eat" (Gagnon, 2011). Fish advisories continually try to warn people of the dangers of consuming "too much" contaminated fish, particularly women of childbearing age. The outreach to Indigenous communities is slightly different, however.

Although Indigenous communities may know about the health risks associated with consuming contaminated fish, the idea that there is a "choice" to not eat the contaminated foods is false. For Indigenous peoples tied to the land – spiritually, culturally, economically – the choice to move is not an option. The choice to eat *other* food is, for many, also not a valid option. As Valoree Gagnon (2011) found in her important study on fish toxins and advisories in the Ojibwa community of Keweenaw Bay, Lake Superior, "fish" and "contaminants" appear differently, based on the perceptions and priorities of those who encounter them. In her study, Gagnon examined the fish contaminant knowledge, impacts on fishing and fish consumption, and the factors that contribute to harvesting decisions and behaviors. She found that the fundamental guidance and essential framework associated with the harvesting beliefs, values, and traditional lifeways were not represented in the fish advisories. In fact, having a fish advisory can lead to a politics of calculation, similar to the ones discussed in Boundary Bay (Chapter 5).

The Ojibwa are the people of the lake; they have relied on the lake's harvest for millennia. To turn their back on the fish is to turn their back on a way of life. Similar to the issues facing the Coast Salish peoples discussed in Chapters 5 and 6, the Ojibwa peoples' ways forward is contextualized by place and custom. The communities are fixed to set territorial boundaries to make their livelihood, yet extraterritorial pollution disproportionately influences the quality of this life (Donatuto, 2008).

So, what does that mean in terms of ways forward? For some, they stay and hope for the best. Some choose to ignore the signs because it is too overwhelming. For others, like Josephine, they make their work trying to do what they can – raising the profile of the issues, raising awareness, increasing allies. For Josephine, this means walking.

Along the way, she tells stories, collects friends, and builds allies. Over the years, a team of people has come to support this annual Journey, and other walks have sprung up in solidarity. With each Journey comes increased awareness with increased concern.

The 2011 Journey described below was perhaps the most highly publicized and the most involved. It is a journey similar to mine – a Journey from the waters of the Salish Sea to the heart of the Great Lakes. This Journey is astounding.

Four Directions Water Walk

In 2011, Grandmother Nokomis Josephine Mandamin embarked on arguably the most ambitious and inspirational walk yet; to gather pails of salt water from the Four Sacred Directions – from Hudson Bay, the Atlantic Ocean, the Gulf of Mexico, and the Pacific Ocean – to meet at the center, on the shores of Lake Superior (see Figure 8.3). The four directions link to the four cardinal points on the Medicine Wheel, beginning in the East and moving clockwise to the West. For the Ojibwa, the directions are represented by the colors yellow, red, black, and white. In addition, the sky above, the earth below, and at the center the self, the physical world, complete the Medicine Wheel, or the wheel of life.

Many teachings are embedded within the Medicine Wheel and the four directions, both spiritually and practically. They are in place to remind people of the need for balance in the world, and the balance that people must achieve in everyday life. The need for "centering" and "grounding" is also explicitly linked to respect for place and respect for others. So, for Grandmother Josephine, extending the Journey to the Four Directions not only was a practical way of widening her message, it was also spiritually grounded in an ancient practice, which served to foster reciprocal and respectful relationships between earth and humans.

Josephine gathered the water in copper buckets at each of the four collection sites. At one site after another, she prepared the water and the volunteers with blessings and promises. Groups of volunteers helped to carry the salt water from each of the four collection sites to the final destination in Lake Superior. The walkers took turns carrying the pail – over mountain passes, across bridges, and along

Table 8.2 Josephine's schedule

April 7:	Approximately 8 a.m., leaving Toronto to Aberdeen, Washington. Ceremonies with the Anishinaabe on 8, 9, and tours
April 10:	Start Send Off with the water and walk until 17
April 18:	Fly out of Spokane, Wa., Gulf of Mexico
April 20:	Start Send Off with the water and walk until 28
April 29:	Fly out of Memphis, Tenn., to Thunder Bay
May 4:	Fly out to Ottawa from SSM; – on to Bangor, Maine
May 7:	Start Send Off with water from Machias until 15 May
May 16:	Fly from Ottawa-SSM, pick up vehicle, drive to Winnipeg
May 18:	Train to Churchill and return to Winnipeg
May 23:	Approximate Send Off from Winnipeg
	and walk with the water up to Kenora
June 1:	Leave to join East Walkers in SSM, Ontario
June 13:	All four pails of salt water to arrive at Madigan Lake, Bad River, Wisconsin

Source: www.motherearthwaterwalk.com/?page_id=2190.

Table 8.3 Walkers from the West

April 10	Aberdeen, Washington send off
April 11	Olympia, Washington
April 15	Leavenworth, Washington
April 19	Spokane, Washington
April 22	St. Regis, Montana
April 25	Whitefish, Montana
April 29	Shelby, Montana
May 2	Havre, Montana
May 5	Malta, Montana
May 9	Cadillac, Saskatchewan
May 12	Assiniboia, Saskatchewan
May 16	Weyburn, Saskatchewan
May 20	Pipestone, Manitoba
May 23	Killarney, Manitoba
May 27	Emerson, Manitoba
May 30	Grand Forks, North Dakota
May 31	Crookston, Minnesota
June 3	Bemidji, Minnesota
June 6	Grand Rapids, Minnesota
June 9	Duluth, Minnesota
June 12	Bad River, Wisconsin

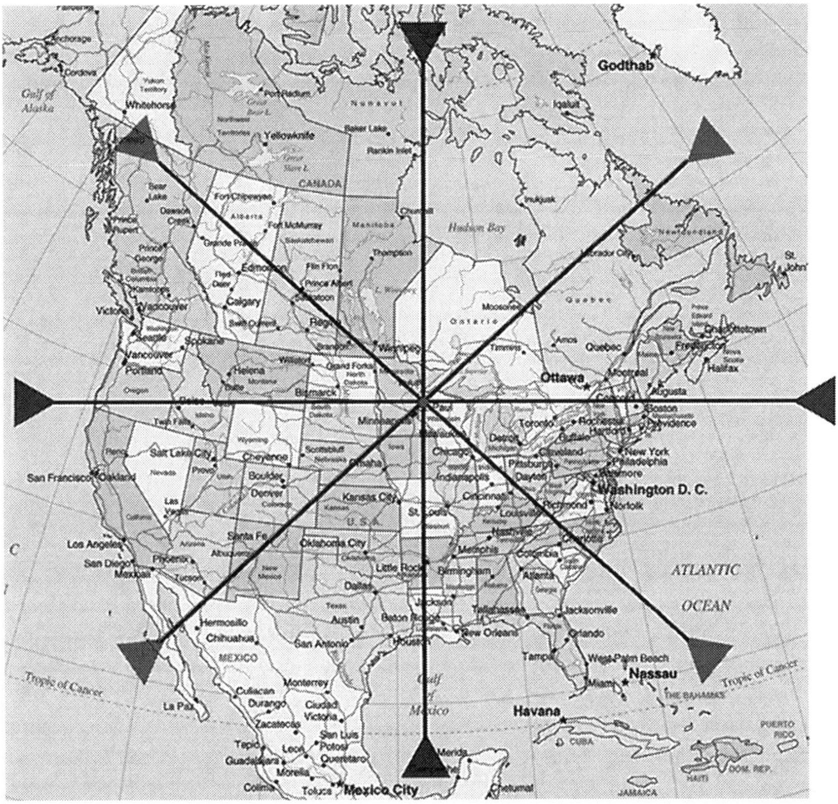

Figure 8.3 Map of Four Directions Water Walk, 2011.

Source: Water Walkers, 2013.

roadsides. This required a team of dedicated people to set up camp, provide food, coordinate public relations, and to make sure everyone was on target for the final convergence.

So, what started out as a singular journey, ballooned into a troop of people who joined the cause. Looking at the schedule makes you realize the logistics associated with this type of event (see Tables 8.2 and 8.3: Josephine's schedule and the Walkers from the West schedule. The other schedules are available in the Appendix.).

After 3 months of walking – and thousands of kilometers – the Anishinaabe Grandmothers, women, men, and youth from Canada and the United States converged in Bad River, Wisconsin to celebrate. The next day all four pails were released – in unison – into Lake Superior. Hundreds of people participated in this journey. However, the journey touched thousands more. For each town they walked through, a public relations volunteer was one day ahead of the Walkers, contacting local media and generally trying to raise awareness about the event. People could also participate virtually. The age of social media, which has shown up over and over in this volume, has helped bring this journey to people from all corners of the world.

Another amazing component of this journey was that people could follow the Water Walkers virtually. With a GPS chip attached to the bucket, people could keep pace with the Walkers, in real-time. The map of the Walkers could be accessed (and still is available) at the website: http://emptyglassforwater.ca/map/. Fundraising campaigns also allowed people to contribute to the cause without physically being part of it.

This movement also motivated award-winning film-maker Jeff Bear from Urban Rez Productions, to produce the documentary, *The Water Walk*. The film follows Josephine's journey from the waters of the Salish Sea to Lake Superior (The Western Walk). The film documents the send-off ceremony from the Skokomish Nation, along the Olympic Peninsula, and the walk through the temperate rainforest through to the first mountain pass. Jeff Bear describes the film and the inspiration behind its creation:

> One elder's passion is lovingly depicted in this portrait of courage, determination and the power of water. Josephine Mandamin has spent the last 10 years on a remarkable journey on foot to raise awareness of the importance, fragility and sacredness of water, including walking around all the Great Lakes down to the mouth of the St. Lawrence River. In 2011, Josephine embarked on her most ambitious walk yet: to collect four pails of water from Hudson Bay, the Atlantic Ocean, the Gulf of Mexico and the Pacific Ocean, ending at the Great Lakes. Her incredible journey from the four directions to Lake Superior is an inspirational testament to the human spirit and the life-giving power of water that nourishes us all.

Conclusions: lessons from the Water Walks

What do these walks mean for water governance, for transborder water governance? What lessons can be gleaned from raising attention to these issues?

When someone starts a journey such as this, you never really know how it is going to be received, what "measurable outcomes" will materialize. However, like most movements, events, or even institutions, a journey starts with a vision, a set of intentions. The original idea no doubt changes along the way, but the key message, if clearly defined, provides guidance. In this case – raising awareness of water issues – the success was overwhelming.

But does raising awareness lead to institutional change? To policy change? To behavior change? By thinking of this as a cascading movement where people are moved to do *what they can, how they can*, might just be enough. The stated goal of the 2011 Mother Earth Water Walk was to "raise consciousness of the need to care for the water, a sacred gift, the source of all life". The Walkers ask, "What will you do for the water?" This question places the onus of water protection not on agencies far away, but on individuals, to do their part in whatever way they can. This relocates the power and responsibility from *someone else*, *somewhere else* to the self. This shift fosters empowerment and self-determination, which is part of the wider goals of wellness and healing. Although extraterritorial pollution remains an issue, and governance structures certainly need to address all people equally, the relocation of responsibility to the self, to the individual, is a sustainable strategy, which ultimately makes the question of "what makes a good upstream neighbor" directly related to taking responsibility within your own self, and your own basin. It also means *knowing* your waterway, connecting with your environment. This approach is also seen in the Canoe Journey described in Chapter 7. Ideally, if everyone took the time to really know their waterways (and their neighbors), many of the issues associated with extraterritorial pollutants would be resolved. Clearly, the need for international governance mechanisms, accountability, and enforceable rules and regulations remains paramount, but working towards inter-basin accountability and connectedness to waterways is a good place to start. Mechanisms such as the United Nations Declaration on the Rights of Indigenous Peoples, Great Lakes Indian Fish and Wildlife Commission, the Binational Lake Superior Forum, the Yukon River Inter-Tribal Council, and the Coast Salish Gathering each play an important role in the transboundary water issues. However, within that mix, the role of the individual should not be lost. The Water Walkers serve as a good reminder for this.

In the next chapter, the penultimate for the book, a charismatic whale named Luna, or *Tsu-xiit*, upsets the notions of borders and water governance that other chapters in this book have grappled with. Luna/*Tsu-xiit* serves as a reminder of the need for greater nuance in our water governance practices. The story, like the ones presented before it, continues to explore characteristics of what makes a good upstream neighbor, while asserting the need to work arduously to promote wider understanding of diverse worldviews and decolonizing practices in transboundary management.

Box 8.1 The story of the Water Song

Told by Beatrice Menase Kwe Jackson, Migizi Clan

This song was written by Doreen Day at the request of her grandson. She attended a conference about the water at which the internationally known speaker, Dr. Masaru Emoto, said that the very least we should do every day, is to speak to the water:

> Water, we love you.
> We thank you.
> We respect you.

So she did this. Every day on their drive to drop Mashkoonce (Little Elk) to school, they passed a body of water. And every day they said these words to the water as they drove by. They made games by saying it in different voices and then would say it as fast as they could. Then one day Mashkoonce said, “Nokomis why can’t we say this in our language?” So, Doreen asked her daughter’s language teacher to write it in Ojibwamowin. Doreen had the words taped to the car visor as they learned the words.

One day this grandson Mashkoonce said, “Nokomis why don’t we sing the words, don’t you think the water would like it to be sung?” So she thought about it and came up with the tune. They sang this song to the water every morning on their drive to school.

It is sung like a lullaby and we don’t use shakers or drums.

Doreen and her grandson, Mashkoonce, give permission for everyone to share this song . . . sing it to the water every day.

Ne-be Gee Zah- gay- e- goo
Gee Me-gwetch -wayn ne- me – goo
Gee Zah Wayn ne- me- goo

A significant aspect of sharing the Water Song – like organizing the Water Walks – is to help contribute to building a collective conscience. Water is a great unifier. Celebrating and honoring the importance of water through song and collective action are ways that communities such as the Ojibwa are contributing to a paradigm shift, which helps people to understand, more viscerally, the unifying principles of water.

Listen to the water song at www.motherearthwaterwalk.com/?page_id =2190.

9 What boundary? What whale? Whose responsibility?

The blurring of political and cultural boundaries in marine governance

In July 2001 a lone juvenile orca was observed in a remote fjord called Nootka Sound on the west coast of Vancouver Island, British Columbia. The orca was a curious sight. After more than 40 years of research, scientists have come to learn that orcas are social creatures that stay with their families (or pods) for life. Even when the animals are fully grown, they are not known to stray far from their mothers. Why, then, was this juvenile whale in isolation? Why did the orca travel 200 miles away from his resident community in the Salish Sea to take up residence in the traditional territory of the Mowachaht/Muchalaht First Nation in British Columbia? To help answer these questions, numerous marine scientists travelled to Nootka Sound to observe this orca, now identified as L98 by the scientific community, or "Luna" to the general public.[1]

Over the next 2 years, Luna became well known for his friendly behavior – frolicking with boats, rubbing against the vessels, and even letting people touch him. However, these remarkable characteristics also made people concerned for Luna's safety and for the safety of others. Although many boaters and observers found much joy in this friendly behavior, researchers and governmental employees warned boaters that it was best to ignore Luna, as the more attention the whale received from humans the less likely it was he would return to his pod. Some local residents grew concerned, others angered, when Luna started to cause damage to their boats.

As it became increasingly clear that Luna would not reunite with his pod "naturally", a transboundary effort to "save Luna" ensued. Scientists and government officials in Canada corresponded with scientists and government officials in the United States to come up with a plan to reunite the orca with his pod in Washington State. This multijurisdictional issue required multi-agency coordination, which required significant cooperation financially and otherwise. A significant financial contribution by Washington State in October 2003, which was matched a few days later by the Canadian government, provided the extra push for the coordinated move (McClure, 2003). In June 2004, after months of discussions, the Department of Fisheries and Oceans Canada (DFO)[2] publicly launched the relocation plan (see Figure 9.1).

The DFO's plan was to lure Luna into a holding pen, close the gates, and then transfer him by truck 200 miles to the southern tip of Vancouver Island. Luna

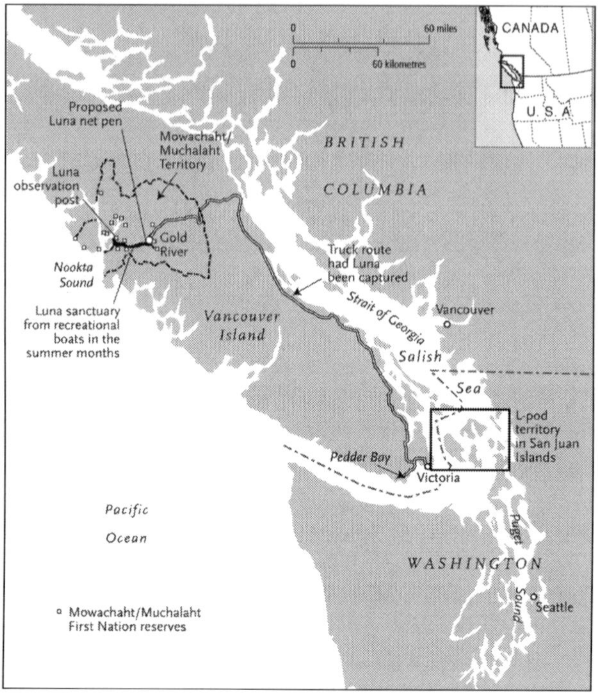

Figure 9.1 Map of relocation plan to Pedder Bay, British Columbia, and Luna's family (L-pod's summer territory in San Juan Island, Washington).

would then be placed in Pedder Bay near the province's capital, Victoria. The hope was that Luna would make acoustic contact with his pod, and swim across the international border and back into the L-pod territory around the San Juan Islands. If, however, the reunification did not occur, a non-public contingency plan to place Luna in an aquarium was planned (Joyce, 2004).

The relocation plan was devised by federal officials (with support from numerous scientists, researchers, and aquarium personnel), but did not include consultation with the Indigenous community whose waters Luna inhabited. Had the agencies included the Mowachaht/Muchalaht First Nation members in the decision-making process, they would have heard a different perspective – that Luna, was not in fact "lost", rather he had returned "home" (James, 2010).

Luna, or in the perception and language of the Mowachaht/Muchalaht First Nation, *Tsu-xiit*, embodied the spirit of their recently deceased chief, Ambrose Maquinna. Before passing, Chief Maquinna had disclosed to Mowachaht/ Muchalaht elder Jerry Jack, that his spirit would return to them in the form of an *oakawin* (orca, or killer whale). About the same time of the chief's passing, *Tsu-xiit* arrived in Nootka Sound, in the traditional territory of Mowachaht/Muchalaht First Nation.[3]

Despite the DFO's lengthy coordination process, the Mowachaht/Muchalaht First Nation was never directly involved in the decision-making process for the transfer. Although the Mowachaht/Muchalaht First Nation had publicly announced *Txu-xiit's* position as the chief incarnate they were not invited to be part of the DFO-led discussions. This lack of meaningful consultation ultimately led to a series of high-profile events, including what is now referred to as the "The Nine Days".

For 9 days, members of the Mowachaht/Muchalaht First Nation and the DFO engaged in what newspapers called a "Tug of Whale". In an effort to halt the plan and to keep *Tsu-xiit* in Nootka Sound, members of the First Nation took to their canoes and diverted *Tsu-xiit* away from the holding pens. During the tense days, the paddlers were able to steer *Tsu-xiit* away from the capture pens by showering him with attention. Striking images of the Mowachaht/Muchalaht members paddling alongside *Tsu-xiit*, rubbing his side, drumming, and singing traditional songs, hit the media by storm and launched the story into the public eye (see Figure 9.2). The Mowachaht/Muchalaht decision to resist the move was important, politically, but it was also a very powerful unifier for the community. This unification also provided a powerful resistance against State authority. The way that the Mowachaht/Muchalaht chose to resist (peacefully through song and canoe) proved to be a powerful performative act. By taking to human-powered canoes rather than motorized fishing boats (which were also available) it presented the situation as a David and Goliath battle. It also helped to frame the issue as deeply rooted in tradition. The physical and mental will of the community to keep *Tsu-xiit* in their water was palpable. The vulnerability of the paddlers (both to the physical elements and also the high-powered motorized craft which the DFO officers had) accentuated the asymmetrical power dynamics. These dynamics, in many ways, worked in the Mowachaht/Muchalaht First Nation's favor.

After Mowachaht/Muchalaht community members started paddling with *Tsu-xiit* it was clear that the DFO would need to devise a new plan. An article published

Figure 9.2 Mowachaht/Muchalaht community members paddling with *Tsu-xiit* during the 9-day stand-off.

Source: Photo taken by Suzanne Chisholm (used with permission).

by the national Canadian newspaper, *Globe and Mail*, 2 days into the stand-off reported:

> Department of Fisheries and Oceans officials could *only stand by and watch* as their quarry swam out toward the sea. The unexpected development *threw a wrench* into a highly publicized and costly plan to capture the whale and truck it 350 kilometers down the coast to a bay near Victoria.
>
> (emphasis mine, Armstrong 2005)

It was not immediately evident, however, that the First Nation would succeed in its efforts to stop the DFO plan. In an article written about the incident, Mowachaht/Muchalaht First Nation member Tyee Ha'wilth Mike Maquinna noted their potentially vulnerable position:

> "The concern we have is that DFO is trying to escalate this into a conflict . . . All we are doing is the same thing we've been doing here for thousands of years; paddling our canoes and singing songs. We have a very special connection with *Tsu-xiit* and we're paddling in support of him," he said. "We're trying to stay out of harm's way, but DFO seems committed to turn this into a battle, even though we've made it clear we don't want that. They have bulletproof vests, guns, and high-powered vessels. We're just paddlers in traditional canoes."
>
> (Wiwchar, 2004)

The Tug-of-Whale ensued. *Tsu-xiit* followed the canoes down the Nootka Sound and then, without notice, would dash off to follow the DFO boat. On the seventh day, the DFO boat successfully led *Tsu-xiit* into the holding pen. Although it seemed that the DFO had captured Luna, the gate was never closed and, after more than 10 dramatic minutes, *Tsu-xiit* swam out of the pen and away with the Mowachaht/Muchalaht paddlers. After this folly, 2 days later, the DFO called off the effort to relocate Luna. However, the DFO maintained the strict position that humans could not interact with Luna and they would prosecute individuals who came within 100 meters of the whale, citing the Marine Mammals Regulations of the Fisheries Act (DFO, 2013). In both Canada and the United States, it is a crime to disturb marine mammals in the wild, and in Canada the offence carries a fine as high as $100,000.

The Mowachaht/Muchalaht First Nation was in a difficult position. Although they had "won" the battle to keep *Tsu-xiit* in his traditional waters (which they did for almost 3 years), the act of keeping *Tsu-xiit* out of harm's way (particularly away from boats and float planes) required ongoing human intervention. This intervention, however, was deemed illegal under the federal Fisheries Act. Thus, the boundaries in this case continued to grow – jurisdictional boundaries, human–animal boundaries, and legal boundaries of contact.

In order for the Mowachaht/Muchalaht First Nation to keep Luna out of harm's way, they were required to work within the system set by the State. To do so, they took measures to interact "legally" with *Tsu-xiit*. They applied for, and

Figure 9.3 Jamie James, Mowachaht/Muchalaht Fisheries Manager and *Tsu-xiit*, October 2004.

Source: Photo by Suzanne Chisholm (used with permission).

received, a temporary DFO permit that allowed their Fisheries Officer, Jamie James, to watch over *Tsu-xiit* during the fall of 2004 (see Figure 9.3). During these months James' full-time job was to "whale-sit" *Tsu-xiit*, going out to the waters every day. In 2005, Jamie set up camp in the remote waters, where his sole job was to socialize with and redirect Luna's "friendly behavior".

But these boundaries remained fuzzy. Although the DFO reissued a permit to the Mowachaht/Muchalaht First Nation in the summer of 2005, a stipulation was attached indicating they could not "initiate contact" with *Tsu-xiit*. After those initial DFO permits expired, however, no further permits were allocated. The decision to once again make socializing with *Tsu-xiit* "illegal" in the eyes of the Canadian government reflects power dynamics related to defining categories and privileging worldviews that materialize in boundary-setting (Sundberg, 2011).

To fill the void left by James' departure, journalists Suzanne Chisholm and Mike Parfitt who came to Nootka Sound to document this story – and ultimately produced the award-winning documentary films, *Saving Luna* (2008) and *The Whale* (2012) – crossed yet another boundary, from "observer" to "actor" by taking over the role as Luna's companion. They, too, applied for a permit to look after Luna "legally" but did not receive approval from the DFO. Running the risk of fines and threats of incarceration, the journalists set up camp on their boat in an attempt to keep Luna out of harm's way. However, accompanying Luna every minute proved impossible. When the couple left the area for a family visit, tragedy struck (Chisholm, 2012).

On a stormy day in March 2006, a large tugboat pulled into Nootka Sound in an attempt to avoid inclement weather. Perhaps curious of the vessel, Luna playfully interacted with the tugboat. As the vessel pulled away, Luna was drawn into the propeller and was instantly killed.

Although Luna's life ended in tragedy, retelling the story provides an opportunity – a *lichtung* in the words of Heidegger – to learn from its public unfolding and explore the edges, "transgressions", and entanglements between animal and human (Philo and Wilbert, 2000; Collard, 2012) and the power dynamics set up between socially created political borders. As James (2010) reflects, "it is not too often in one's life that you can be part of the unfolding of a legend. Now that the drama is over, it is our responsibility to take the lessons presented to us and let them inform our actions". This chapter is written with that aim.

Lessons from Luna

At first brush, the story of this lost whale (known as Luna, L98, or *Tsu-xiit* depending on your position) seems a familiar tale: a "lost" juvenile whale fending for himself in the wild and a group of environmentally-minded citizens banding together to "save" the whale by reuniting him with his family, and repositioning him to his "natural place". Stories of successful reunification of stray, friendly whales have, after-all, been on the rise since the Warner Brothers' hit movie *Free Willy*. In fact, a year after Luna arrived in Nootka Sound, another whale – known as Springer – was "rescued" in the Puget Sound of Washington, having separated from her pod. Responding to concerns that the young whale would die in the congested waters of Puget Sound, officials devised a plan to net Springer and reunite her with her pod in Canada – a plan that, miraculously, worked.

However, as the story unfolds, it becomes increasingly clear that Luna's tale is far from straightforward, as seemingly uncontested categories such as "animal", "human", "lost", and "found" become challenged at every turn. Part of the messiness is that there are multiple boundaries in question. They involve several political jurisdictions (national, state, provincial, reserve/non-reserve), as well as cultural, species, and epistemological. By drawing on Luna's story and the multiple discourses generated around its unfolding, this chapter explores how current governance systems are often ill-equipped to transcend boundaries.

Analyzing the discourses created around Luna sheds light on the complex power dynamics and value systems embedded in the bounding of space and the ideologies associated with transboundary governance practices. Thus, in this chapter, I explore the following interrelated questions:

- How are managers – who are fixed to national standards, protocols, and rules – able to transcend bounded spaces? Relatedly, how possible is it for resource managers to transcend boundaries of human–animal transmogrification?
- Who holds the power to decide what, and whose, interpretation of the natural world should be taken up as policy?
- Ultimately, whose perspective is naturalized and privileged as the "rightful" voice, which translates to the "rightful place"?

In grappling with these questions, I argue that greater attention to power dynamics and embedded belief systems is essential – and often undervalued – in current environmental management practices and decision-making processes.

To help tease out power dynamics in belief systems, scholars such as Whatmore (2002) suggest viewing "nature" and "society" as a hybrid relationship. That is, the relationship is reflexive, with each mutually constituting the other and influencing each other at different times and spaces. Other scholars take this a step further and try to move away from an anthropocentric framing, by inserting a "posthumanist" perspective into the concept of hybridity (see Haraway, 2008; Lulka, 2009; Sundberg, 2011; Collard, 2012). For example, Lulka (2009, p. 378) proposes a "thick hybridity" which commonly occurs outside the "direct purview of society". Lulka suggests that, rather than reifying nature, thick hybridity provides an impetus for people to embrace this uncertainty. Similarly, Collard (2012) explores this hybrid relationship between nature and society by discussing "the entanglements" between animal and human, while Haraway (2008) calls the relationship "queer messmates".

This chapter contributes to these discussions through the intriguing, and complex case of a juvenile whale that was simultaneously "lost" and "found" and between multiple borders. This fleshy being – who meant many different things to different people – provides an opportunity to think critically about how worldviews are ascribed onto and built into management practices. This case complicates issues around transboundary water governance management by providing an opportunity to explore how concepts of hybridity materialize and interface with management practices.

To help in this analysis, I engage in three sets of geographic literature: border studies, animal geographies, and Indigenous studies. Bringing these literature sets into conversation with each other helps to untangle belief systems (and power systems) that are often implicit within governance systems, particularly when these systems transcend multiple borders.

Engaging with this literature also affords a widening interpretation of "borders" from jurisdictional (managing units) to include forms of being (i.e. animal–human transmogrification) and epistemological. As such, this chapter contributes to the ongoing discussions exploring "hybridity" within critical animal geography. The case reinforces the arguments presented on the social construction of borders (Balibar, 2004; Fall, 2005, 2010; Agnew, 2007; Popescu, 2012) and enriches this line of reasoning with insights from animal geographies. I conclude by arguing that greater attention to the "agency" or "fleshiness" of the being helps to cut through the conceptual pitfalls of the constructed, but very real, boundaries.

Theorizing the edges through animal geographies

Over the past 20 years, the field of animal geography has made progress in exploring the boundaries between, and the dynamic relationship of, animals and humans.[4] Notably, Wolch and Emel's (1998) insights were pivotal in the development of contemporary animal geographies. Their argument that animals have been so interwoven into the basic affairs of human life and so indispensable to the scaffolding of "progress" that humans have not been able (or willing) to fully see them remains valid today. Disentangling "animal rights" from "agency", for example, helped to show how seemingly progressive environmental groups, whose efforts aim to champion animal rights, tend to commodify animals rather than give them agency. Since their groundbreaking work, other scholars have explored the power dynamics/ethics associated with the process of "othering" animals and creating a hybrid-relationship between animals and humans in which animals are left without agency (Whatmore, 2002; Bear, 2011; Sundberg, 2011). Recent scholarship extends the work in animal geographies away from the "collective" or "herd" to the "individual" animal (Bear, 2011). This subtle difference provides space to challenge what humans conceive as animals.

As part of this reframing, scholars from across disciplines have found Foucault's work on biopower applicable to human–animal relationships (Holloway, 2007; Haraway, 2008; Cadman, 2009; Holloway *et al.*, 2009; Shukin, 2009; Collard, 2012). In particular, Collard's (2012, p. 29) article on the "entanglements" between cougars and humans in Vancouver Island, Canada, helped advance the idea "that interspecies relationships produce space and are expressed biopolitically". Furthermore, Lulka's (2009) conceptualization of "thick hybridity" provides space to explore the reflexive relationship between animals and humans, and articulate the agency of animals in these relationships. Looking at the interspecies relationships between Luna and the many actors surrounding him, illuminates how dynamics change when the dominant discourse, which normalizes the placement of animals in society, is called into question.

Thus, this chapter widens the focus of transboundary water governance found in the previous chapter and contributes to the burgeoning discussions on animality and materiality in human geography (e.g. Haraway, 2008; Panelli, 2010; Bear, 2011; Sundberg, 2011; Collard, 2012) by arguing that greater sensitivity to power-dynamics is needed for the governance of animals between diverse cultural frameworks and across bounded geographic spaces. This contributes, particularly, to Sundberg's (2011) work, which advanced the need to account for nonhumans as political actors and (re)conceptualize agency through a posthumanist framework.

Although the concept of the social construction of nature is well established in the academy (and posthumanist thinking increasingly so), Luna's case highlights the lack of carry-over into the daily practice of environmental management. As Castree (2004) notes, "the dichotomy of society–nature continues to inform lay and expert discourse", which remains true a decade after its original claim. That is, much work needs to occur to destabilize these fixed categories and treat the relationship between animals and humans as both hybrid and reflexive.

Complicating the decision-making process is the multiplicity of positions from which the decisions are made. As this case shows, Luna holds many meanings. Luna is seen both as an animal that needs to be managed and as a chief incarnate that has returned home. The latter version holds particular challenges for contemporary environmental managers. As Wolch (1998, p. 121) reflects:

> In many parts of the world beliefs in transmogrification or transmigration of souls provide a basis for beliefs in human–animal continuity (or even coincidence). But in the Western world animals have for many centuries been defined as fundamentally different and ontologically separate from humans, and although explicit criteria for establishing human difference have changed over time, all criteria routinely use humans as the standard for judgment.

The varying definitions, interpretations, and worldviews, undoubtedly, have impacts on how people determine what is "right" for a particular being in question, and ultimately how they interact through their governance decisions. Similarly, literature related to animals in zoos, for example, has argued for a new species of animal to be designated (Anderson, 1995; Wolch, 1998; Philo and Wilbert, 2000; Calarco, 2008; Chrulew, 2011). Increasingly, questions related to the impacts and ethics of observation are also being applied to "over-observed" animals in nature as well (Collard, 2012).

Because the multiple constructions are so pronounced, Luna's story provides opportunities to explore the complex intermingling of worldviews, politics, and power, in the governance and management policies of living things.

(De)constructing Luna (seeing Luna/knowing Luna)

A fundamental challenge in governing living beings is that the established set of policies and practices reflect and reify a dominant worldview. Starting with the position that the animal is its own being (with its own agency) is rarely the starting point for governance frameworks. Rather, it is the interpretations of people's perceptions of the animal that frame the interaction, although the reflexive nature of the relationship continues to shape the interaction.

Luna meant many things to many people. In many ways, Luna functioned as a mirror reflecting variant perceptions of nature. To the marine scientists, Luna was L98, a stray orca whale that exhibited "atypical" behavior. To the Mowachaht/Muchalaht First Nation, *Tsu-xiit* was the incarnation of their chief. To the casual boater, Luna was a friendly animal that rubbed against their boat. To the commercial fisher, Luna was a liability to their assets. To the governmental official, Luna was an international incident that required coordinated efforts and federal funds. And, to the environmentalist, Luna was an endangered animal that needed to be protected.

These multiple constructions are indicative of the variations in worldview that each actor brings to the table. Thus, neither Luna, specifically, nor orca, in general, are neutral terms. Yet, the material existence of Luna mutually constitutes the interpretations of his existence. Bringing the *fleshiness* of the being to the fore helps to break through these narrow (and humanist) interpretations (Sundberg, 2011).

Framing the notion of whales as a singular identity has political consequences. Not recognizing the existence of these multiple constructions and perspectives is, in fact, at the heart of many struggles over the environment. As discussed above, these miscommunications are based on fundamentally different ways of viewing, and interacting with, the natural environment. Considering these divergent frameworks requires a willingness to consider multiple worldviews in the decision-making process and a built-in flexibility in governance systems to respond to issues that transgress nested identities and fixed jurisdictional spaces.

Another poignant example of how constructed identities impact governance is found with the logging controversies that focus on Canada's west coast. Like Luna, the fate of the temperate rainforest has "pitted environmentalist against industry, First Nations against the state, environmentalists against First Nations, even the state against industry, in a complex shifting matrix of political actors" (Braun and Wainwright, 2001, p. 50). As Braun and Wainwright note, the controversy was not about the "rainforest" as singular; rather it was about the politics of the discursive practices that produced the ideology surrounding the "rainforest". Hence, in environmental politics – regardless of the issue – it is the act of framing nature rather than nature itself that has political consequences (Braun, 2002, 2005).

A striking difference between the socially-created identities in this case is the divergent views of Luna as a "lost whale" that needed to be reunited with his family and the view that Luna had "come home" in the form of *Tsu-xiit* (the chief incarnate). As discussed in the previous section, these conceptions are very bound up with notions of nature as "out there" versus nature as "everywhere" or as inseparable from humans. In the first instance, Luna was seen as transgressing a boundary between nature and culture, and in the second, he was seen as "coming home".

The public juxtaposition of these opposing worldviews presents a paradox in which the ordering of nature is called into question (and, in essence, the divergent epistemologies of science and nature are called into question). What often goes unrecognized in the daily practices of "environmental management" are the power dynamics implicit in ordering nature. Thus, environmental management requires ongoing translation between cultures and "a way of life"; if that work is not conducted, misunderstandings are inevitable (Nadasdy, 2004). As discussed in the previous section, critical scholarship in animal geographies contributes to a greater understanding of how dominant narratives prescribe the "rightful" places for animals and how these are reinforced through policies and governance practices.

In particular Philo and Wilbert (2000), Sundberg (2011), and Collard (2012) each discuss how humans' attempts to "order animals" have had mixed consequences.

Part of the messiness of Luna's story is the overlapping of worldviews co-existing in such close proximity. Just as Luna existed in-between worlds, so do the Mowachaht/Muchalaht, who are bound geographically by a dominant Western culture. The multiple identities of Luna as an animal and a human, as a whale and a chief, and as a victim and a victor, help challenge these binaries. "Animal geographies have opened up space to examine the coexistence of humans and animals in a way that acknowledges the 'otherness and difference' of animals" (Cloke and Perkins, 2005). However, as Luna's story so poignantly reveals, these nuances rarely make it into the daily practice of environmental management, not because individuals within the system are narrow-minded, rather that the Western epistemology reinforces a fundamental distinction between humans and animals/nature as separate entities. Ultimately this dominant worldview plays out in the managing systems and public discourses that influence decision-making.

Knowing Luna

The construction of Luna's identity is intricately tied to the production of knowledge and belief systems created around his species. Orcas or "Killer Whales" have captivated people's imaginations for thousands of years. Well-documented accounts of encounters in the sea appear in ancient Greek mythology (Pliny the Elder) and play centrally in Indigenous mythology throughout the world. In recent history, public perception of orcas (in a Western context) has changed dramatically.

The growing aquarium industry brought orcas to public attention, primarily through the icon and branding of "Shamu" (Munro, 2001; Murray, 2009). Criticisms from animal rights activists, however, have somewhat tempered the appetite for "entertainment in a pen" and "plucking" whales from the ocean. This phenomenon has taken on national significance through films such as *Blackfish*, which exposes the dark side of the operations at Sea World. Although aquarium shows are still popular, and bring public attention to the species, efforts are made to reinforce that the whales in captivity are "rescued" whales rather than "captured" whales (Murray, 2009).

For example, the whale-watching industry transforms entertainment in the pen to entertainment in the wild. Through what Cindi Katz (1998) refers to as "greenateering", new forms of "environmentally friendly entertainment" have developed throughout the world. Off the coast of British Columbia and Washington, this greenateering has provided tourists with the option to appreciate orcas in their natural habitat. Tourists are able to view the whales through a number of eco-outfitters ranging from rustic kayak tours to high-speed boat tours to luxury dinner cruises. The activities are packaged as "eco-friendly" adventures in which the tourists are promised a thrilling experience.

Not surprisingly, the prolific (and profitable) eco-tours are now under criticism for "loving the animals to death", as swarms of nature-loving tourist vessels crowd the whales as they emerge to the surface for breath. The activities, perceived as passive and animal-friendly, may harm animals. Studies reveal that harassment from whale-watching, essentially chasing the whales, and the air pollution of the hovering boat traffic, may cause much stress to the animals in questions (Jelinski *et al.*, 2002; and Williams *et al.*, 2002). Thus, the tourist eager to learn about, and bear witness to, animals in their natural habitat becomes a hybrid space between "wild" and "harassed" (Cloke and Perkins, 2005; Besio *et al.*, 2008; Murray, 2009).

Another part of the process of "knowing" Luna, specifically, or orcas more generally, is the development of a science industry that has grown around studying the behavior of orcas. For the past 40 years, scientists throughout the world have spent considerable time and effort learning about the behavior of orcas (Baird, 2001). During the course of these studies, scientists have learned what constitutes the "normal" behavior of orcas, generally, and in the coastal waters off British Columbia and Washington (Duffus and Deardon, 1993; Ford *et al.*, 2000; Baird, 2001; Filatova *et al.*, 2004; and Miller *et al.*, 2004). For example, it is known that orcas in this region are social creatures, have distinct calls, stay with their mothers for life, and are members of either a transient, resident, or offshore pod. These studies also document how orcas are affected by anthropogenic behavior: that the noise of engines affects their ability to find fish through echolocation, that overfishing of salmon and global warming are reducing food sources, and that toxic waste and polychlorinated biphenyls are causing damage to their immune systems (Jelinski *et al.*, 2002; Wartzok *et al.*, 2003; Ford *et al.*, 2004; Lusseau *et al.*, 2004).

Not only are the general characteristics of the orcas known but, also, every resident orca in the Salish Sea study area is documented through comprehensive census studies, led by the Center for Whale Research on San Juan Island. Through this constant monitoring and documentation, the genealogies of the orcas are known in stunning detail. The whales are known through unique markings behind their dorsal fins called "saddle patches" and the shape of the fins, recorded through photographs. The whales are assigned unique alphanumeric designations depending on which pod they are in and when they were born. Books and brochures are published with this information so that anyone interested (from scientists to tourists) can easily identify the orcas. Scientists know Luna as L98. That is, he is a member of the resident L-pod population, and he was the ninety-eighth whale born to that pod since scientists started systemically recording their genealogy.[5] For example, this statement about Luna's lineage was posted on the Reunite Luna (2012) website:

> When Luna was born, in September 1999, Marine Biologists were unsure who his mother was. He was often seen swimming with Splash (L67), but also with Kiska (K18). Eventually he was observed being nursed by Splash, and it is believed that Kiska, whose calf had died, was treating Luna as her own.

The classification systems allow scientists to recognize aberrant behavior, or matters out of place. Thus, when Luna strayed from his "rightful" path, scientists knew *where* he should be and *whom* he should be with. The close monitoring also feeds directly into policy decisions related to status of the southern resident pod populations.[6]

The public nature of Luna's journey reinforced the idea of needing to put Luna back in his "rightful" place. For example, the website "Reunite Luna" diligently reported on the happenings of Luna, publicly advocated for his placement back with L-pod, and amplified this story to the wider world. Numerous posts documented the happenings of Luna, including what boats he had been mingling with:

> *Report from Nootka Sound*
>
> Luna has been spending a huge amount of his time with two large boats lately. Most of his attention has been given to a 130-foot-long landing craft that hauls supplies and fuel to work camps along the Sound . . . 2005–10–26

When he was making calls to other pods:

> *LunaLive Stewardship Program detects Luna vocalizing with transient orcas*
>
> YUQUOT, BC, Canada – Luna, the solitary killer whale of Nootka Sound, entertained some guests last night. At 2:41 AM, Allan Muir, a LunaLive researcher based nearly half-way around the world in Scotland, detected the calls of a pod of transient orca intermixed with those of Luna. "This is a very rare event. In over 30 years of studying Orca vocalizations, we've only ever heard residents and transient vocalizing simultaneously in the same acoustic space three other times," said Paul Spong, director of OrcaLab on Hanson Island. 2005–11–18

And, even, how he is suspected to feel on his birthday:

> *Luna's Lonely Sixth Birthday*
>
> September 19, 2005 marks Luna's sixth birthday, and his fourth year separated from his pod. Birthdays are supposed to be a time for family celebration. But the only thing that Luna can celebrate this year is that he made it through another busy boating season. It hardly seems worth lighting a candle for. 2005–09–19

Members of the Mowachaht/Muchalaht First Nation have their own explanations to describe the relationships to the world they live in. Their observations about orcas and the marine life date back thousands of years and co-evolve with the natural environment – the traditional waters of *a'aminqas* now known as the Nootka Sound (Drucker, 1951). The contemporary governance mechanisms in place to "manage" the natural environment, rarely, however, reflect traditional worldviews and how "science informs policy".

This leads us to the dilemma that I described at the beginning of the book: who, then, holds the power to decide what, and whose, interpretation of the natural world should be taken up as policy? And whose perspective is naturalized and privileged as the "rightful" voice, which translates to the "rightful place"? The traditions and beliefs *outside* of the Western scientific tradition have been historically marginalized as Western beliefs are reified (and institutionalized) through policies and nation-building projects (Harris, 2002). Newcomer worldviews define the policies that have not only carved the physical landscape of the country, but also defined human relationships with nature. The case of Luna is particularly powerful because it brings the possibility of destabilizing constructed dualisms of humans and nature, and identifying the power dynamics embedded in established governance systems.

By embracing Luna as their chief incarnate, the Mowachaht/Muchalaht First Nation was exercising their sovereign right over the seascape, but also challenging Western worldviews where society–nature are separate entities. The controversial and highly publicized Makah whale hunt off the Olympic Peninsula in the summer of 1999 posed similar challenges to Western worldviews (Cote, 2010). Similarly, for the Ojibwa communities of the Great Lakes, the wolf is an integral part of the Anishinaabe culture.

The reaction of the Canadian government, halting its plans to move Luna, indicates that a power shift has occurred – where the State no longer acts with disregard to those "outside" the dominant structure. Thus, the story of Luna is not just a story of a lost orca whale; it is a story of power, race, and privilege reified through State policies and subverted through the First Nation's actions.

Whose story? Discourse analysis and discussion

Examining how Luna's story unfolded in the public eye sheds light on embedded power dynamics. To better understand this dynamic, I analyzed the unfolding of Luna's story in the print media between 2001 and 2006, representing 172 articles from newspapers throughout North America (with a concentration in British Columbia and Washington). I approached the articles curious to see *how* the story unfolded, whose voice was being amplified, and whose voices were being silenced.[7]

The exercise confirmed that the dominant narrative of the public unfolding of Luna's case was presented mostly from a governmental agency perspective, with minimal attention to inclusion of the First Nation's perspective (except for when the story became "heated" with the 9-day stand-off).

Overall, of the 172 articles analyzed, 30 percent were told from the perspective of the Department of Fisheries and Oceans, while only 8 percent were reported from the Mowachaht/Muchalaht First Nation's perspective. The breakdown was as follows: Department of Fisheries and Oceans, Canada (30 percent), National Oceanic and Atmospheric Administration, U.S. (21 percent), Whale conservancies, U.S. (20 percent), Environmental Stewardship Groups, Canada represented (11 percent), Aquariums, Canada and the U.S. (10 percent), and the Mowachaht/Muchalaht First Nation (8 percent).

The analysis also revealed that, temporally, the First Nation was not included in the public unfolding (through print media) in any substantive manner until 2004, which marked the start of the 9-day stand-off. Viewing the story backwards, the late arrival of the Mowachaht/Muchalaht voice in the narrative is striking considering the significance of Luna's arrival to the Mowachaht/Muchalaht First Nation.

In general, the dominant narrative of the media situates Luna's behavior as aberrant and relates to the "vulnerability" of the individual whale, and the subsequent efforts to "reunite" and "save" Luna. Luna is given no agency in the discussions. The idea that Luna may have chosen to travel to Nootka Sound is rarely considered in the print media, thereby reinforcing a dominant discourse of "normalized" and dominant voice.

From policy to practice – navigating boundaries

The discourse analysis helped tease apart the many "voices" that aimed to speak for Luna and interpret what was best for the animal. The narrative was developed as a reflexive conversation between the actors presenting – and asserting – their interpretation. The many years of scientific studies on J, K, and L pods (and orcas in general) found Luna's behavior to be "aberrant". The storyline of the chief coming back to the community in the form of a sacred whale – in this case *Tsu-xiit* – was less visible.

The normalization of a storyline that reinforces a dominant discourse – "A lost whale that needs to be found", rather than a whale who has "come home" to his family – is, at its essence, about the normalization of the "louder" and "more practiced" voice. It is this more visible voice that the general public has looked to for guidance and authority. In this case, the scientific community, the governing agencies, and the state/provincial politicians and bureaucrats all reinforced the dialogue that Luna was in need of "saving" and "out of place".

The authoritarian voice is reinforced by how the stories are presented in the media. The genealogy of the unfolding and the emphasis of topics and perspectives presented in the articles provide insights into how science, policy, and environmental management mutually constitute (and reinforce) each other. However, looking more closely at the timeline of the event shows that the plan to move Luna was a powerful combination of public pressure to "remove" Luna (as a nuisance and public safety issue for boaters) and "reunite" Luna (as a need to both protect the endangered orcas and to save the "at risk" juvenile whale). Thus, the story, in essence, has a subtext of power and privilege – that of the commercial fishers' needs (and the role of the DFO to mediate these needs). Parsing the timing of events helps to shed light on the privileging.

Tsu-xiit had, after all, resided in the traditional waters of the Mowachaht/Muchalaht territory for a full year with little fanfare. During this time, *Tsu-xiit* exhibited no behavior indicating an intention to return to his resident community in Puget Sound. His food sources were plentiful, he inhabited waters much cleaner than those found in the southern waters of the L pod into which he was born, and he found company with which to socialize.

However, the increased pressures from local boat-owners who worried that the whale's "friendly" behavior would cause expensive property damage, the (perceived) public safety concerns, coupled with the endangered status of the Southern Resident orcas, pressured the Canadian government to remove the "problem" whale from Nootka Sound. This is when the DFO stepped in. Thus, the original decision to move *Tsu-xiit* had less to do with the whale itself, and rather more with the political pressures from boaters and international environmental groups (McClure, 2005). The international nature of the situation brought added media attention as the decision-making required coordination between government officials.

By looking at the whale as an individual – a fleshy being – the justifications for "rescuing him" become less clear. The opaqueness is evident when examining the rationales to *protect* Luna. As one DFO official commented in a public interview, "We knew that the more Luna socialized with boats, the more in danger he was putting himself. We felt that the best thing to do was to first stop the socialization and then to help him relocate with his pod in the southern waters". However, the rationale did not carry throughout the entire plan.

For example, James (2010) outlined several reasons why *Tsu-xiit* should not be moved, beyond the belief that the whale was their chief incarnate. For one, the plan did not respect *Tsu-xiit's* decision to reside in his chosen territory – a choice worthy of both respect and consideration. Second, the plan to transfer Luna did not assure the whale's safety, nor did it solve the "boat problem". In fact, the southern waters were much more congested with boats – and far more polluted – than the relatively quiet Nootka Sound. Third, and most striking, was that there were no funds allocated for a return trip if the reunification failed. Rather, the standing plan was for Luna to go to an aquarium.

The failure to consult with First Nations highlights ongoing power-dynamics that resurface throughout processes of environmental management. As James (2010) reflected, "They had their own agenda . . . they didn't consult with us and we found it was a disrespect not only to our cultural beliefs but also just to the animal itself". Mike Maquinna, Grand Chief of the Mowachaht/Muchalaht First Nation, further explained that capturing the whale would be disrespectful:

> What we've been saying all along is that nature must be allowed to take its course, but nature has been lost in all of the process. We're standing with the whale, and will do everything we can to ensure its safety.
>
> (Wiwchar, 2004)

The sentiments identified above support the idea of "letting be" or "letting go", which is largely missing in much of the environmental management and animal geography work on ethics (Collard, 2012), and is ripe for further analysis.

Thus, for the Mowachaht/Muchalaht First Nation, transferring *Tsu-xiit* was viewed as a violent affront to his well-being that did not respect his choice to reside by his people. By way of compromise, Chief Maquinna offered to lead a reunification plan that was seen as less harmful to *Tsu-xiit* and still respected his choice. The plan included Mowachaht/Muchalaht canoes leading *Tsu-xiit* out of Nootka Sound, and down the west coast of Vancouver Island to the San Juan Islands. The DFO rejected the plan as too dangerous. Thus, Luna was in troubled waters – allowed to stay in the traditional waters with his people, but still putting himself (and others) at danger; free to choose, but not fully protected; between multiple boundaries: jurisdictional, cultural, species, and epistemological. Ultimately, this middle ground led to Luna's demise.

Conclusion

> *[N]ature is something imagined and real, external yet made, outside history but fiercely contested at every turn.*
>
> —Castree and Braun, 2001

In this chapter, I examined the case of Luna, a single whale with multiple identities, whose very existence challenged the concept of transboundary governance. Luna's story highlights the tensions associated with governing a single being that transgresses multiple and often competing categories. Analyzing the public unfolding of Luna's story illustrates how contemporary environmental governance frameworks are often ill-equipped to handle these transgressions – jurisdictional, species, cultural, or epistemological.

Although the concept of social construction of nature is well established in the academy, much work is needed to translate these ideas to the practice of environmental management. Analyzing the discourses created around Luna sheds light on the complex power dynamics and value systems embedded in the "bounding" of space and the "ideologies" associated with governance practices and how these "well-practiced" narratives influence policy decisions. The dominant narrative of the "whale as out of place and in need of 'saving'" was rationalized in many ways – through scientific studies on behavior, through economic concern for property loss, through governmental protocols and fixed jurisdictions. The less-practiced narrative of the "whale coming home" as the chief incarnate challenged multiple conceptual, ideological, and jurisdictional boundaries. This transgression opened up space to insert a strong Indigenous worldview into the narrative, which had previously been largely unconsidered. A key outcome of these tensions (and the clearing or *lichtung* that they created) is the need to reposition Luna as an individual, *fleshy being* with agency.

I sought to answer questions related to managing species across borders and the power dynamics associated with privileging the "rightful voice", which translates to the "rightful place". The engagement with these inquiries led to three key insights:

- Governance systems require greater flexibility to accommodate multiple boundaries and worldviews.
- A significant need remains for governmental and non-governmental agencies to prioritize sustained and meaningful consultation with First Nations in matters relating to traditional territories and cultural beliefs.

- Greater attention to the agency or "fleshiness" of the being may help cut through competing constructions of nature and open up space for less represented perspectives to be seen.

Although examining the transgressions and fleshiness of Luna/*Tsu-xiit* tells us much about the politics of governing across postcolonial and posthumanist boundaries, much work remains in the project of opening up space (conceptually and materially) for the inclusion of multiple worldviews and perspectives in the practice of environmental management.

The following questions can serve to guide this process:

- What steps are required to ensure that government agencies engage in consistent and meaningful consultation with Indigenous communities?
- How can mainstream governance frameworks become more aware of the power dynamics related to dominant frameworks, and recognize the importance of respecting alternative ways-of-knowing?
- What are the practical implications of viewing animals consistently as "fleshy beings"?
- How does conceptualization of a posthumanist framework materialize in practice?
- What are the possibilities of locating concepts such as "letting be" or "letting go" more centrally in animal geographies and environmental governance?

This chapter continues the discussion of the importance of greater sensitivity to power dynamics in governance of shared waters and contributes to the need for greater understanding of governance of animals between diverse cultural frameworks and across bounded geographic spaces. It is my hope that asking the simple question "was Luna lost or was he found?" will help to inspire further discussion.

Notes

1 The whale was positively identified as L98 in November 2001 and the identity was made public in January 2002. The name Luna was suggested by a 10-year-old girl from Bellingham, Washington, who responded to a competition hosted as a public relations event at the Whale Museum on San Juan Island.

2 Fisheries and Oceans Canada was formerly, and remains commonly, known as the Department of Fisheries and Oceans, or simply, DFO.

3 This type of animal–human transition is not uncommon in Indigenous communities on the outer Coast of Vancouver Island (or in other belief systems around the world). This type of transmogrification is well-documented both in oral histories and written text (Drucker, 1951).

4 Anderson, 1995; Cloke and Perkins, 1998, 2005; Wolch and Emel, 1998; Philo and Wilbert, 2000; Whatmore, 2002; Wolch, 2002; Lulka, 2004, 2009; Hobson, 2007; Campbell and O'Neal, 2007; Campbell, 2008; Haraway, 2008; Besio *et al.*, 2008; Hovorka, 2008; Johnston, 2008; Bear and Eden, 2011; Sundberg, 2011; Collard, 2012.

5 There are three resident pods: J, K, and L.

6 In Canada, the pods are listed as "endangered" but the governmental agencies have limited authority to enforce their protection under the Canadian Species at Risk Act;

in the U.S. the southern resident pod's status shifted from "depleted" to "endangered" in February 2006 under the Marine Mammal Protection Act.

7 Three upper-division college students from Northwest Indian College repeated the process independently. This process served two purposes: to train the students in methods of critical discourse analysis and to validate results. Although discourse analysis is certainly not a "precise methodology" (largely because the categories are so slippery), the process helps to identify trends and dominant voices. In all four reviews, the trends were consistent.

10 Conclusion and reflections

What makes a good upstream neighbor?

In this book, I asked three interrelated questions: "How are governance mechanisms changing to address the social, political, and ecological aspects of transboundary water?", "How are the Indigenous-led governance mechanisms linked to the twinned goals of ecosystem protection and processes of self-determination, empowerment, and decolonization?" and, simply, "What makes a good upstream neighbor?"

To help answer these questions, I investigated how the mechanisms in place to govern the transboundary waters between Canada and the United States have changed over the last century. Specifically, I analyzed how Indigenous communities have become increasingly involved in redefining transboundary water governance.

In the following pages, I reflect on these questions, offer a summary of my key theoretical contribution, and query "where do we go from here?"

How are governance mechanisms changing to address the social, political, and ecological aspects of transboundary water?

In the book's first Part, I identified changing patterns of transboundary water governance along the Canada–U.S. border. Notably, I showed a shift from federally controlled and mandated institutions – including a devolution of responsibility to state/provincial governmental entities – to increased stakeholder participation of environmental issues on the rise since the 1960s. These trends are widely cited in environmental governance literature (e.g. Bulkeley, 2005) and are applicable to trends in transboundary water governance along the Canada–U.S. border (Norman and Bakker, 2009).

What is less studied – and a major contribution of this book – is how changing patterns of governance reflect wider social and political trends related to processes of decolonization in the North American borderland. In order to connect processes of environmental governance with decolonization, I first provide an overview of representational institutional mechanisms for transboundary water governance along the Canada–U.S. borderland (Part One) and then explore the contributions of Indigenous-led mechanisms to transboundary water governance (Part Two).

In Part One, I identify links between borders (colonial bordering), water governance, and the politics of scale. I then outline key transboundary water governance mechanisms in the Canada–U.S. context and highlight how one of the original binational institutions – the International Joint Commission – has implemented changes to address changing environments and political cultures. The development of IJC's International Watersheds Initiative, for example, reflects a commitment to greater inclusion of non-State actors in the governance of shared waters (and a commitment to proactive rather than reactive governance). Despite these changes, the IJC is still a federally run institution that operates through the binational Boundary Waters Treaty. The IJC changes are still under the architecture of a binational, federal agency, which alone is not able to fully reflect the demands for wider participation. For example, there has been no IJC commissioner with First Nations or Native American heritage. Rectifying this deficit by prioritizing more diverse representation at IJC – particularly, but not solely, in relation to Indigenous peoples – would undoubtedly enrich the Commission and contribute to a new vantage point from which to address shared water issues.

The creation of regionally focused state and provincial organizations such as the British Columbia–Washington Environmental Cooperation Council are also important factors in the shifting patterns of transboundary governance, but, like the IJC, are still subject to the framings of nation-state. This became very apparent when the ECC had a 5-year hiatus in operations largely due to state and provincial budget cuts.

A key contribution of this volume is to widen the discussion of rescaling to include the recent surge in Indigenous-led, transboundary mechanisms. As I explore in Part Two, the development of these organizations is indicative of wider trends of decolonization and self-determination. A key argument throughout my analysis is that when the primary mechanism for transboundary water governance is state or federally controlled, the nation-state boundaries are inherently reified. Even if the stated purview of the state/federal agency is "transboundary", they are defined by systemic nation-state boundaries and associated policies that are colonial relics. The work towards collaborating with partners on the *other* side of the border continues to reinforce national identities and national interpretations of landscape. They do not (and cannot) genuinely include connected ecosystems, nor traditional territories for Indigenous communities.

Thus, the increase of Indigenous-led transboundary governance mechanisms such as the Yukon River Inter-Tribal Council, the Coast Salish Gatherings, and the Great Lakes Indian Fisheries Commission are positive examples of rescaling governance to place Indigenous communities at the center of the governance structure, which reflects core beliefs. This rescaling is poignant particularly along the border (at the site of the colonial constructions), where Indigenous communities were fragmented and reorganized in accordance with new nation-building projects – in this case the construction of Canada and the United States as separate nations.

How are the Indigenous-led governance mechanisms linked to the twinned goals of ecosystem protection and processes of self-determination, empowerment, and decolonization?

Through cases – or parables of change – I explore the second question: how Indigenous-led mechanisms are meeting goals of environmental protection and self-determination. I examine the cultural politics of transboundary water governance, as it pertains to Indigenous communities that live "between borders". I first highlighted the ongoing impacts of colonial bordering and how contemporary governance mechanisms fall short in protecting Indigenous communities (particularly as these mechanisms are rooted in a nation-state framework and treat borders as fixed). I also highlighted environmental issues that impact all people, but particularly impact Indigenous communities, because of the traditional reliance on marine-based resources for sustenance.

Part Two highlights Indigenous-led movements that are designed to contribute to ecosystem protection. The cases include both governance structures (such as the Coast Salish Gatherings of Chapter 6) as well as performative techniques that strengthen communities, build allies, and contribute to raising a collective conscience around water (such as the intertribal Canoe Journey of Chapter 7 and the Water Walkers of Chapter 8). The cases also examine how counter-hegemonic techniques such as "strategic essentialism", "performativity", and "critical cartography" are changing the dynamics of transboundary water governance. In addition, the focus on preparing youth for leadership positions – and to "walk between worlds" – is also a fundamentally important aspect of the Indigenous-led initiatives.

The case of Luna/*Tsu-xiit*, the "lost whale", demonstrates the complexities of boundaries, both in terms of political boundaries and cultural (animal–human) boundaries. Luna's story provides an opportunity to think critically about how worldviews are ascribed onto and built into management practices, and how these management practices reinforce dominant narratives of the State and Science. Engaging with notions of hybridity helps to tease out the social constructions that are so largely unchallenged and unseen: the constructions of physical political borders (between nation-states) as well as those between "nature" and "society" (which Luna helps with). All cases encourage a more nuanced approach of and critical inquiry into transboundary governance.

Highlighting examples of Indigenous-led governance mechanisms provided a counter-narrative to dominant systems of governance that are defined by the State. The cases highlight how goals of ecosystem protection are part of wider counter-hegemonic activities that can contribute to decolonizing activities, self-determination, and empowerment. I engaged with lessons from the Canada–U.S. border – a deceptively neutral border – but the lessons are universally applicable. Ultimately, I advocate for creating governance mechanisms commensurate to a scale that makes sense both ecologically and culturally.

My hope is that this volume will help to reframe the dominant narrative related to transboundary water governance. This reframing helps to unpack the "border" in transborder as an active colonizing act, which continues to shape and influence water policy and decision-making. Reframing the narrative so that Indigenous communities are in the center of the discussion (rather than the periphery or not in the dialogue at all) provides an avenue to explore how governance of water (a lifesource) can lead to wider projects such as decolonization and self-determination. Mainstream dialogue reinforces colonial borders as fixed, ahistorical, and unproblematized, while Indigenous spaces are often seen as a historical relic. Thus, through narrative, I aim to gently recenter the dialogue and open up conceptual space for a more critical look at transborder water governance.

What makes a good upstream neighbor?

The last question I posed is: "What makes a good upstream neighbor?" This question is generalizable to communities around the world. I started the discussion listing established characteristics of "good upstream neighbors":

- transparency
- communication
- respect
- empathy
- equality
- equity.

The cases presented in this book contribute to another set of core principles that foster neighborly riparian relationships. These principles help prepare actors for uncertain futures, or unexpected bends in the river:

- a commitment to ongoing problem-solving and innovation (even in times of non-crisis);
- knowledge of place;
- inter-generational education;
- working together (pulling together);
- honoring water;
- daily reflection on priority areas;
- matching action with values;
- doing what you can, individually;
- being part of the solution (everyone takes ownership of issues);
- using most available technology, but grounding it in culture;
- incorporating "old ways" and "new ways" in problem-solving;
- strength in diversity – diverse worldviews help solve problems;
- ability to see both locally and globally (frog's eye view and bird's eye view).

These are accomplished by:

- hard work
- preparation

- foresight
- flexibility
- commitment to diversity
- collective conscience – unifying principle of water.

Lessons from the intertribal Canoe Journey show that a "good neighbor" is one that "pulls together" for the common cause. The participants pulling in unison highlight how crucial communication, equality of actors, and clear vision is to achieving shared goals. The Journey itself recognizes the importance of knowledge of place, respect for waters, and inter-generational education – investing in youth and respecting elders.

In addition, many of the cases show how important diverse ways of seeing (and knowing) are in the management of shared waters. For example, using water probes and GPS units in the Canoe Journeys of the Yukon and the coastal Pacific brings together different technologies and ways of knowing. This "hybrid space" between traditional practice and modern technologies brings people together for a common cause – one that is linked to knowing, protecting, and respecting our shared waters. This type of sustained action is critical for ongoing collaboration.

The Grandmother Water Walkers showed that importance of reverence for water. By honoring water – and not taking water for granted – you become cognizant of how daily actions impact a lifesource. A key lesson from the Water Walkers is that you *do what you can*. For some, this means raising awareness. For others it means scientific inquiry or technical innovations. One lesson from the walk is that *each person should be part of the solution in a way that is meaningful to him or her.*

Another significant aspect of the Water Walk and the sharing of the Water Song is the contribution to building a collective conscience. Water is a great unifier. Celebrating and honoring the importance of water through song collective action are ways that Indigenous communities are contributing to a paradigm shift, which helps people to understand – more viscerally – that our universal reliance on water makes us more similar than different, and that protecting your upstream neighbor is protecting yourself. Water helps to blur the false dichotomy of "us" and "them"; and contributes to a collective understanding of greater purpose and understanding.

To make a good "upstream neighbor" you cooperate in times of both non-crisis and crisis. One of the key points raised by people operating within a state-run transboundary organization is that the motivation to support transboundary institutions is highest in times of crisis. However, as shown by the Indigenous-led transboundary institutions, the wider goals of self-determination and self-governance (in addition to ecosystem protection) provide an impetus for ongoing participation in times of "non-crisis".

The case of Luna provides a more nuanced set of reflections on the very nature of borders; how governance is even more difficult when the being itself is contested. Governing across political jurisdictions certainly raises a set of key challenges. However, it is also important to analyze governance challenges between worldviews. The different interpretations of Luna/*Tsu-xiit* are a telling example of widening these borders to include cultural considerations and seeing the politics, understanding that borders are often more complex than originally conceived.

Moving forward

At the beginning of the book, I likened the process of analyzing transboundary water governance to a roadside geologist where, at the site of an international border, you can see the nested scales of governance: federal, tribal, provincial, state, and municipal, each operating within (seemingly) neatly defined responsibilities and purviews. In the pages that followed, I blurred these scales, suggesting that the governance process being considered as a complex hydrosocial process, explicitly engaging with the cultural, political, and ecological aspects of *bordering*, provides a greater understanding of transborder water governance (something that is largely missing in the literature). This engagement, therefore, leads to an increased recognition of how institutions and governance mechanisms influence and reify established power-dynamics and colonially interpreted landscapes.

Analyzing the rescaling of environmental governance mechanisms through an exploration of water governance is an important exercise, as the "slippery" characteristics of water are, for the most part, non-allegiant to state boundaries. Unlike trees, which are rooted in place and can easily be characterized as part of one side or the other, water flows through, over, and under political delineations. As the stories in this book remind us, water blurs borders of all kind.

The undeniable fact that all life requires water raises the stakes. Some argue that the next wars will be fought over water. I, however, suggest that water provides a great opportunity to address fundamental issues related to governance, and cultural and environmental politics. This is both an academic and a practical task.

Academically, this is accomplished by closer attention to discursive practices, by opening up conceptual space for alternative dialogues and ways of seeing, by remembering our history, and learning from our past. This work is ongoing. Although great strides have no doubt occurred in decolonizing practices over the past century, much work remains. The work now is for people to "see" the invisible.

Practically, on an individual level, this means incorporating the core lessons of respect and integrity into daily practice. This includes respect and integrity for the resources that sustain us: for water – our lifesource, and for the treatment of others – our neighbors. It is also about knowing (and learning from) our own story, and the stories of our ancestors. It means thinking beyond the scope of your own lifetime, to think about the generations ahead of us.

Although the task is big, I remain hopeful. Water, after all, is a great unifier. It helps us realize that we are literally and metaphorically "all in the same boat" and "all upstream to someone". Putting this knowledge into practice is the next step.

Appendix A

Tribal and First Nations Treaty Accord, signed 23 November 2004 at Sault St. Marie, Michigan

Note: the following two images are reprinted with permission from Chief Dean Sayers (Batchewana First Nation), President Levi Carrick (Bay Mills Chippewa Indian Community), Chairman Aaron Payment (Sault Sainte Marie Tribe of Chippewa), and Chiefs Sayers (Garden River First Nation).

TREATY BETWEEN THE SAULT STE. MARIE TRIBE OF CHIPPEWA INDIANS, and GARDEN RIVER FIRST NATION, and BAY MILLS INDIAN COMMUNITY, and BATCHEWANA FIRST NATION

Regarding the preservation, protection and enhancement of the waters of the St. Mary's River ecosystem

THE SOVEREIGN NATIONS OF THE SAULT STE. MARIE TRIBE OF CHIPPEWA INDIANS, AND THE GARDEN RIVER FIRST NATION, AND THE BAY MILLS INDIAN COMMUNITY AND THE BATCHEWANA FIRST NATION:

A. **ACKNOWLEDGING** that our collective ancestors have inhabited the lands surrounding the waters of the St. Mary's River since long before any current geopolitical boundaries were established; and
B. **RECOGNIZING** that the waters of the St. Mary's River have served, and continue to serve, as the life blood for the region which supports each of our collective Nations; and
C. **REAFFIRMING** our commitment and responsibility as protectors of the waters for the next seven generations and beyond; and
D. **UNDERSTANDING** that the waters of the St. Mary's River and its ecosystem have undergone significant abuse and mistreatment resulting from the introduction of toxic substances and aquatic alien invasive species; and
E. **ACKNOWLEDGING** that many of these toxic substances and invasive species enter the waters of the Great Lakes, including the St. Mary's River, from the air, groundwater infiltration, sediments in the lake and river beds, runoff of non-point sources, and shipping operations; and
F. **AWARE** that the governments of Canada and the United States, together with their respective political subdivisions, have established certain commitments toward the revitalization, preservation and protection of the waters of the Great Lakes, including the St. Mary's River; and
G. **RECOGNIZING** the need for strengthened efforts from each of our Nations to address the continuing contamination of the waters of the St. Mary's River ecosystem; and
H. **CONTINUING** to recognize the sovereign rights of each of our Nations and our ability to interact with other political bodies on a government to government basis; and
I. **RECOGNIZING** that our Nations are uniquely able to influence other governments to respond and take action because of our inherent sovereignty; and
J. **REAFFIRMING** the spirit of friendship, cooperation, and pledged commitment to work together to secure a healthy future for the Great Lakes, including the St. Mary's River, under the Tribal and First Nations Great Lakes Water Accord, signed November 23, 2004; and
K. **CONCLUDING** that our Nations' mutual interests regarding the St. Mary's River are better served when our Nations' efforts and influence are united to serve a common goal.

HAVE AGREED AS FOLLOWS:

ARTICLE I
PURPOSE

The purpose of this Treaty is to unite the efforts and influence of our Nations to restore and maintain the chemical, physical, and biological integrity of the waters of the St. Mary's River. In order to achieve this purpose, we agree that we will use maximum effort to:

A. Develop programs and practices necessary for a better understanding of the St. Mary's River and its ecosystem; and
B. Eliminate or reduce to the maximum extent practicable the discharge of toxic substances and introduction of invasive species; and
C. Influence the Governments of the United States and Canada, and their respective political subdivisions and agencies, to abide by existing commitments to revitalize, preserve, and protect the waters of the St. Mary's River; and
D. Encourage the Governments of Canada and the United States, and their respective political subdivisions and agencies, to develop additional programs and practices to achieve these results.

ARTICLE II
OBJECTIVES

Our Sovereign Nations shall work together on these general objectives pertaining to the St. Mary's River:

A. It is our collective goal that the waters of the St. Mary's River be free from:
   1. Substances that settle to form objectionable sludge deposit or adversely effect aquatic life or waterfowl;
   2. Floating materials such as debris, oil, or scum in amounts that are unsightly or deleterious;
   3. Thermal pollutants that produce color, odor, or taste that interferes with beneficial uses;
   4. Materials and thermal pollutants that produce harmful or toxic conditions to human, animal, or aquatic life and which interfere with beneficial uses;
   5. Nutrients in amounts that create growths of aquatic life, which interferes with beneficial uses; and
   6. Alien aquatic invasive species that are harmful to naturally occurring aquatic life or interfere with beneficial uses.
B. It is our collective goal that each of our Nations continue our respective cultural heritage and traditional teachings to promote understanding of the importance or protection of the waters of the St. Mary's River, as well as other waters of the Great Lakes, as the life blood of our region.
C. It is our collective goal to work together to identify specific objectives and strategies to achieve the general objectives we have identified.

ARTICLE III
TRIBAL AND FIRST NATION JOINT COMMISSION

Our Sovereign Nations shall form a Tribal and First Nation Joint Commission. The Commission shall be comprised of one representative of each of our Nations to facilitate open communication between and coordination among each of our Nations.

A. The Commission shall:
   1. Meet at least biannually;
   2. Develop specific objectives to be accomplished;
   3. Develop joint strategies for recommendation to each of our Nations' Governments; and
   4. Investigate issues regarding chemical, physical, and biological integrity of the waters of the St. Mary's River and make recommendations regarding actions in response to these issues.
B. Any of our Nations may provide additional technical or financial assistance to the Commission, including staff or other resources. The commission may request such additional assistance; however, any additional assistance provided shall be at the sole discretion of each of our respective Nations.
C. The Commission has no authority to independently bind any of our Nations' Governments individually, except as specifically authorized by all Nations consistent with each Nations' respective laws.

SIGNED AT THE BAY MILLS INDIAN RESERVATION ON NOVEMBER 8, 2006.

FOR THE SAULT STE. MARIE TRIBE OF CHIPPEWA INDIANS,
BY:
ITS:

FOR THE BAY MILLS INDIAN COMMUNITY,
BY:
ITS:

FOR THE GARDEN RIVER FIRST NATION,
BY:
ITS:

FOR THE BATCHEWANA FIRST NATION,
BY:
ITS:

TREATY BETWEEN
THE SAULT STE. MARIE TRIBE OF CHIPPEWA INDIANS, and
GARDEN RIVER FIRST NATION, and
BAY MILLS INDIAN COMMUNITY, and
BATCHEWANA FIRST NATION
Regarding the preservation, protection and enhancement of the waters of the St. Mary's River ecosystem

WITNESSES:

Appendix B

Substances covered under the Rotterdam Convention

- 2,4,5-T and its salts and esters
- alachlor
- aldicarb
- aldrin
- asbestos – actinolite, anthophyllite, amosite, crocidolite, and tremolite only
- benomyl (certain formulations)
- binapacryl
- captafol
- carbofuran (certain formulations)
- chlordane
- chlordimeform
- chlorobenzilate
- dichlorodiphenyltrichloroethane (DDT)
- dieldrin
- dinitro-ortho-cresol (DNOC) and its salts
- dinoseb and its salts and esters
- 1,2-dibromoethane (EDB)
- endosulfan
- ethylene dichloride
- ethylene oxide
- fluoroacetamide
- hexachlorocyclohexane (mixed isomers)
- heptachlor
- hexachlorobenzene
- lindane
- mercury compounds including inorganic and organometallic mercury compounds
- methamidophos (certain formulations)
- methyl parathion (certain formulations)
- monocrotophos
- parathion
- pentachlorophenol and its salts and esters
- phosphamidon (certain formulations)

- polybrominated biphenyls (PBB)
- polychlorinated biphenyls (PCB)
- polychlorinated terphenyls (PCT)
- tetraethyl lead
- tetramethyl lead
- thiram (certain formulations)
- toxaphene
- tributyl tin compounds
- tris (2,3-dibromopropyl) phosphate (TRIS)

Appendix C

The full schedule of the Water Walkers

Walkers from the North

May 21	Churchill, Manitoba send off (train departs 7:30pm)
May 23	Winnipeg, Manitoba
May 24	Richer, Manitoba
May 25	Hadashville, Manitoba
May 26	Falcon Lake
May 27	Royal Lake
May 28	Kenora, Ontario
May 29	Sioux Narrows, Ontario
May 30	Nestor Falls, Ontario
June 1	Manitou Rapids, International Falls
June 7	Duluth, Minnesota
June 10	Bad River, Wisconsin

Walkers from the South

April 20	Gulfport, Mississippi send off
April 22	Hattiesburg, Mississippi
April 24	Jackson, Mississippi
April 26	Grenada, Mississippi
April 28	Memphis, Tennessee
April 29	Wilson, Arkansas
April 30	Yarbro, Arkansas
May 1	Marston, Missouri
May 2	Chaffee, Missouri
May 3	Perryville, Missouri
May 4	Festus, Missouri
May 6	Ofallon, Missouri
May 8	Hannibal, Missouri
May 9	Winchester, Missouri
May 10	Fort Madison, Iowa

May 11	Mediapolis, Iowa
May 12	Muscatine, Iowa
May 13	Davenport, Iowa
May 16	Dubuque, Iowa
May 17	Fennimore, Wisconsin
May 18	Readstown, Wisconsin
May 19	Sparta, Wisconsin
May 20	Pidegeon Falls, Wisconsin
May 21	Cadott, Wisconsin
May 22	Ladysmith, Wisconsin
May 23	LCO!, Wisconsin
May 24	Drummond, Wisconsin
May 25	Ashland, Wisconsin
June 12	Bad River, Wisconsin

Walkers from the East

May 7	Machias, Maine send off
May 8	Skowhegan, Maine
May 9–10	Armstrong, Quebec
May 11	Vallee Jonction
May 12	Levis, Quebec
May 13	Victoriaville, Quebec
May 14	Drummondville, Quebec
May 15	Longueuil, Quebec
May 16	Montreal, Quebec
May 17, 18	Cornwall, Ontario
May 19, 20	Ottawa, Ontario
May 21	Pembroke, Ontario
May 22	Deep River, Ontario
May 23	Stonecliffe, Ontario
May 24	Mattawa, Ontario
May 25	North Bay, Ontario
May 26, 27	Sudbury, Ontario
May 28	McKerrow, Ontario
May 29	Serpent River, Ontario
May 30	Thessalon, Ontario
May 31, June 1	Sault Ste. Marie, Ontario
June 2, 3	Newberry, Michigan
June 4, 5	Munising, Michigan
June 6, 7	Marquette, Michigan
June 8	Ishpeming, Michigan
June 9	Ironwood, Michigan
June 10	Bad River, Wisconsin

Walkers from the West

April 10	Aberdeen, Washington send off
April 11	Olympia, Washington
April 15	Leavenworth, Washington
April 19	Spokane, Washington
April 22	St. Regis, Montana
April 25	Whitefish, Montana
April 29	Shelby, Montana
May 2	Havre, Montana
May 5	Malta, Montana
May 9	Cadillac, Saskatchewan
May 12	Assiniboia, Saskatchewan
May 16	Weyburn, Saskatchewan
May 20	Pipestone, Manitoba
May 23	Killarney, Manitoba
May 27	Emerson, Manitoba
May 30	Grand Forks, North Dakota
May 31	Crookston, Minnesota
June 3	Bemidji, Minnesota
June 6	Grand Rapids, Minnesota
June 9	Duluth, Minnesota
June 12	Bad River, Wisconsin

Four Directions Water Walk – For more information: www.motherearthwaterwalk.com/?page_id=2190. www.fourdirectionsteachings.com/

Bibliography

Absolon K. (2011) *Kaandossiwin: How we come to know.* Blackwood, Nova Scotia: Fernwood.

Abukhater A. (2013) *Water as a catalyst for peace: Transboundary water management and conflict resolution.* London: Routledge.

Adamson R. (2005) Law, sovereignty, and transnationalism: Delivering social goods using a functional approach to borders. In: Nicol H and Townsend-Gault I (eds) *Holding the line: Borders in a global world.* Vancouver, BC: UBC Press.

AFN. (2007) *Traditional foods: Are they safe for First Nations consumption?* Ottawa, ON: Environmental Stewardship Group, Assembly of First Nations.

Agarwal A. (1982) *State of India's environment report.* New Delhi, India: Centre for Science and Environment.

Agarwal T. (2009) Concentration level, pattern and toxic potential of PAHs in traffic soil of Delhi, India. *Journal of Hazardous Materials* 171: 894–900.

Agnew J. (1994) The territorial trap: The geographical assumptions of international relations theory. *Review of International Political Economy* 1: 53–80.

Agnew J. (1997) The dramaturgy of horizons: Geographical scale in the "Reconstruction of Italy" by the new Italian political parties. *Political Geography* 16: 99–121.

Agnew J. (2007) No borders, no nations: Making Greece in Macedonia. *Annals of the Association of American Geographers* 97: 398–422.

Agnew J. (2010) Still trapped in territory. *Geopolitics* 15: 779–784.

Agnew J. (2012) Putting politics into economic geography. In: Barnes TJ, Peck J, and Sheppard E (eds) *Wiley-Blackwell companion to economic geography.* Malden, MA: Wiley-Blackwell, 567–580.

Alcantara C and Nelles J. (2014) Indigenous Peoples and the State in Settler Societies: Toward a more robust definition of multilevel governance. *Publius: The Journal of Federalism* 44: 183.

Allen E. (1976) Intergroup ties and exogemy among Northern Coast Salish. *Northwest Anthropological Research Notes* 10: 161–172.

Alper D and Monahan R. (1986) Regional transboundary negotiations leading to the Skagit River Treaty: Analysis and future application. *Canadian Public Policy* 21: 163–174.

Alper DK. (1996) The idea of Cascadia: Emergent transborder regionalisms in the Pacific Northwest-Western Canada. *Journal of Borderlands Studies* 10: 1–22.

Alper DK. (1997) Transboundary environmental relations in British Columbia and the Pacific Northwest. *American Review of Canadian Studies* 27: 359–383.

AMAP. (2011) *Arctic pollution 2011 (mercury).* Oslo, Norway: Arctic Monitoring and Assessment Programme.

Anderson B. (1991) *Imagined communities: Reflections on the spread and origins of nationalism.* London: Verso Press.

Anderson EW. (1992) The political and strategic significance of water. *Outlook on Agriculture* 21: 247–253.

Anderson K. (1995) Culture and nature in the Adelaide Zoo: At the frontiers of "human" geography. *Transactions of the Institute of British Geographers, New Series* 20: 275–294.

Anderson K. (2007) *Race and the crisis of humanism.* London: Routledge.

Anderson M. (1996) *Frontiers: Territory and the state in the modern world.* Cambridge, UK: Polity.

Angelbeck W. (2009) "They recognize no superior Chief": Power, practice, anarchism and warfare in the Coast Salish past. *Department of Anthropology.* Vancouver, BC: University of British Columbia.

Armstrong J. (2005) A whale of a solution: Give Luna human link. *Globe and Mail,* Ottawa, ON, 11 August.

Audley JJ. (1997) *Green politics and global trade: NAFTA and the future of environmental politics.* Washington, DC: Georgetown University Press.

Awuah-Nyamekye S and Sarfo-Mensah P. (2011) Ensuring equitable distribution of land in Ghana: Spirituality or policy? A case study from the Forest-Savanna Agroecological Zone of Ghana. *The International Indigenous Policy Journal* 2: 1–24.

Baird R. (2001) Status of killer whales: Orcinus orca in Canada. *Canadian Field-Naturalist*: 676–701.

Bakker K. (2003a) From public to private to . . . mutual? Restructuring water supply governance in England and Wales. *Geoforum* 34: 359–374.

Bakker K. (2003b) *An uncooperative commodity: Privatizing water in England and Wales.* Oxford; New York: Oxford University Press.

Bakker K. (2005) Neoliberalizing nature? Market environmentalism in water supply in England and Wales. *Annals of the Association of American Geographers* 95: 542–565.

Bakker K. (2010) *Privatizing water: Governance failure and the world's urban water crisis.* Ithaca, NY: Cornell University Press.

Bakker K. (2013) Constructing "public" water: The World Bank and water as an object of development. *Environment andPlanning D* 31: 280–300.

Balibar E. (2004) *Politics and the other scene.* London: Verso Books.

Bankes N and Bourget L. (2013) Apportionment of the St. Mary and Milk River. In: Norman ES, Cohen A, and Bakker K (eds) *Water without borders? Canada, the United States and shared waters.* Toronto: University of Toronto Press, 159–178.

Barber J. (1983) *Blessed are the peace makers: A commemoration of the 200th anniversary of the Treaty of Paris.* Washington, DC: National Portrait Gallery by the Smithsonian Institution Press.

Barman J. (1999) What a difference a border makes: Aboriginal racial intermixture in the Pacific Northwest. *Journal of the West* 38: 14–20.

Bear C. (2011) Being Angelica? Exploring individual animal geographies. *Area* 43: 297–304.

Bear C and Eden S. (2011) Thinking like a fish? Engaging with nonhuman difference through recreational angling. *Environment and Planning D: Society and Space* 29: 336–352.

Bear LL. (2000) Jagged worldviews colliding. In: Battiste M (ed.) *Reclaiming Indigenous voice and vision.* Vancouver, BC: UBC Press, 77–85.

Bellah, R. (1977) Foreword. In: Rabinow P. (1977) *Reflections on field work in Morocco.* Berkeley, CA: University of California Press, ix–xiii.

Berkes F. (1999) *Sacred ecology: Traditional ecological knowledge and resource management.* Philadelphia, PA: Taylor & Francis.

Berry KD, Saito L, Kauneckis D, and Berry KA. (2012) Understanding perceptions of successful cooperation on water quality issues: A comparison across six Western U.S. interstate watersheds. *Regions and Cohesion* 2: 57–82.

Besio K, Johnston L, and Longhurst R. (2008) Sexy beasts and devoted mums: Narrating nature through dolphin tourism. *Environment and Planning A* 40: 1219–1234.

Biermann F, Pattberg P, van Asselt H, and Zelli F. (2009) The fragnentation of global governance architectures: A framework for analysis. *Global Environmental Politics* 9: 14–40.

Bierwert CB. (1999) *Brushed by Cedar, living by the River: Coast Salish figures of power.* Albuquerque, NM: University of New Mexico Press.

Biswas AK. (2004) Integrated water resources management: A reassessment – A water forum contribution. *Water International* 29: 248–256.

Blatter J, Ingram H, and Levesque SL. (2001) Expanding perspectives on transboundary water. In: Blatter J and Ingram H (eds) *Reflections on water: New approaches to transboundary conflicts and cooperation.* Cambridge, MA: The MIT Press.

Borrows J. (2002) *Recovering Canada: The resurgence of Indigenous Law.* Toronto: University of Toronto Press.

Boxberger D. (1989) *To fish in common: The ethnohistory of Lummi Indian salmon fishing.* Seattle, WA: University of Washington Press.

Boxberger DL. (1993) Lightning Boldts and sparrow wings: A comparison of Native fishing rights in British Columbia and Washington State. *Native Studies* 9.

Boxberger DL and Miller B. (1997) Evolution or history? A response to Tollefson. *Ethnohistory* 44: 135–138.

Boyd D. (2012) *The right to a healthy environment: Revitalizing Canada's Constitution.* Vancouver, BC: University of British Columbia.

Brady MP. (2000) The fungibility of borders. *Nepantla: Views from South* 1: 171–190.

Brandson N and Hearne R. (2013) Devils Lake and Red River Basin. In: Norman ES, Cohen A, and Bakker K (eds) *Water without borders? Canada, the United States and shared waters.* Toronto: University of Toronto Press, 179–192.

Braun B. (2000) Producing vertical territory: Geology and governmentality in the late Victorian Canada. *Ecumene* 7: 7–46.

Braun B. (2002) *The intemperate rainforest: Nature, culture, and power on Canada's West Coast.* Minneapolis, MN: University of Minnesota Press.

Braun B. (2005) Environmental issues: Writing a more-than-human urban geography. *Progress in Human Geography* 29: 635–650.

Braun B and Wainwright J. (2001) Nature, poststructuralism, and politics. In: Castree N and Braun B (eds) *Social nature: Theory, practice, and politics.* Malden and Oxford: Blackwell, 41–63.

Brenner N. (1997) State territorial restructuring and the production of spatial scale: Urban and regional planning in the Federal Republic of Germany, 1960–1990. *Political Geography* 16: 273–306.

Brenner N. (2001) The limits to scale? Methodological reflection on scalar structuration. *Progress in Human Geography* 25: 591–614.

Brenner N. (2004) *New state spaces: Urban governance and the rescaling of statehood.* Oxford: Oxford University Press.

Brenner N, Jones M and MacLeod G. (2003) State space in question. In: Brenner N, Jessop B, Jones M, and MacLeod G. (eds) *State/space: A reader.* Oxford: Blackwell, 1–26.

Brichieri-Colombi S. (2009) *The world water crisis: The failures of resource management.* London; New York. I.B. Tauris.

Briggs K and Alexander A. (2006) Paths of Our Ancestors. *Editorial: Seattle Times*. August 10, 2006.

Brooks I. (2007) International Watersheds Initiative: Building capacity for an integrated ecosystem approach to transboundary watersheds. *American Water Association Newsletter – Washington Section*, November–December 2007: 5.

Brown CJ and Purcell M. (2005) There's nothing inherent about scale: Political ecology, the local trap, and the politics of development in the Brazilian Amazon. *Geoforum* 36: 607–624.

Bryan J. (2009) Where would we be without them? Knowledge, space and power in Indigenous politics. *Futures* 41: 24–32.

Budds J. (2008) Whose scarcity? The hydrosocial cycle and the changing waterscape of La Ligua River Basin, Chile. In: Goodman M, Boykoff M, and Evered K (eds) *Contentious geographies: Environment, meaning, scale*. Aldershot: Ashgate, 59–68.

Budds J. (2009) Contested H_2O: Science, policy and politics in water resources management in Chile. *Geoforum* 40: 418–430.

Budds J and Hinojosa L. (2012) Restructuring and rescaling water governance in mining contexts: The co-production of waterscapes in Peru. *Walter Alternatives* 5: 119–137.

Bulkeley H. (2005) Reconfiguring environmental governance: Towards a politics of scales and networks. *Political Geography* 24: 875–902.

Butler J. (1997) *Excitable speech: A politics of the performative*. New York: Routledge.

Cadman L. (2009) Life and death in our posthuman(ist) times. *Antipode* 41: 133–158.

Cajete G. (2000) *Native Science: Natural laws of interdependence*. Sante Fe, NM: Clear Light.

Calarco M. (2008) *Zoogeographies: The question of the animal from Heidegger to Derrida*. New York: Columbia University Press.

Campbell M. (2008) An animal geography of avian feeding habits in Peterborough, Ontario. *Area* 40: 472–480.

Campbell M and O'Neal M. (2007) An animal geography of avian ecology in Glasgow. *Applied Geography* 27: 78–88.

Carlson KT. (2001) *A St'o:lo-Coast Salish Historical Atlas*. Vancouver, BC: Douglas & McIntyre Ltd.

Carroll JE. (1981) Patterns old and new. In: Spencer R, Kirton J, and Nossa KR (eds) *The International Joint Commission seventy years on*. Toronto: University of Toronto, 43–59.

Castree N. (2004) Nature is dead! Long live nature! *Environment and Planning A* 36: 191–194.

Castree N and Braun B. (2001) *Social nature: Theory, practice, and politics*. Malden and Oxford: Blackwell.

CEC. (2013) *Commission for Environmental Cooperation Ministerial Statement*. Available at: www.cec.org/Page.asp?PageID=122&ContentID=2179&SiteNodeID=357 (Accessed 10 July 2014).

Chandhoke N. (2003) Governance and the pluralisation of the state: Implications for democratic citizenship. *Economic and Political Weekly* 38: 2957–2968.

Chisholm S. (2012) Personal communication with author. Victoria, BC.

Chisholm S and Parfit M. (2012) Mountain Side Film. 74.

Chrulew M. (2011) Managing love and death at the zoo: The biopolitics of endangered species preservation. *Australian Humanities Review* 50:137–157.

Clamen M. (2013) The IJC and transboundary water disputes: Past, present, and future. In: Norman ES, Cohen A, and Bakker K (eds) *Water without borders? Canada, the United States and shared waters*. Toronto: University of Toronto Press, 70–87.

Clamen, M. (2014) Personal communication with author via email, 20 February 2014.

Clarkson T and Magos L. (2006) The toxicology of mercury and its chemical compounds. *Critical Review of Toxicology* 36: 609–662.

Clayton D. (2000) *Islands of truth: The imperial fashioning of Vancouver Island*. Vancouver, BC: The University of British Columbia Press.

Cloke P and Perkins H. (1998) Cracking the canyon with the awesome foursome: Representations of adventure tourism in New Zealand. *Environment and Planning D: Society and Space* 16: 185–218.

Cloke P and Perkins H. (2005) Cetacean performance and tourism in Kaikoura, New Zealand. *Environment and Planning D: Society and Space* 23: 903–924.

Coast Salish Gathering. (2008) Coast Salish Gathering 2008 Program. Sequim, Washington, DC.

Coast Salish Gathering. (2012) Coast Salish Gathering 2010 Program, Tulalip. Tulalip, Washington, DC.

Coates P. (2013) *A story of six rivers: History, culture and ecology*. London: Reaktion Books.

Cohen A. (2012) Rescaling environmental governance: Watersheds as boundary objects at the intersection of science, neoliberalism, and participation. *Environment and Planning A* 44.

Cohen A and Davidson S. (2011) The watershed approach: Challenges, antecedents, and the transition from technical tool to governance unit. *Water Alternatives* 4: 521–534.

Cohen A and Harris LM. (2014) Performing watersheds: Performativity and the production of scale. In: Rose-Redwood R and Glass M (eds) *Performativity, space, and politics*. London: Routledge.

Cohen A and McCarthy J. (2014) Reviewing rescaling: Strengthening the case for environmental considerations. *Progress in Human Geography*, 7 March 2014, doi: 10.1177/0309132514521483.

Colbern T, Dumansoki D, and Meyers J. (1996) *Our stolen future: Are we threatening our fertility, intelligence, and survival? A scientific detective story*. New York: Plume.

Collard R-C. (2012) Cougar-human entanglements and the biopolitical un/making of safe space. *Environment and Planning A: Society and Space* 30.

Conca K. (2006) *Governing water: Contentious transnational politics and global institution building*. Cambridge, MA: MIT Press.

Corti G. (1997) All commons are local: The Antarctic Treaty System as a regional model for effective environmental management. In: Susskind LE, Moomaw WR, and Gallagher K (eds) *Innovations in international environmental negotiation*. San Francisco, CA: Jossey-Bass, 24–40.

Cote C. (2010) *Spirits of our whaling ancestors: Revitalizing Makah and Nuu-chah-nulth traditions*. Seattle, WA: University of Washington Press.

Crampton JW and Elden S. (2006) Space, politics, calculation: An introduction. *Social and Cultural Geography* 7: 681–685.

Crang P, Cloke P, and Cook I. (2004) *Practising human geography*. London: Sage.

Davidson D. (2013) Environmental Cooperation Council email correspondence with author.

de Loë RC, Varghese J, Ferreyra C, and Kreutzwiser RD. (2007) *Water allocation and water security in Canada: Initiating a policy dialogue for the 21st century*. Guelph, ON: Guelph Water Management Group, University of Guelph, 76.

Dean M. (1999) *Governmentality: Power and rule in modern society*. London: Sage.

Delaney D and Leitner H. (1997) The political construction of scale. *Political Geography* 16: 93–97.

Deloria V. (1984) *The Nations within: The past and future of American Indian sovereignty*. Austin, TX: University of Texas.

Deloria V and Wilkins DE. (1999) *Tribes, treaties, and constitutional tribulations*. Austin, TX: University of Texas Press.

Demeritt D. (2001) Scientific forest conservation and the statistical picturing of nature's limits in the Progressive-era United States. *Environment and Planning D: Society and Space* 19: 431–459.

DFO. (2013) Be whale wise – marine wildlife guidelines for boaters, paddlers and viewers. Available at: www.pac.dfo-mpo.gc.ca/fm-gp/species-especes/mammals-mammiferes/view-observer-eng.htm (Accessed 16 August 2014).

Diaz-Bautista A, Alper D and Martinez K. (2008) Energy policy and economic growth in the Pacific border region of North America. In Loucky J, Alper DK and Day JC (eds) *Transboundary policy challenges in the Pacific border regions of North America*. Calgary, AB: University of Calgary Press, 63–92.

DiMento J and Doughman P. (1998) Soft teeth in the back of the mouth: The NAFTA Environmental Side Agreement implemented. *Georgetown International Environmental Law* 3: 651–752.

Dinar A. (2004) Exploring transboundary water conflict and cooperation. *Water Resources Research* 40: article no. W05S01, doi:10.1029/2003WR002598.

Donatuto J. (2008) When seafood feeds the spirit yet poisons the body: Developing health indicators for risk assessment in a Native American fishing community. *Resource Management and Environmental Studies*. Vancouver, BC: University of British Columbia.

Donzelot J. (1997 [1977]) *The policing of families*. Baltimore, MA: Johns Hopkins University Press.

Dore J and Lebel L. (2010) Deliberation and scale in Mekong Region water governance. *Environmental Management* 46: 60–80.

Dreisziger N. (1981) Dreams and disappointments. In: Spencer R, Kirton J, and Nossal KR (eds) *The International Joint Commission seventy years on*. Toronto: University of Toronto, 8–23.

Drucker P. (1951) The Northern and Central Nootkan Tribes. *Bureau of American Ethnology Bulletin* 144. Washington, DC: Smithsonian Institution.

Duffus DA and Deardon T. (1993) Recreational use, valuation, and management of killer whales (Orcinus orca) on Canada's Pacific Coast. *Environmental Conservation Journal* 20: 149–156.

Duncan J. (2002) Embodying colonialism? Domination and resistance in 19th century Ceylonese coffee plantations. *Journal of Historical Geography* 28: 317–338.

ECC. (2013) British Columbia/Washington Environmental Cooperation Council. Available at: www.env.gov.bc.ca/spd/ecc/ (Accessed 16 August 2014).

El-Hayek YH. (2007) Mercury contamination in Arctic Canada: Possible implications for Aboriginal health. *Journal on Developmental Disabilities* 13: 67–90.

Elden S. (2006) *Speaking against number: Heidegger, language and the politics of calculation*. Edinburgh: University of Edinburgh.

Elden S. (2007) Governmentality, calculation, territory. *Environment and Planning D: Society and Space* 25: 562–580.

Epstein S. (1978) *The politics of cancer*. San Francisco, CA: Sierra Club Books.

Espey M and Towfique B. (2004) International bilateral water treaty formation. *Water Resources Research* 40.

Ettlinger N. (2011) Governmentality as epistemology. *Annals of the Association of American Geographers* 101: 537–560.

European Commission. (2000) *2000 Directive 2000/60/EC of the European Parliament and the Council of 23rd October 2000 establishing a framework for Community action in the field of water policy*. Brussels: European Commission.

Evenden MD. (2004) *Fish versus power: An environmental history of the Fraser River.* New York: Cambridge University Press.

Evenden L and Turberville DL. (2006) The Pacific Coast borderland and frontier. In: Evans S (ed.) *The borderlands and the American and Canadian Wests: Essays on regional history of the Forty-ninth Parallel.* Lincoln: University of Nebraska Press, 42–48.

Fall J. (2005) *Drawing the line: Nature, hybridity and politics in transboundary spaces.* Burlington, VT: Ashgate.

Fall J. (2010) Artificial States? On the enduring geographical myth of natural borders? *Political Geography* 29: 140–147.

Feitelson E and Fischhendler I. (2009) Spaces of water governance: The case of Israel and its neighbors. *Annals of the Association of American Geographers* 99: 728–745.

Filatova O, Burdin A, Hoyt E, and Sato H. (2004) A catalogue of discrete calls of resident killer whales (Orcinus orca) from the Avacha Gulf of Kamchatka Peninsula. *Zoologichesky Journal* 83: 1169–1180.

Findlay JM and Coates P. (2002) *Parallel destinies: Canadian-American relations west of the Rockies.* Seattle, WA: University of Washington Press.

Fischhendler I and Feitelson E. (2005) The formation and viability of a non-basin water management: The U.S.–Canada case. *Geoforum* 36: 792–804.

Ford J, Ellis G and Balcomb K. (2000) *Killer whales: The natural history and genealogy of Orcinus orca in British Columbia and Washington.* Seattle, WA: University of Washington Press.

Ford J, Horne J and Allman K. (2004) Echolocation signals of free-ranging killer whales (Orcinus orca) and modeling of foraging for Chinook salmon (Oncorhynchus tshawytscha). *Journal of the Acoustical Society of America* 115: 901–909.

Foucault M. (1979 [1976]) *History of sexuality, Volume 1: An introduction.* New York: Random House.

Foucault M. (2007) *Security, territory, population (lectures at the College De France).* New York: Palgrave.

Furlong K. (2006) Hidden theories, troubled waters: International relations, the "territorial trap", and the Southern African Development Community's transboundary waters. *Political Geography* 25: 438–458.

Furlong K. (2007) Municipal water supply governance in Ontario, ON: Neoliberalization, utility restructuring, and infrastructure management. Ph.D. thesis. University of British Columbia, 418.

Furlong K and Bakker K. (2010) The contradictions of "good" governance: Business models, alternative service delivery, and sustainability in municipal water supply. *Environment and Planning C* 28: 349–368.

Gadgil M, Berkes F and Folke C. (1993) Indigenous knowledge of biodiversity conservation. *Ambio* 22: 151–156.

Gagnon VS. (2011) Fish contaminants through the tribal perspective: An ethnography of the Keweenaw Bay Indian Community's tribal fish harvest. *Department of Social Sciences.* Houghton, MI: Michigan Technological University.

Gibbs D and Jonas AEG. (2001) Rescaling and regional governance: The English Regional Development Agencies and the environment. *Environment and Planning C: Government and Policy* 19: 269–288.

Gilbert H. (2007) Leaky borders and solid citizens: Governing security, prosperity and quality of life in a North American partnership. *Antipode* 39: 77–98.

Gilbert H and Tompkins J. (1996) *Post-colonial drama: Theory, practice, politics.* London: Routledge.

Giordano M, Giordano M and Wolf A. (2002) The geography of water conflict and cooperation: Internal pressures and international manifestations. *The Geographical Journal* 168: 293–312.

Gleick P. (2007) *The world's water: The biennial report on freshwater resources 2006–2007.* Washington, DC: Island Press.

Gleick PH. (2000) The changing water paradigm – A look at twenty-first century water resources development. *Water International* 25: 127–138.

Gleick PH, Chalecki EL and Wong A. (2002–2003) Measuring water well-being: Water indicators and indices. In: Gleick PH and Pacific Institute for Studies in Development Environment and Security. (eds) *The world's water: The biennial report on freshwater resources.* Washington, DC: Island Press, 87–112.

Goldman M. (2009) Constructing connectivity: Conservation corridors and conservation politics in East African rangelands. *Annals of the Association of American Geographers* 99: 335–359.

Gregory D. (2004) *The colonial present.* Cambridge, MA: Blackwell.

Griffiths T and Robbins L. (1997) *Ecology and empire.* Edinburgh, UK and Seattle, WA: Keele University Press and University of Washington Press.

Grove R. (1997) *Green imperialism, colonial expansion, tropical island Edens and the origins of environmentalism.* Cambridge: Cambridge University Press.

Guha R and Spivak GC. (1988) *Selected subaltern studies.* New York: Oxford University Press.

Hannah MG. (2000) *Governmentality and the mastery of territory in nineteenth-century America.* Cambridge: Cambridge University Press.

Hannah MG. (2009) Calculable territory in the West German census boycott movements of the 1980s. *Political Geography* 28: 66–75.

Haraway D. (2008) *When species meet.* Minneapolis, MN: University of Minnesota Press.

Harcourt M. (2007) Phone interview with Mike Harcourt.

Harmon A. (2000) *Indians in the making: Ethnic Relations and Indian identities around Puget Sound.* Berkeley, CA: University of California Press.

Harris C. (2002) *Making native space: Colonialism, resistance, and reserves in British Columbia.* Vancouver, BC: University of British Columbia Press.

Harris DC. (2000) Territoriality, aboriginal rights and the Heiltuk spawn-on-kelp fishery. *UBC Law Review* 34: 195–238.

Harris DC. (2001) *Fish, law, and colonialism: The legal capture of salmon in British Columbia.* Toronto, ON: University of Toronto Press.

Harris LM. (2006) Irrigation, gender, and social geographies of the changing waterscapes of southeastern Anatolia. *Environment and Planning D: Society and Space* 24: 187–213.

Harris LM. (2009) Gender and emergent water governance: Comparative overview of neoliberalized natures and gender dimensions of privatization, devolution and marketization. *Gender, Place and Culture: A Journal of Feminist Geography* 16: 387–408.

Harris LM and Alatout S. (2010) Negotiating hydro-scales, forging states: Comparison of the upper Tigris/Euphrates and Jordan river basins. *Political Geography* 29: 148–156.

Harris L and Hazen H. (2006) Power of maps: (Counter)-mapping for conservation. *Acme International E-journal of Critical Geographies* 4: 99–130.

Harris DC and Millerd P. (2010) Food fish, commercial fish, and fish to support a moderate livelihood: Characterizing Aboriginal and Treaty Rights to Canadian Fisheries. *Arctic Review on Law and Politics* 1: 82–107.

Harris L, Goldin J and Sneddon C. (2013) *Contemporary water governance in the Global South: Scarcity, marketization and participation.* London: Routledge.

Healy R, VanNinjnatten DL and Lopez-Vallejo M. (2014) *Environmental policy in North America: Approaches, capacity, and the management of transboundary issues*. Toronto: University of Toronto Press.

Hele KS. (2005) *Lines drawn upon the water: First Nations and the Great Lakes borders and borderlands*. Waterloo, ON: Wilfrid Laurier University Press.

Heynen NC. (2003) The scalar production of injustice within the urban forest. *Antipode* 35: 980–998.

Hobson K. (2007) Political animals? On animals as subjects in an enlarged political geography. *Political Geography* 26: 250–267.

Holifield R. (2012) Environmental justice as recognition and participation in risk assessment: Negotiating and translating health risk at a superfund site in Indian Country. *Annals of the Association of American Geographers* 102: 591–613.

Holifield RB. (2010) Regulatory science and risk assessment in Indian Country: Taking tribal publics into account. *Geographies of Science* 3: 250.

Holifield R, Porter M and Walker G. (2009) Spaces of environmental justice: Frameworks for critical engagement. *Antipode* 41: 591–612.

Holloway L. (2007) Subjecting cows to robots: Farming technologies and the making of animal subjects. *Environment and Planning D: Society and Space* 25.

Holloway L and Morris C. (2007) Exploring biopower in the regulation of farm animal bodies: Genetic policy interventions in UK livestock. *Genomics, Society and Policy* 3: 82–98.

Holloway L, Morris C, Gilna B, and Gibbs D. (2009) Biopower, genetics and livestock breeding: (Re)constituting animal populations and heterogeneous biosocial collectivities. *Transactions of the Institute of British Geographers* 34: 394–407.

Holmes JW. (1981) Introduction. In: Spencer R, Kirton J and Nossa KR (eds) *The International Joint Commission seventy years on*. Toronto: University of Toronto, 43–59.

Hovorka A. (2008) Transspecies urban theory: Chickens in an African city. *Cultural Geographies* 15: 95–117.

Howitt R. (1998) Scale as relation: Musical metaphors of geographical scale. *Area* 30: 49–58.

Howitt R. (2002) Scale and the other: Levinas and geography. *Geoforum* 33: 299–313.

Huang H-C, Lee C-L, Lai C-H, Fang M-D, and Lai I-C. (2012) Transboundary movement of polycyclic aromatic hydrocarbons (PAHs) in the Kuroshio Sphere of the western Pacific Ocean. *Atmospheric Environment* 54: 470–479.

Huhndorf S. (2009) *Mapping the Americas: The transnational politics of contemporary Native culture*. Ithaca, NY: Cornell University Press.

IJC. (1977) *Water Quality in the Saint John River Basin*. Washington, DC and Ottowa: International Joint Commission (Accessed 7 January 2014).

IJC. (1997) *The IJC and the 21st Century*. Washington, DC and Ottawa, ON: International Joint Commission.

IJC. (2000) *Transboundary Watersheds*. Washington, DC and Ottawa, ON: International Joint Commission.

IJC. (2005) *A discussion paper on International Joint Commission and Transboundary Issues*. Washington, DC and Ottawa, ON: International Joint Commission.

IJC. (2014) International Joint Commission's International Watersheds Initiative. Available at: www.ijc.org/en_/IWI (Accessed 7 January 2014).

Ivey JL, de Loë RC, and Kreutzwiser RD. (2006) Planning for source water protection in Ontario. *Applied Geography* 26: 192–209.

Jackson RH and Owens P. (2005) The evolution of world society. In: Baylis J and Smith S (eds) *The globalization of world politics: An introduction to international relations*. Oxford: Oxford University Press, 13–30.

James J. (2010) Personal communication with author. Gold River (Tsaxana), British Columbia.

Jelinski D, Krueger C, and Duffus D. (2002) Geostatistical analyses of interactions between killer whales (Orcinus orca) and recreational whale-watching boats. *Applied Geography* 22: 393–411.

Jepson W. (2013) Measuring "no-win" waterscapes: Experience-based scales and classification approaches to assess household water security in *colonias* on the US-Mexico border. *Geoforum* 51: 107–120.

Jepson W and Brown H. (2014) If no gasoline, no water: Privatizing drinking water quality in South Texas *colonias*. *Environment and Planning A* 46: 1032–1048.

Jessop B. (2004) Hollowing out the "nation-state" and multilevel governance. In: Kennett P (ed.) *A handbook of comparative social policy*. Cheltenham, UK: Edward Elgar, 11–25.

Johnson P-M and Beaulieu A. (1996) *The environment and NAFTA: Understanding and implementing the new continental law*. Washington, DC: Island Press.

Johnston C. (2008) Beyond the clearing: Towards a dwelt animal geography. *Progress in Human Geography* 32: 633–649.

Jolly C. (1998) The British Columbia-Washington Environment and the founding of the Environmental Cooperation Council. International Environmental Law lecture, University of Washington, Seattle, 29 January 1998.

Jonas A. (2006) Pro scale: Further reflections of the "scale debate" in human geography. *Transactions of the Institute of British Geographers* 31: 399–406.

Joyce M. (2004) Luna memo – Document released under the Access to Information Act. In email correspondence between Georges Cormier, Marilyn Joyce, Robert Jones, Patrice Simon, and Brian Wong (Document released under the Access to Information Act). Ottawa, ON: DFO.

Kaika M. (2003) Constructing scarcity and sensationalising water politics: 170 days that shook Athens. *Antipode* 35: 919–954.

Kaiser R and Nikiforova E. (2008) The performativity of scale: The social construction of scale effects in Narva, Estonia. *Environment and Planning D: Society and Space* 26: 537–562.

Katz C. (1998) Whose nature, whose culture. In: Braun B and Castree N (eds) *Remaking reality*. London; New York: Routledge, 46–63.

Kauanui JK. (2008) *Hawaiian blood: Colonialism and the politics of sovereignty and indigeneity*. Durham, NC: Duke University Press.

Kennedy D. (2007) Quantifying "two sides of a coin": A statistical examination of Central Coast Salish Network. *BC Studies: The British Columbian Quarterly* 153: 3–34.

Kliot N, Shmueli D, and Shamir U. (2001) Institutions for management of transboundary water resources: Their nature, characteristics and shortcomings. *Water Policy* 3: 229–255.

Knight DB. (1982) Identity and territory: Geographical perspectives on nationalism and regionalism. *Annals of the Association of American Geographers* 72: 514–531.

Kostovicova D. (2005) *Kosovo: The politics of identity and space*. Oxford: Routledge.

Kovach M. (2010) *Indigenous methodologies: Characteristics, conversations, and contexts*. Toronto: University of Toronto Press.

KuKanich B, Papich M, Huff D, and Stoskopf M. (2004) Comparison of amikacin pharmacokinetics in a killer whale (Orcinus orca) and a beluga whale (Delphinapterus leucas). *Journal of Zoo and Wildlife Medicine* 35: 179–184.

Kuus M and Agnew J. (2008) Theorizing the state geographically: Sovereignty, subjectivity, territoriality. In: Cox K, Low M, and Robinson J (eds) *SAGE handbook of political geography*. Thousand Oaks, CA: Sage, 95–106.

La Duke W. (1999) *All our relations: Native struggles for land and life*. Cambridge, MA: South End Press.

Langston N. (2010a) *Toxic bodies: Hormone disrupters and the legacy of DES*. New Haven, CT: Yale University Press.

Langston N. (2010b) Toxic inequities: Chemical exposure and Indigenous Communities in Canada and the United States. *Natural Resources Journal* 50: 393–406.

Larsen EM and Richardson SA. (1990) Some effects of a major oil spill on wintering shorebirds at Grays Harbor, Washington. *Northwestern Naturalist*: 88–92.

Latour B. (1999) *Pandora's hope*. Cambridge, MA: Harvard University Press.

Lautz J and Giordano M. (2005) Transboundary water law in Africa: Development, nature, and geography. *Natural Resources Forum* 45: 1053–1087.

Leach WD and Pelkey N. (2001) Making watershed partnerships work: A review of the empirical literature. *Journal of Water Resources Planning and Management* 127: 378–385.

Leitner H and Miller B. (2007) Scale and the limitations of ontological debate: A commentary on Marston, Jones and Woodward. *Transactions of the Institute of British Geographers* 32: 116–125.

LeMarquand D. (1993) The International Joint Commission and changing Canada-United States boundary relations. *Natural Resources Journal* 33: 59–91.

Linton J. (2010) *What is water? The history of a modern abstraction*. Vancouver, BC: University of British Columbia Press.

Little Bear L. (2000) Jagged worldviews colliding. In: Battiste M (ed.) *Reclaiming Indigenous voice and vision*. Vancouver, BC: UBC Press, 77–85.

Liverman D. (2004) Who governs, at what scale and at what price? Geography, environmental governance, and the commodification of nature. *Annals of the Association of American Geographers* 94: 734–738.

Locke H and McKinney M. (2013) The Flathead River Basin. In: Norman ES, Cohen A and Bakker K (eds) *Water without borders? Canada, the United States and shared waters*. Toronto: University of Toronto Press, 193–220.

Loftus A. (2007) Working the socio-natural relations of the urban waterscape. *International Journal of Urban and Regional Research* 3: 41–59.

Loftus A and Lumsden F. (2008) Reworking hegemony in the urban waterscape. *Transactions of the Institute of British Geographers* 33: 109–126.

Lohmann R, Breivik K, Dachs J, and Muir DG (2007) Global fate of POPs: Current and future research directions. *Environmental Pollution* 150: 150–165.

Lulka D. (2004) Stabilizing the herd: Fixing the identity of nonhumans. *Environment and Planning D: Society and Space* 22: 439–463.

Lulka D. (2009) The residual humanism of hybridity: Retaining a sense of the earth. *Transactions of the Institute of British Geographers, New Series* 34: 378–393.

Lusseau D, Williams R, Wilson B, Grellier K, Barton TR, Hammond PS, and Thompson PM. (2004) Parallel influence of climate on the behaviour of Pacific killer whales and Atlantic bottlenose dolphins. *Ecology Letters*: 1068–1076.

McCaffrey SC. (1996) The Harmon Doctrine one hundred years later: Buried, not praised. *Natural Resources Journal* 36: 725–767.

McCaffrey SC. (1997) Water scarcity: Institutional and legal responses. In: Brans EHP (ed.) *The scarcity of water: Emerging legal and policy responses*. London and Boston, MA: Kluwer Law International, 43–58.

McCarthy J. (2005) Scale, sovereignty, and strategy in environmental governance. *Antipode* 37: 731–753.

McClure R. (2003) Canada pledges money to return Luna to pod. *Seattle Post-Intelligencer*. Seattle, WA.

McClure R. (2005) Efforts to protect orcas may have wide impact: Public urged to comment on the conservation plan. *Seattle: Post-Intelligencer.* Seattle, WA.

McGinnis MV. (1999) Making the watershed connection. *Policy Studies Journal* 27: 497–501.

MacKinnon D. (2011) Reconstructing scale: Towards a new scalar politics. *Progress in Human Geography* 35: 21–36.

McManus S. (2005) *The line which separates: Race, gender, and the making of the Alberta-Montana borderlands.* Lincoln, NE: University of Nebraska Press.

McNeil K. (2008) Native rights case law. In: Bailey G (ed.) *Handbook of North American Indians, Volume 2, Indians in contemporary society.* Washington: Smithsonian Institution, 166–176.

Malkin E. (2000) Commentary: Taking the green out of NAFTA. *Business Week (International Edition).*

Manson SM. (2008) Does scale exist? An epistemological scale continuum for complex human-environment systems. *Geoforum* 39: 776–788.

Marchak P. (1998) Environment and resource protection: Does NAFTA make a difference?. *Organization and Environment* 11: 133–157.

Marston SA. (2000) The social construction of scale. *Progress in Human Geography* 24: 219–242.

Marston SA, Jones JP, and Woodward K. (2005) Human geography without scale. *Transactions of the Institute of British Geography* 30: 416–432.

Massey D. (2003) Imagining the field. In: Pryke M, Rose G and Whatmore S (eds) *Using social theory: Thinking through research.* vols. London: Sage, 71–88.

Matson R (ed.) (2010) The Crescent Beach site and the place of the Locarno Beach phase. UBC Laboratory of Archaeology, Vancouver, BC. Available at: http://anth.ubc.ca/the-crescent-beach-site-and-the-place-of-the-locarno-beach-phase/ (Accessed 16 August 2014).

Menzies CR and Butler C. (2006) Understanding ecological knowledge. In: Menzies CR. (ed.) *Traditional Ecological Knowledge and Natural Resource Management.* Lincoln, NE: University of Nebraska Press, 1–17.

Miller B. (1996–1997) The "really real" border and the divided Salish Community. *BC Studies: The British Columbian Quarterly* 112: 63–79.

Miller B. (2003) *Invisible indigenes: The politics of nonrecognition.* Lincoln, NE: University of Nebraska Press.

Miller B. (2006) Conceptual and practical boundaries: West Coast Indians/First Nations on the border of contagion in the post-9/11 era. In: Evans S (ed.) *The Borderlands of the American and Canadian Wests: Essays on the Regional History of the 49th Parallel.* Norman, NE: University of Nebraska Press, 299–308.

Miller P, Shapiro A, Tyack P, and Solow A. (2004) Call-type matching in vocal exchanges of free-ranging resident killer whales, Orcinus orca. *Animal Behaviour* 67: 1099–1107.

Mirosa O and Harris L. (2012) Human right to water: Contemporary challenges and contours of a global debate. *Antipode* 44: 932–949.

Mitchell B. (1990) Integrated water management. In: Mitchell B (ed.) *Integrated water management: International experiences and perspectives.* London: Bellhaven Press, 1–21.

Mitchell B. (2004) Integrated Water Resources Management: A reassessment. *Water International* 29: 398–399.

Mitchell B. (2006) IWRM in practice: Lessons from Canadian experiences. *Journal of Contemporary Water Research and Education*: 51–55.

Mitchell D. (2000) *Cultural Geography: A Critical Introduction.* Oxford and Malden, MA: Blackwell.

Mitchell T. (1991) *Colonising Egypt.* Berkeley, CA: University of California Press.

Mitchell T. (1999) Society, economy, and the state effect. In: Steinmetz G (ed.) *State/Culture: State-formation after the Cultural Turn.* Ithaca, NY: Cornell University Press.

Mitchell T. (2002) *Rule of Experts.* Berkeley, CA: University of California Press.

Molle F. (2006) Planning and managing water at the river basin level: Emergence and evolution of a concept. *Comprehensive Assessment of Water Management in Agriculture.* Colombo, Sri Lanka: International Water Management Institute.

Molle F. (2009) River-basin planning and management: The social life of a concept. *Geoforum* 40: 484–494.

Montgomery DR, Grant GE, and Sullivan K. (1995) Watershed analysis as a framework for implementing ecosystem managment. *Journal of the American Water Resources Association* 31: 369–386.

Mountz A. (2010) Refugees – performing distinction: The paradoxical positionings of refugees. In: Cresswell T and Merriman P (eds) *Mobilities: Practices, spaces, and subjects.* Aldershot, UK: Ashgate, 255–270.

Muehlmann S. (2013) *Where the River Ends: Contested Indigeneity and the Colorado River Delta.* Durham, NC: Duke University Press.

Mumme S. (1999) Managing acute water scarcity on the U.S.–Mexico border: Institutional issues raised by the 1990's drought. *Natural Resources Journal* 39: 149–168.

Munro R. (2001) Whales in captivity: Let's end this ugly business. *The Seattle Times.* Seattle, WA.

Munton D. (1980–81) Dependence and interdependence in transboundary environmental relations. *International Journal [Canada]* 36: 139–184.

Murray S. (2009) Cashing in on whales: Cetaceans as symbol and commodity along the Northern Pacific Coast, 1959–2008. *History Department.* Burnaby, British Columbia Canada: Simon Fraser University.

Myrdal G. (1944) *An American dilemma: The Negro problem and modern democracy.* New York: Harper Brothers.

Nadasdy P. (1999) The politics of TEK: Power and the "integration" of knowledge. *Arctic Anthropology* 36: 1–18.

Nadasdy P. (2004) *Hunters and bureaucrats: Power, knowledge, and Aboriginal-State relations in the Southwest Yukon.* Vancouver, BC: UBC Press.

Nadasdy P. (2005) Transcending the debate over the ecologically noble Indian: Indigenous peoples and environmentalism. *Ethnohistory* 52: 291–331.

Nadasdy P. (2006) The case of the missing sheep: Time, space and the politics of "trust" in co-management practice. In: Menzies CR (ed.) *Traditional ecological knowledge and natural resource management.* Lincoln, NE and London: University of Nebraska Press, 127–151.

Nater E and Grigal D. (1992) Regional trends in mercury distribution across the Great Lakes states, north central USA. *Nature* 358: 139–141.

Neering R. (2011) *The Pig War: The last Canada–U.S. border conflict.* Surrey: Heritage House.

Nelles J and Alcantara C. (2011) Strengthening the ties that bind? An analysis of aboriginal–municipal inter-governmental agreements in British Columbia. *Canadian Public Administration* 54: 315–334.

Nevarez L. (1996) Just wait until there's drought: Mediating environmental crisis for urban growth. *Antipode* 28: 246–272.

Newman D. (2002) Boundaries. In: Agnew J, Mitchell K, and Toal G (eds) *A companion to political geography.* Oxford, UK: Blackwell, 123–137.

Newman D. (2006) The lines that continue to separate us: Borders in our "borderless" world. *Progress in Human Geography* 30: 143–161.

Norman, ES (2009) Navigating bordered geographies: Water governance along the Canada–U.S. border. Unpublished Dissertation, Department of Geography, University of British Columbia. Advisors: Matthew Evenden and Karen Bakker.

Norman ES. (2013) Who's counting? Spatial politics, ecocolonisation, and the politics of calculation in Boundary Bay. *Area* (Royal Geographical Society) 45: 179–187.

Norman ES. (2014) Locating the border in Boundary Bay: Non-point pollution, contaminated shellfish, and transboundary governance. In: Jones R and Johnson C (eds) *Placing the border in everyday Life*. London: Ashgate Press, 67–92.

Norman ES and Melious J. (2008) Hidden waters: Transboundary environmental management across the 49th Parallel. In: Alper D, Day C, and Loucky J (eds) *Border bio-regions and coastal corridors: Transnational policy challenges in Western North America*. Calgary, AB: University of Calgary Press, 195–218.

Norman ES and Bakker K. (2009) Transgressing scales: Transboundary water governance across the Canada –U.S. border. *Annals of the Association of American Geographers* 99: 99–117.

Norman ES, Bakker K, and Cook C. (2012) Introduction to the themed section: Water governance and the politics of scale. *Water Alternatives* 5: 52–61.

Norman ES, Cohen A, and Bakker K. (2013) *Water without borders? Canada, the United States, and shared waters*. Toronto: University of Toronto Press.

Norman ES, Cook C, and Cohen A. (2015) Introduction: Why the politics of scale matter in the governance of water. In: Norman ES, Cook C, and Cohen A (eds) *Negotiating water governance: Why the politics of scale matters*. London: Ashgate, 1–25.

Nuzzo JB. (2006) The biological threat to U.S. water supplies: Toward a national water security policy. *Biosecurity and Bioterrorism-Biodefense Strategy Practice and Science* 4: 147–159.

NWIFC. (2010) "Shellfish" Northwest Indian Fisheries Commission. Available at: http://nwifc.org/about-us/shellfish/ (Accessed 15 August 2010).

Ó Tuathail G. (1996) *Critical geopolitics*. London: Routledge.

Obrist D. (2012) Mercury distribution across 14 U.S. forests. Part II: Patterns of methyl mercury concentrations and areal mass of total and methyl mercury. *Environmental Science and Technology* 46: 5921–5930.

Ohmae K. (1995) *The end of the Nation State: The rise of regional economies*. New York: The Free Press.

Paasi, A. (1999) 'Boundaries as social processes: Territoriality in the world of flows'. In: Newman D (ed.) *Boundaries, territory and postmodernity*. London: Frank Cass, 69–88.

Paasi A. (2002) Territory. In: Agnew J, Mitchell K, and Toal G (eds) *A companion to political geography*. Oxford, UK: Blackwell, 109–112.

Paasi A. (2009) Bounded spaces in a "borderless world": Border studies, power and the anatomy of territory. *Journal of Power* 2: 213–234.

Pacific Coast Collaborative. (2013) Available at: www.pacificcoastcollaborative.org/Pages/Welcome.aspx (Accessed 5 November 2013).

Panelli R. (2010) More-than-human social geographies: Posthuman and other possibilities. *Progress in Human Geography* 34: 79–87.

Pentland R and Hurley A. (2007) Thirsty neighbors: Canada transboundary governance. In: Bakker L (ed.) *Eau Canada: The future of Canada's water*. Vancouver, BC: UBC Press.

Perlinger JA. (2005) New approaches to measure atmospheric PBT concentration and flux in the Great Lakes. UESPA Great Lakes National Protection Office, Chicago, IL, 1 December 2005.

Perlinger JA, Tobias DE, Morrow PS, and Doskey PV. (2005) Evaluation of novel techniques for measurement of air-water exchange of persistent bioaccumulative toxicants in Lake Superior. *Environmental Science and Technology* 39: 8411–8419.

Perlinger JA, Gorman J, Norman ES, Obrist D, Selin N, Urban N, and Wu S. (2014) The evolution of science and policy related to atmosphere-surface. Working Paper. Houghton, MI: Michigan Technological University.

Perreault T. (2003) Making space. *Latin American Perspectives* 30: 96–121.

Perreault T. (2005) State restructuring and the scale politics of rural water governance in Bolivia. *Environment and Planning A* 37: 263–284.

Perreault T. (2008) Custom and contradiction: Rural water governance and the politics of "usos y costumbres" in Bolivia's irrigators' movement. *Annals of the Association of American Geographers* 98: 835–854.

Phare M-A. (2009) *Denying the source: The crisis of First Nations water rights*. Surrey, BC: Rocky Mountain Books.

Phare M-A. (2013) Indigenous peoples and water: Governing across borders. In: Norman ES, Cohen A and Bakker K (eds) *Water without borders? Canada, the United States and shared waters*. Toronto: University of Toronto Press, 27–46.

Phare M-A. (2014) Personal communication via email. 28 February 2014.

Philo C and Wilbert C. (2000) *Animal spaces, beastly places: New geographies of human–animal relations*. London: Routledge.

Picot C, Nguyen TA, Roudot AC and Parent-Massin D. (2011) A preliminary risk assessment of human exposure to phycotoxins in shellfish: a review. *Human and Ecological Risk Assessment* 17: 328–366.

Pierre J and Peters BG. (2000) *Governance, politics, and the state*. New York: St. Martin's Press.

Popescu G. (2012) *Bordering and ordering the twenty-first century: Understanding borders*. Lanham, MD: Rowman & Littlefield.

Price G. (1967) *Origins of the war with Mexico: The Polk-Stockton intrigue*. Austin, TX: University of Texas Press.

Rabinow P. (1977) *Reflections on field work in Morocco*. Berkeley, CA: University of California Press.

Raibmon P. (2005) *Authentic Indians: Episodes of encounter from the late-nineteenth century northwest coast*. Durham, NC: Duke University Press.

Ranco DJ, O'Neill CA, Donatuto J and Harper BL. (2011) Environmental justice, American Indians and the cultural dilemma: Developing environmental management for tribal health and well-being. *Environmental Justice* 4: 221–230.

Reo NJ. (2011) The importance of belief systems in Traditional Ecological Knowledge initiatives. *The International Indigenous Policy Journal* 2: 1–25.

Reunite Luna. (2012) Available at: www.reuniteluna.com/news_release.php?id=571 (Accessed 5 March 2014).

Rieu-Clarke A. (2005) *International law and sustainable development: Lessons from the law of international watercourses*. London: IWA.

Rivers without Borders. (2013) Available at: http://riverswithoutborders.org/ (Accessed 5 November 2013).

Robbins P. (2012) *Political ecology: A critical introduction*. New York: John Wiley & Sons.

Rose G. (2000) Practicing photography: An archive, a study, some photographs and a researcher.*Journal of Historical Geography* 26: 555–571

Rose-Redwood R. (2011) Rethinking the agenda of political toponymy. *ACME: An International E-Journal for Critical Geographies* 10: 34–41

Rose-Redwood R. (2012) With numbers in place: Security, territory, and the production of calculable space. *Annals of the Association of American Geographers* 102: 295–319.

Sack RD. (1986) *Human territoriality*. Cambridge: Cambridge University Press.

Said E. (1979) *Orientalism*. New York City, New York: Vintage Books.

Sarma UK and Barpujari I. (2011) Eco-cosmologies and biodiversity conservation: Continuity and change among the Karbis of Assam. *The International Indigenous Policy Journal* 2: 1–23.

Savelle M. (1940) *The diplomatic history of the Canadian boundary, 1759–1763*. New Haven, CT: Yale University Press.

Sayre N. (2005) Ecological and geographical scale: Parallels and potential for integration. *Progress in Human Geography* 29: 276–290.

Sayre N. (2009) Scale. In: Castree N, Demeritt D, Liverman D, and Rhoads B (ed.) *A companion to environmental geography*. Oxford, UK: Blackwell, 95–108.

Schantz SL, Widholm JJ, and Rice DC. (2003) Effects of PCB exposure on neuropsychological function in children. *Environmental Health Perspectives* 111: 357–376.

Schmeier S. (2013) *Governing international watercourses: River basin organizations and the sustainable governance of internationally shared rivers and lakes*. London: Routledge.

Schmidt SK. (2007) Mutual recognition as a new mode of governance. *Journal of European Public Policy* 14: 667–681.

Seiler RM. (2002) Selling patriotism/selling beer: The case of the "I AM CANADIAN!" commercial. *The American Review of Canadian Studies* 32: 45–66.

Selin H. (2010) *Global governance of hazardous chemicals: Challenges of multilevel management*. Cambridge, MA: MIT Press.

Selin NE. (2011) Science and strategies to reduce mercury risks: A critical review. *Journal of Environmental Monitoring* 13: 2389–2399.

Selin NE, Jacob DJ, Yantosca RM, Strode S, Jaeglé L, and Sunderland EM. (2008) Global 3-D land-ocean-atmosphere model for mercury: Present-day vs. pre-industrial cycles and anthropogenic enrichment factors for deposition. *Global Biogeochemical Cycles*, 22, GB2011, doi:10.1029/2007GB003040.

Shah T and van Koppen B. (2007) *IWRM challenges in developing countries: Lessons from India and elsewhere*, Colombo, Sri Lanka: International Water Management Institute.

Shukin N. (2009) *Animal capital: Rendering life in biopolitical times*. Minneapolis, MN: University of Minnesota Press.

Shurts J and Paisley R. (2013) The Columbia River Treaty. In: Norman ES, Cohen A, and Bakker K (eds) *Water without borders? Canada, the United States and shared waters*. Toronto: University of Toronto Press, 139–159.

Sigman H. (2005) Transboundary spillovers and decentralization of environmental policies. *Journal of Environmental Economics and Management* 50: 82–101.

Simpson A. (2000) Paths toward a Mohawk Nation: Narratives of citizenship and nationhood in Kahnawake. In: Ivison D, Patton P, and Sanders W (eds) *Political Theory and the Rights of Indigenous Peoples*. Cambridge: Cambridge University Press, 113–136.

Simpson A. (2007) On ethnographic refusal: Indigeneity, "voice" and colonial citizenship. *Junctures: The Journal for Thematic Dialogue* 9.

Singleton S. (2002) Collaborative environmental planning in the American West: The good, the bad and the ugly. *Environmental Politics* 11: 54–75.

Smith LT. (2012) *Decolonizing methodologies: Research and Indigenous peoples*. 2nd edition. New York: Zed Books.

Smith N. (1992) Geography, difference and the politics of scale. In: Doherty J, Graham M, and Malek M (eds) *Postmodernism and the Social Sciences*. New York: St. Martin's Press, 57–79.

Smith N. (1993) Homeless/global: Scaling places. In: Bird J, Curtis B, Putnam T, Robertson G, and Tickner L (eds) *Mapping the futures: Local cultures, global change*. London: Routledge, 87–119.

Smith N. (2000) Scale. In: Johnston RJ, Gregory D, Pratt G, and Watts M (eds) *The dictionary of human geography* (fourth edition). Oxford: Blackwell, 724–727.

Sneddon C and Fox C. (2006) Rethinking transboundary waters: A critical hydropolitics of the Mekong Basin. *Political Geography* 25: 181–202.

Spalding MK. (1999) Governance issues under the Environmental Side Agreement to the NAFTA. In: Spalding MK (ed.) *Sustainable development in San Diego-Tijuana: Environmental, social, and economic implications of interdependence.* La Jolla, CA: Center for U.S.-Mexican Studies: University of California, San Diego.

Sparke M. (1998) A map that roared and an original atlas: Canada, cartography, and the narration of nation. *Annals of the Association of American Geographers* 88: 463–495.

Sparke M. (2006) A neoliberal nexus: Economy, security and the biopolitics of citizenship on the border. *Political Geography* 25: 151–180.

Spivak GC. (1987) *In other worlds: Essays in cultural politics*. London: Methuen.

Spivak GC. (1988) Can the subaltern speak. In: Nelson C and Grossberb L (eds) *Marxism and the interpretation of culture*. Basingstoke, UK: Macmillan Education, 271–315.

Spivak GC. (1996) *The Spivak reader: Selected works of Gayatri Chakrovorty Spivak.* London: Routledge.

Steinberg PE. (2009) Sovereignty, territory, and the mapping of mobility: A view from the outside. *Annals of the Association of American Geographers* 99: 467–495.

Stephenson M. (2013) The challenge of the Canoe Journey: Paddle to Quinault. *North Kitsap Herald*. North Kitsap, Washington, 18 July.

Strange S. (1996) *Retreat of the State: The diffusion of power in the world economy*. Cambridge: Cambridge University Press.

Stumpff LM. (2010) Back to the bison: The confederated Salish and Kootenai Tribes and the National Bison Range. Available at: http://nativecases.evergreen.edu/collection/cases/back-to-the-bison.html (Accessed 7 December 2010).

Sullivan C. (2002) Calculating a water poverty index. *World Development* 30: 1195–1210.

Sundberg J. (2004) Identities in the making: Conservation, gender and race in the Maya Biospere Reserve, Guatemala. *Gender, Place, and Culture* 11: 43–66.

Sundberg J. (2008) "Trash-talk" and the production of quotidian geopolitical boundaries in the United States – Mexico borderlands. *Social and Cultural Geography* 9: 871–890.

Sundberg J. (2011) Diabolic caminos in the desert and cat fights on the Río: A posthumanist political ecology of boundary enforcement in the United States–Mexico borderlands. *Annals of the Association of American Geographers* 101: 318–336.

Susskind L. (1994) *Environmental diplomacy: Negotiating more effective global agreements*. Oxford: Oxford University Press.

Sutherland J. (2000) The coexistence of sustainable development and Aboriginal fishing rights in Canada. *Indigenous Law Bulletin* 4: 18–20.

Suttles W. (1954) Post-contact culture among the Lummi Indians. *British Columbia Historical Quarterly* XVII: 29–102.

Suttles W. (1960) Affinal ties, subsistence, and prestige among the Coast Salish. *American Anthropologist* 62: 296–305.

Suttles W. (1963) The persistence of intervillage ties among the Coast Salish. *Ethnology* 2: 512–525.

Suttles W. (1974) *Coast Salish and western Washington Indians: The economic life of the Coast Salish of Haro and Rosario Straits*. New York: Garland.

Suttles W. (1990) Central Coast Salish subsistence. *Northwest Anthropological Research Notes* 24: 147–152.

Swyngedouw E. (1997) Neither global nor local: "Glocalization" and the politics of scale. In: Cox K (ed.) *Spaces of globalization: Reasserting the power of the local.* New York: Guilford Press, 137–166.

Swyngedouw E. (1999) Modernity and hybridity: Nature, *regeneracionismo*, and the production of the Spanish waterscape, 1890–1930. *Annals of the Association of American Geographers* 89: 443–465.

Swyngedouw E. (2004*) Social power and the urbanization of water: Flows of power.* New York: Oxford University Press.

Swyngedouw E. (2005) Governance innovation and the citizen: The Janus face of governance-beyond-the-state. *Urban Studies* 42: 1991–2006.

Swyngedouw E. (2006) Circulations and metabolisms: (Hybrid) natures and (cyborg) cities. *Science as Culture* 15: 105–121.

Swyngedouw E. (2009) The political economy and political ecology of the hydro-social cycle. *Journal of Contemporary Water Research and Education* 142: 56–60.

Swyngedouw E and Heynen N. (2003) Urban political ecology, justice and the politics of scale. *Antipode* 35: 898–918.

Taylor J. (1999) *Making salmon: An environmental history of the Northwest Fisheries crisis.* Seattle, WA: University of Washington Press.

Thom B. (2009) The paradox of boundaries in Coast Salish Territories. *Cultural Geographies* 16: 179–205.

Thom B. (2010) The anathema of aggregation: Towards 21st-century self-government in the Coast Salish world. *Anthropoligica* 52: 33–48.

Tucker B. (2013) Inventing the Salish Sea: Exploring the performative act of place naming off the Pacific Coast of North America. MA thesis, University of Victoria.

United Nations. (2013) The Millennium Development Goals Report – 2013. *WHO/ UNICEF Joint Monitoring Programme for Water Supply and Sanitation.* Geneva: United Nations.

USGS. (2008) Tribal Canoe Journey to help restore Salish Sea resources. Interview with Eric Grossman. Available at: http://gallery.usgs.gov/audios/52 (Accessed 14 February 2008).

USGS. (2013) U.S. Geological Survey Western Fisheries Research Center. Available at: http://wfrc.usgs.gov (Accessed 15 December 2013).

van Houtum H, Kramsch O, and Zierhofer W. (2005) *B/ordering Space* (eds). Aldershot: Ashgate.

Van Rooy A. (1997) The frontiers of influence: NGO lobbying at the 1974 World Food Conference, the 1992 Earth Summit and Beyond. *World Development* 25: 93–114.

Van Rooy A. (2004) *The global legitimacy game: Civil society, globalization, and protest.* New York: Palgrave Macmillan.

Verma B. (1956) The Squamish: A study of changing political organization. *Department of Anthropology.* Vancouver, BC: University of British Columbia.

Visser M. (2007) *Cold, clear, and deadly: Unraveling a toxic legacy.* Lansing, MI: Michigan State University Press.

Visser M. (2014). Personal communication. May 10, 2014.

Vogel E. (2012) Parcelling out the watershed: The recurring consequences of organising Columbia river management within a basin-based territory. *Water Alternatives* 5: 161–190.

von der Porten S and de Loë RC. (2013a) Water governance and Indigenous governance: Towards a synthesis. *Indigenous Policy Journal* 23: 1–12.

von der Porten S and de Loë RC. (2013b) Collaborative approaches to governance for water and Indigenous peoples: A case study from British Columbia, Canada. *Geoforum* 50: 149–160.

Vouri M. (2008) *The Pig War*. Charleston, SC: Arcadia.

Wainwright J and Bryan J. (2009) Cartography, territory, property: Postcolonial reflection on Indigenous counter-mapping in Nicaragua and Belize. *Cultural Geographies* 16: 153–178.

Wania F and Mackay D.(1996) Tracking the distribution of persistent organic pollutants. *Environmental Science and Technology* 30: A390–A396.

Wania F, Axelman J, and Broman D. (1998) A review of processes involved in the exchange of persistent organic pollutants across the air-sea interface. *Environmental Pollution* 102: 3–24.

Warner JF and Johnson CL. (2007) "Virtual water" – Real people: Useful concept or prescriptive tool? *Water International* 32: 63–77.

Warry W. (2008) *Ending denial: Understanding Aboriginal issues*. Toronto, ON: University of Toronto Press.

Wartzok D, Popper A, Gordon J, and Merrill J. (2003) Factors affecting the responses of marine mammals to acoustic disturbance. *Marine Technology Society Journal* 37: 6–15.

Watson N. (2007) Collaborative capital: A key to the successful practice of integrated water resources management. In: Warner J (ed.) *Multi-stakeholder platforms for integrated water management*. Aldershot, England; Burlington, VT: Ashgate, 31–48.

Watson TL. (2009) Ho`i Hou iā Papahānaumoku: A history of ecocolonization in the Pu`uhonua of Wai`anae. Ph.D. thesis. University of Hawaii.

Westra L. (2008) *Environmental justice and the rights of Indigenous Peoples*. Abingdon, Oxford.

Whatmore S. (1999) Human geographies: Rethinking the "human" in human geography. In: Massey D, Allen J, and Sarre P (eds) *Human Geography Today*. Cambridge: Polity Press, 22–39.

Whatmore S. (2002) *Hybrid geographies: Natures, cultures, spaces*. London: Sage.

Whatmore S. (2003) Generating materials. In: Pryke M, Rose G, and Whatmore S (eds) *Using Social Theory*. London: Sage, 89–105.

White JP, Murphy L, and Spence N. (2012) Water and Indigenous Peoples: Canada's paradox. *The International Indigenous Policy Journal* 3: 1–23.

White R. (1995) *The organic machine: Remaking of the Columbia River*. New York: Hill & Wang.

Wildcat D. (2004) Traditional Ecological Knowledge. Bellingham, WA, Lecture, Northwest Indian College.

Wildcat D. (2011) *Red Alert: Saving the Planet with Indigenous Knowledge*. Golden, CO: Fulcrum.

Wilkinson CF. (1987) *American Indians, time, and the law: Indigenous societies in a modern constitutional democracy*. Hartford, CT: Yale University Press.

Williams R, Trites A, and Bain D. (2002) Behavioural responses of killer whales (orcinus orca) to whale-watching boats: Opportunistic observations and experimental approaches. *Journal of Zoology* 256: 255–270.

Willoughby WR. (1981) Expectations and experience 1909–1979. In: Spencer R, Kirton J, and Nossal KR (eds) *The International Joint Commission seventy years on*. Toronto, ON: University of Toronto, 24–42.

Wilson S. (2008) Research is ceremony: Indigenous research methods. Blackwood, NS: Fernwood.

Wirth JD. (1996) The Trail Smelter Dispute: Canadians and Americans confront trans-boundary pollution, 1927–41. *Environmental History* 1: 1 –34.

Wiwchar D. (2004) Mowachaht/Muchalaht keep Tsu-xiit free. *Ha-Shilth-Sa Newspaper*. Nuu-chah-nulth, British Columbia.

Wolch J. (1998) Zoopolis. In: Wolch J and Emel J (eds) *Animal geographies: Place, politics, and identity in the nature-culture borderlands*. London; New York: Verso, 119–138.

Wolch J. (2002) Anima urbis. *Progress in Human Geography* 26: 721–742.

Wolch J and Emel J. (1998) *Animal geographies: Place, politics, and identity in the nature-culture borderlands*. London; New York: Verso.

Wolf AT. (1999) "Water wars" and water reality: Conflict and cooperation along international waterways. In: Lonergan S (ed.) *Environmental change, adaptation, and human security*. Dordrecht: Kluwer Academic, 251–265.

Wynn G. (2010) Mapping a Continent: Historical Atlas of North America: 1492–1814 (Review). *University of Toronto Quarterly* 79: 542–543.

Yoffe S, Wolf AT, and Giordano M. (2003) Conflict and cooperation over international freshwater resources: Indicators of basins at risk. *Journal of the American Water Resources Association* 39: 1109–1126.

YRITWC. (2013) *Yukon River Inter-Tribal Watershed Council*. Available at: www.yritwc.org/.

Zeitoun M and Warner J. (2006) Hydro-hegemony – a framework for analysis of transboundary water conflicts. *Water Policy* 8: 435–460.

Zeitoun M and Allan T. (2008) Applying hegemony and power theory to transboundary water analysis. *Water Policy* 10: 3–12.

Zeitoun M and Mirumachi N. (2008) Transboundary water interaction: Reconsidering conflict and cooperation. *International Environmental Agreements* 8: 297–316.

Zeitoun M, Eid-Sabbagh K, Talhami M, and Dajani M. (2013) Hydro-hegemony in the Upper Jordan waterscape: Control and use of the flows. *Water Alternatives* 6: 86–106.

Zimmer A and Sakdapolrak P. (2012) The social practices of governing: Analysing waste water governance in a Delhi slum. *Environment and Urbanization in Asia* 3: 325–341.

Zimmerer KS and Bassett TJ. (2003) *Political ecology: An integrative approach to geography and environment-development studies*. New York: Guilford Press.

Index